The Foundations of Palatial Crete

States and Cities of Ancient Greece

Edited by
R. F. WILLETTS

The Foundations of
Palatial Crete

A survey of Crete in the Early Bronze Age

Keith Branigan BA PhD
Lecturer in Archaeology, University of Bristol

London
Routledge & Kegan Paul

First published 1970
by Routledge & Kegan Paul Limited
Broadway House, 68–74 Carter Lane
London, E.C.4
Printed in Great Britain
by Western Printing Services Ltd.
Bristol
© Keith Branigan 1970
SBN 7100 6617 1

TO LITTLE NONG

Contents

List of plates

List of figures in the text

Acknowledgements for plates

I am indebted to M. Christian Zervos for so kindly allowing me to reproduce plates 1, 3a, 4, 5, 6, 9, 10b, 11a, 12, 14a, from his superb 'L'Art de la Crete'. Plates 7b, 8, 10a, 11b, 13, 14b were kindly supplied by Professor M. Hirmer. The remaining plates were generously offered to me by the following good friends, Sinclair Hood (pls. 2, 7a), Mervyn Popham (pl. 3b), Professor Doro Levi (pls. 15 and 16), Dr. A. Zoes (pl. 6a).

Preface

The civilization which Evans called Minoan lasted for something like fourteen hundred years. The last six hundred years of this era have received a great deal of attention from scholars and laymen alike and many books and thousands of learned articles have been written about them. This is not surprising, for the period of six hundred years from 2,000 B.C. to 1,400 B.C. is that in which Minoan civilization reached maturity; it is the period of the great palaces and all the riches that they held. What is surprising however, is that the previous eight hundred years have been relatively ignored. Apart from excavation reports there are no books about the Minoan Early Bronze Age, and relatively few articles. Pendlebury, Hutchinson, and Schachermeyr have all written chapters which deal with the period, but only briefly and in outline. Both student and layman alike are therefore unable to read a comprehensive account of Early Minoan Crete. This book is an attempt to remedy the situation.

It is not intended however to be a textbook in which each and every problem concerning our knowledge and understanding of the period is discussed and a solution suggested. Rather the book is written around a central theme – the debt of palatial Crete to the Early Bronze Age civilization. Each chapter is designed to trace the development of one particular aspect of that civilization from the sub-Neolithic period to the erection of the palaces in MM I.

The term 'Early Bronze Age' is used throughout to cover the period occupied by EM I, EM II, EM III and MM Ia; that is to say, I regard the MM Ia phase as a part of the Early Bronze Age and inseparable from any discussion of it. My reasons for doing so will, I hope, become apparent as the book progresses. Evans's terminology and ceramic framework for the period has been adhered to with one or two changes in the duration and positioning of certain pottery fabrics within that framework.

Preface

In order to avoid punctuating the text with a large number of footnotes, references have been grouped together under a single footnote wherever this has been possible. The chapter bibliography which follows the general bibliography will allow the reader to quickly find the books and articles most relevant to any subject which he may wish to pursue further. In selecting figures and plates I have tried to achieve a balance between the important but already well-illustrated objects and less well-known objects published only in expensive or unobtainable books.

Inevitably during eight years of study I have received a great deal of help, encouragement, advice, information and stimulation from an ever-widening circle of friends and colleagues. To all of these I owe a debt of gratitude which I am pleased to have the opportunity to acknowledge. In particular I must express my thanks to Mr. Peter Gelling, who first introduced me to the archaeology of Crete, and to Dr. F. J. Tritsch for encouragement and stimulation throughout the period of my studies. To Mr. Mark Cameron must go the credit and thanks for rescuing me from a seedy Iraklion guest-house and introducing me to the pleasures and benefits of life at the Taverna, Knossos. It was he too who introduced me to Dr. Peter Warren who has proved a firm friend and constant stimulation to re-thinking my understanding of Early Minoan Crete. To these, and other students of the British School at Athens, I owe much. I should like to acknowledge the kindness and help afforded to me by Dr. Alexiou and his assistant, Dr. Sakellarakis, at Iraklion Museum, and by the staff of the British School at Athens, in London, Athens, and Knossos. Finally I wish to thank Mr. R. F. Willetts for considerable help and advice in preparing this book for publication, and the publishers for their willing co-operation.

KEITH BRANIGAN   *Bristol, March 1968*

1 Background to the enquiry

Man's discovery of copper ore and the means by which it could be turned into metal was one of the major discoveries in history. Where it was first made we cannot be sure, but in our present state of knowledge it seems likely that the discovery was made in Anatolia sometime during the sixth millennium B.C. Native copper had already been used for beads in the early seventh millennium B.C. at Catal Huyuk in the Konya plain, and the earliest copper tools occur in level XXI at Mersin in the early fifth millennium B.C.[1] By the second half of the fifth millennium copper was being used for chisels and axes, for needles, pins, awls, and daggers. The Anatolian Bronze Age proper may begin in the middle of the fourth millennium B.C. although the dating of the relevant sites is at present controversial. Certainly by the beginning of the third millennium B.C., there were flourishing Bronze Age cultures at Troy, Poliochni, Thermi, and Emporio in north-west Anatolia, Beycesultan in the south-west, and Tarsus in Cilicia.[2] These are large settlements, in many cases well defended by thick walls and providing evidence of a rich ruling class. Tomb deposits such as those from Alaja and Dorak illustrate just how much wealth some rulers could accumulate, and similar evidence is provided by the treasure discovered by Schliemann at Troy.[3] Anatolia of course is a vast country and not surprisingly there are great differences between the western cultures, looking towards the Aegean and south-eastern Europe, and those of the east which looked to Syria and Mesopotamia.

One imagines that the working of copper must have begun in Syria not much later than it did in Cilicia, the two lands being

[1] Garstang *1953* 76, fig. 50.
[2] Blegen et al *1950*; Bernabo-Brea *1964*; Lamb *1936*; Hood *1955*, *1962*; Mellaart *1959*, Lloyd and Mellaart *1962*; Goldman *1956*.
[3] Dorak: Mellaart *1959a*; Alaja: Kosay *1951*; Troy: Schliemann *1880*.

adjacent. Evidence is scarce however, although Professor Schaeffer's publication of the Neolithic, Chalcolithic and Early Bronze Age levels at Ras Shamra adds to the knowledge already gleaned from sites like Alalakh and its environs in the Amuq plain.[1] In Syria certainly there was a group of developing cities in the fourth millennium B.C., of which Ras Shamra, Byblos and Alalakh are the best known, all three eventually becoming successful Bronze Age cities. It was once suggested that Byblos in fact was the place where bronze was first produced, but this can no longer be maintained.[2] In the third millennium B.C. Byblos was an important trading centre, and Egyptian ships made regular voyages to it to purchase cedar wood and other commodities. The Egyptians themselves had been using copper since the Badarian period, and objects of bronze appear in First Dynasty tombs.[3] Whilst they could obtain copper from the mines of Sinai, they had no ready source of tin and it may well be that tin was amongst the commodities brought from Byblos, having originally come from Anatolia. Egyptian civilization developed very rapidly at the end of the fourth millennium B.C. The Badarian, Amratian and Gerzean cultures had all developed smoothly though occasionally with a stimulus from beyond the Nile valley. About three thousand B.C. however two kingdoms arose, one controlling Upper Egypt and the other Lower Egypt. Hostilities seem to have broken out between these two kingdoms with the result that the whole of Egypt was united under the kings of Upper (southern) Egypt. After an unsettled period in which the supremacy of the south seems to have been challenged several times, Egypt at last entered into an era of peace about 2,700 B.C. with the accession of Nebka, the first king of the Third Dynasty.[4] Over the course of the next five centuries Egyptian civilization developed those unique artistic and architectural traditions which lasted throughout antiquity. The picture presented by the discoveries made in both tombs and towns of this period is one of great prosperity, the result not only of the fertility of the Nile valley but also of foreign trade with Syria and Palestine.

[1] Ras Shamra: Schaeffer et al *1962*; Byblos: Dunand *1950* and *1956*; Alalakh and environs: Woolley *1953*; General: Braidwood *1953* and *1955*.

[2] Wainwright *1944a*, 100ff.

[3] e.g. Mosso *1910* 218.

[4] The relationship between Khasekhemui, Nebka, and Djoser is obscure, but it now looks as if Nebka succeeded Khasekhemui and founded the Third Dynasty. See Stevenson Smith *1962* 3–10.

Palestine lay between the civilizations of Syria and Egypt, and by the third millennium B.C. it had already developed the political pattern which it was to maintain for the next two thousand years. The use of copper had come to Palestine at the start of the fourth millennium B.C. Probably the earliest cultures using copper here were those of Ghassul in the south and the coastal region in the north, but there were several other localized cultures which soon emerged.[1] At the end of the fourth millennium the Chalcolithic sites in the north assume an urban character, whilst those in the south are generally abandoned. The full flowering of urban civilization in Palestine is contemporary with the start of the Bronze Age, about 3,000 B.C. From this time onwards Palestine is a complex of small city-states, vulnerable to attack from the more powerful kingdoms which had emerged to north, east and south. For this reason the cities of Early Bronze Age Palestine are surrounded by great defensive walls. Nevertheless, despite the insecurity in which they existed, these cities too seem to have prospered and produced many interesting public buildings, particularly temples.[2]

Whilst the beginning of the third millennium saw the start of Bronze Age civilization and the rapid expansion of contacts between the new centres of culture in the Near East, there was no such development at the other end of the Mediterranean basin. Here, people were still in the Neolithic stage of development and some of them would remain so right through the third millennium. At the start of the third millennium B.C. there were two broad cultural groups in the western Mediterranean, the one embracing north-western Italy, the extreme south of France, and the eastern seaboard of the Iberian peninsula, and the other covering southern Italy, Sicily, and Malta. Both of these groups represent the climax

[1] Ghassul: A. Mallon *1933* and R. Koeppel et al *1940*; the other localized Chalcolithic groups are known mainly from surface finds and include a group of about thirty sites around the Wadi Shallale, a small group of sites (principally caves) in the Judaean desert, and another group centred on Beersheba and noted for unusual figurine types and a relative abundance of copper objects. In the north, the Neolithic Coastal culture merges into a Chalcolithic culture of similar distribution and notable for its house-urns. Further inland another culture with clear Neolithic affinities was centred on the Plain of Esdraelon. A brief summary of some of these cultures can be found in Kenyon *1960*.

[2] e.g. the temples at Megiddo, Ai, and possibly the granary-like building at Beth-Yerah.

of the Neolithic period in the western Mediterranean. About 2,300 B.C. the first Chalcolithic cultures appear. In peninsular Italy there are several localized cultures – Remedello, Rinaldone, Gaudho, and Cellino, whilst in Sicily the variety of cultures is even more numerous.[1] All of these cultures however, both in Italy and Sicily, show signs of influence from the eastern Mediterranean and it is widely agreed that the arts of metallurgy were probably introduced to the west from the east. The important sites of Los Millares in Spain, Vila Nova San Pedro in Portugal, and Lebous in southern France suggest that there may perhaps have been actual immigrants from the regions further east who came attracted by the mineral wealth of the west.[2] Nevertheless the contrast between east and west at the end of the third millennium B.C. was still very marked indeed. The west could boast no civilization such as had appeared in Egypt and Syria, nor even city-states of the type which had emerged in Palestine. The people of the western Mediterranean had reached the technological stage of development which we call Chalcolithic, but they were still a very long way indeed from achieving the political, economic, and social progress which had accompanied the technological development in the Near East.

Between these two extremes, both geographically and historically, lay the Early Bronze Age cultures of the Aegean. One cultural group, that of the north-western coast of Anatolia, has already been mentioned. On the opposite side of the Aegean, connections with the cities of the Troad can be detected. The Late Neolithic period in Thessaly had already produced fortified villages like those of Dimini and Sesklo and houses of so-called 'megaron' type.[3] The last phases of the Neolithic in Thessaly – the Larissa and Rakhmani phases – are now thought perhaps to represent a Chalcolithic phase of development.[4] No such phase is discernible further south in Boeotia, Euboea, Attica, and the Peloponnese. In these areas the transition from Neolithic to Bronze Age seems to come quite sharply, perhaps a little before 2,700 B.C. The influence of both the Troad and the Cyclades can be noted amongst contemporary pottery and there can be little doubt that it was from these areas that the secrets

---

[1] For up-to-date accounts see Trump *1966* and Bernabo-Brea *1957*.

[2] But like Renfrew (*1967*) I have reservations about the Aegean and eastern 'colonies' in the west Mediterranean.

[3] Tsountas *1908*.

[4] Milojcic *1959* 1–56.

of metallurgy were introduced. The second phase of the Early Bronze Age, beginning perhaps before 2,500 B.C. was a prosperous one which saw the establishment of many small towns of which the best known are Agios Kosmas (Attica) Zygouries and Lerna (both in the Argolid).[1] About 2,100 B.C. many of these towns were destroyed by fire.[2] The subsequent occupation of these sites shows quite clearly that the destructions were the work of an immigrant people, although we cannot say whence they came. Their architecture is somewhat more simple than that found in the EH II communities and should perhaps be connected with Late Neolithic dwellings in Thessaly and beyond. The transition to Middle Helladic I from this EH III phase is remarkably smooth at Lerna and it would perhaps be fair to say that there is a greater distinction between EH II and EH III than there is between EH III and MH I.[3]

In the Cyclades the pattern of development differs somewhat, and certainly the material culture of the islands is quite distinct from that of the Greek mainland. Until recently the existence of a Cycladic Neolithic could not be proven, but the excavations by Professor Caskey on Keos and Evans and Renfrew on Antiparos have revealed settlements of this period. Both belong to the Late Neolithic phase.[4] In the Cyclades the change over to the Early Bronze Age may well have taken place by the start of the third millennium B.C. The first phase of the Cycladic Early Bronze Age, usually called the 'Pelos' phase, is still little understood, but it seems highly likely that it began by the beginning of the third millennium, for sherds of the succeeding EC II phase (the principal cultural group being the Keros-Syros one) have been found in EH I associations on the mainland.[5] As with the Troad and the Greek mainland, the second phase of the Cycladic Early Bronze Age seems to be long and prosperous. Settlements of the period have not yet been properly investigated, with the exception of Chalandriani on Syros.[6] Here a rocky hill was occupied and surrounded

---

[1] Mylonas *1959*; Blegen *1928*; Caskey, Interim Reports in Hesperia *1954–59*.
[2] Caskey *1960*.
[3] See particularly Caskey *1960*.
[4] Caskey *1962* and *1964a*; Renfrew and Evans *1968*.
[5] Blegen *1921* (Korakou); Blegen *1928* (Zygouries); Goldman *1931* (Eutresis).
[6] Bossert *1960*. The settlement itself was not excavated, but Tsountas excavated a very large cemetery here and plans of a few houses and part of the defence wall are available.

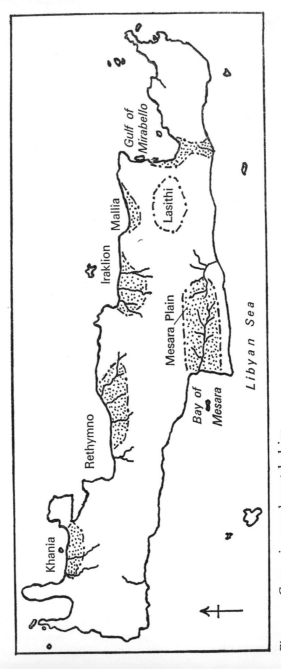

Figure 1 Crete: rivers and coastal plains

by a thick defence wall with bastions, comparable with the defences of EH II Lerna. Although EC II may have begun earlier than EH II there is clear evidence that they overlap considerably. The characteristic marble figurines and frying pans appear on EH II sites on the mainland, and equally the EH II sauceboats are found in the EC II settlements and tombs.[1] As far as we know there was no violent end to the Keros-Syros phase in the Cyclades, but there does not seem to be a continuity of occupation at Chalandriani. The best deposits of EC III material are from the first city of Phylakopi on Melos.[2] Here the EC III phase appears to have been a long one and to have lasted perhaps until the Middle Helladic period had already begun on the mainland.

The final element in Aegean civilization of the third millennium B.C. was that with which we are principally concerned, the Minoan. Crete, more than any other island or region in the Aegean, lay both geographically and historically mid-way along the line of the diffusion of metallurgy in the Mediterranean basin. Crete's position in the Mediterranean is such that in the early days of navigation and sea-faring the island became a focus of intercontinental trade and contact. On the one hand it lay along the sea-route from east to west, and on the other it lay across the sea-route from south to north. That is to say, it was the point through which both commodities and ideas from and to Asia, Africa and Europe were channelled. In the Bronze Age this meant that Crete 'sat upon the lines of communication along which the arts and crafts of the great civilizations of two continents reached the barbarian people of a third'.[3]

Crete itself is predominantly mountainous, with a limestone 'backbone' which stretches from east to west (fig. 1). The coastal plains of the west, the valleys of the centre and east, and the Mesara plain of the south are of limestone, sandstone, and conglomerate. Metamorphic rocks which are mainly covered by the great limestone masses crop out in many localities, particularly in the west of the island. The mineral wealth yielded by these various rocks is not very great: fair amounts of iron, some low grade copper, several

---

[1] Cycladic figurines on the mainland occur at Sounion, Styra, Eleusis, Piraeus, Athens, Brauron, Manika, Zygouries, Agios Kosmas, Neraida, and Ay. Andreas. Sauceboats are found on Kea, Syros, Mykonos, Naxos and Keros.
[2] Atkinson *1904*.
[3] Branigan *1968* 9.

small sources of lead, and unconfirmed reports of tungsten, manganese, zinc, and gold. Several types of stone were utilized by the Minoans however for the manufacture of stone vases, particularly serpentine.[1]

In the west of the island the mountains dominate the scenery and for five thousand years they have dominated the pattern of human settlement. There are few areas where reasonably flat ground may be agriculturally exploited and much of the mountainous terrain is of little use except for summer pasturage. Only in the fertile plain of Khania was there any scope for prehistoric man to develop socially beyond the village stage (pl. 7a). Further east another small plain opens out around the town of Rethymno, and in the centre of the island a third such plain lies behind the town of Heraklion. It is at the southern end of this plain that the palace of Knossos stands. A thin and irregular coastal strip connects this plain to a smaller one further east, in which stands another palace, Mallia. At this point the mountains again reach to the sea. Beyond them lies the Gulf of Mirabello with a thin lowland strip around its western edge. To the east is a high and barren limestone tableland which stretches to the east coast. The narrow lowland strip around the western rim of the Gulf of Mirabello however turns southwards and runs between the mountains towards the south coast and the town of Ierapetra. Unlike the north coast which provides many good natural harbours – Amnisos, and Mochlos for example – the south coast has few protected anchorages. On the other hand it has many sandy beaches suitable for beaching ships. All along the south coast the mountains sweep right down to the sea, but in the bay of Mesara the sandy beaches give way to the flat and fertile plain of Mesara (pl. 1). For the rest of the island, those parts which can support village life are composed of valleys running north-south through the limestone masses. There is one notable exception and that is the upland plain of Lasithi. The area is thickly populated today and in the 1930's John Pendlebury carried out a survey which showed that the same was true in antiquity.[2]

Because of its exceptional altitude Lasithi has quite severe winters, but the lowland plains have a mild climate with rain only through the six winter months. The lack of spring and summer rains means that permanent rivers are scarce and there are perhaps no more than

[1] On Minoan deposits of serpentine see Warren *1965*, and his forthcoming book on Minoan stone vases.   [2] Pendlebury *1936*.

half a dozen throughout the island. The seas surrounding Crete however are full of sea-food and the native fauna include deer, agrimi, pigeons and partridge. In addition the natural vegetation provides quince, almonds, mulberry, asparagus, lettuce, celery, and a variety of herbs.

When the first Neolithic settlers arrived in Crete they thus found an island which could provide them with a varied diet, but one which lacked wild species of sheep and cattle and wild forms of the edible grass crops. The settlers must therefore have brought these animals and plants with them. Only one occupation site of this Early Neolithic period is yet known in Crete, and that is the site of Knossos.[1] The earliest deposit on this site is dated by a C. 14 sample to c. 6,000 B.C. This makes it contemporary with the Early Neolithic settlements recently discovered at Nea Nikomedia and Elateia (in Macedonia and Phocis respectively).[2] The earliest level of occupation at Knossos contained no solid walls, but only post holes and beaten earth floors with traces of hearths. The material equipment included simple beads of clay, stone, and shell, flint and obsidian blades, and bone awls and spatulas, but no pottery. Weinberg therefore believes that the first settlers in Crete were aceramic, and certainly their dwellings, material equipment and crops (emmer and barley) are comparable to those of the aceramic peoples of Thessaly.[3] The excavator of the site, John Evans, offers a different interpretation of the evidence. He believes that this first occupation deposit belongs to the camp site used by the settlers when they arrived at Knossos. The deposit is very thin, only about 8″ thick, and represents a very short period of time. There is no sign of an abandonment following this phase of occupation but pottery becomes increasingly abundant in the levels overlying the earliest stratum. The many advanced features of this pottery indicate quite clearly that those who made it had a well-established ceramic tradition when they arrived in the island and there is no question of them having developed from the aceramic stage to that seen in the first level overlying the earliest deposit.

However it is the advanced nature of this earliest pottery at Knossos which is the stumbling block to those who, like myself, believe that an excavator's opinion as to the archaeological circumstances of his discoveries should not be lightly set aside. If we accept

---

[1] Evans J. D. *1964*.   [2] Rodden *1964* and *1964a*; Weinberg *1962*.
[3] Weinberg *1965* 51ff.

Professor Evans's testimony that there was no evidence of an abandonment between the non-pottery level and the level overlying it, and if we accept that the C. 14 date for this lowest stratum is correct at c. 6,000 B.C., then we find we are dealing with a corpus of pottery which is between two and three thousand years in advance of anything else at present known in the Aegean and eastern Mediterranean. For this reason Weinberg has suggested that in fact the lowest stratum represents a completely different and much earlier group of settlers than the levels immediately above it, and that when the later settlers arrived, in levelling off the site to build their village they removed the evidence of an abandonment and very probably a great deal of the occupation material belonging to the first settlement. Furthermore he rejects the C. 14 date for the end of the Early Neolithic phase (c. 5,000 B.C.). Thus Weinberg postulates an initial aceramic occupation at Knossos c. 6,000 B.C., followed by an abandonment of more than a millennium, in turn followed in the second half of the fifth millennium B.C. by the Early Neolithic settlement. The importance of Weinberg's theory, if we accept it, to our survey of Crete in the third millennium B.C. is that the history of human settlement in Crete prior to the third millennium is reduced by a half and the nature and origins of the Cretan population at the start of the third millennium B.C. are changed.

There is no easy solution to the problem, and certainly I would not claim to be able to solve it. I suspect that the problem may eventually be solved by the dates for the start of the Early and Middle Neolithic of the mainland being moved back to the middle of the seventh and sixth millennia respectively, and that for the end of the Knossian Early Neolithic being lowered well into the fifth millennium B.C. The four metres of deposit argue for a very long Early Neolithic at Knossos, whilst the Early Neolithic deposits at Nea Nikomedia with a carbon date of c. 6,200 B.C. include painted pottery, ceramic shapes which are not primary, and some advanced stone work. These all suggest that the Early Neolithic settlement at Nea Nikomedia may not belong to the start of the Early Neolithic in northern Greece.

As I have said, this digression into the complexities of the Early Neolithic in the Aegean is necessary because one should be aware of the controversy which surrounds the ancestry of the Early Bronze Age occupants of Crete. Whatever one's solution of the chronological problems, there can be no doubt that the Early Neolithic culture of Crete is quite distinct from the cultures of the Greek mainland. The black burnished pottery is decorated in pointille, incised and scribble burnish patterns, and is remarkable for the advanced handle forms – wishbone, ring, pronged and trumpet lugs. Stone was used to produce axes, maceheads, bracelets, beads, blades and pot lids. Spindle whorls and shuttles attest to the appearance of spinning. Male and female figurines and some animal ones including bulls confirm that the earliest settlers held some sort of religious belief. The houses in which they lived were rectangular, built of mud-brick on stone foundations and covered with a brushwood roof. In the succeeding Middle Neolithic phase the houses feature stone benches, rectangular living platforms, rectangular cupboards, plastered walls and perhaps small court-yards. There is little change in the material culture except amongst the pottery. Ripple burnish decoration is very common whilst pointille decoration declines rapidly. Apart from Knossos, three Middle Neolithic sites are known. One is the farmstead at Kat-sambas and the others are unexcavated sites at Mitropolis in the Mesara, and Melidhoni in the Apokoronas district, near Khania.[1]

In contrast to this scarcity of sites, between thirty and forty Late Neolithic sites are known.[2] Many of them belong to the very end of the Neolithic period and might fairly be described as sub-Neolithic. The block of houses excavated by Sir Arthur Evans at Knossos however seem to belong to the Late Neolithic proper for at Knossos the latest Neolithic and earliest Early Minoan deposits were swept away during the building of the first palace.[3] Late Neolithic pottery at Knossos is uninspiring; there is only a little badly exe-cuted pointille decoration, handles are unimaginative, and shapes are simple. Indications of the sudden flowering of ceramic art that was to come with the start of the Early Bronze Age are only to be found on those sites of the very late Neolithic, or sub-Neolithic as we should perhaps call them. At Phaistos there is a flourishing sub-Neolithic phase in which pattern burnishing, burnished buff fabrics, and red ochre decorated fabrics all appear.[4] In the moun-tains south-west of Phaistos the cave at Miamou yielded an

---

[1] Alexiou *1954* (Katsambas); Evans J. D. *1964a* 57; Hood *1965* 112.

[2] Weinberg *1965* map 3.

[3] Evans A. J. *1928* 1–21; Evans J. D. *1964* 138, 188.

[4] Levi *1965*.

interesting group of material including a square-mouthed pot which we might connect with the Lagozza culture of north-western Italy, which flourished in the early third millennium B.C.[1] As far as we can tell this is about the date of the material from Phaistos and Miamou and other 'sub-Neolithic' sites in Crete. An accurate date cannot be given for the start of the Early Bronze Age simply because it began at various times in different parts of the island. At Phaistos however there would seem to be uninterrupted occupation of the site through the sub-Neolithic period into the EM I period and this site may probably be taken as representative of the rest of the Mesara at least, in terms of chronology. On our present evidence many of those who have recently been conducting research into various aspects of the Early Minoan culture believe that the EM I period began in the early third millennium B.C., probably c. 2,800 B.C., within a century either way.

The importance of the transition to the Early Bronze Age at Phaistos is considerable, since Phaistos stands in the middle of the Mesara and it is from the Mesara that such a vast amount of our material of the Early Minoan period has been recovered. On his first visit to Crete in 1893 Sir Arthur Evans saw the material from Agios Onouphrios – only five minutes' walk from Phaistos – and at once drew comparisons between this rather mixed collection of artifacts and Egyptian material of the Fourth and Sixth Dynasties.[2] Amongst the Agios Onouphrios collection there was of course the painted jug which gave the site's name to one of the characteristic pottery fabrics in use during the EM I period. Within a few years of Evans's first visit the Cretan rebellion had given him the chance to obtain permission to begin his excavations at Knossos. As well as revealing the great palace erected in MM I, destroyed in MM IIb and reconstructed again in MM III, these excavations also produced small stratified deposits of Early Minoan material. On the evidence of these Evans was able to formulate the basis of his Early Minoan chronology in 1904.[3]

Already however the Italians had begun their exploration of the Mesara. The first tholoi were discovered and excavated at Agia Triadha and in the excavations on the nearby palace of Phaistos further small deposits of Early Minoan pottery were being discovered.[4] Then, in 1904, Xanthoudides excavated the first of his

[1] Taramelli *1897* fig. 14   [2] Evans A. J. *1895.*
[3] Evans A. J. *1904* 18, fig. 7.   [4] Banti *1933*; Pernier *1935.*

tholoi, at Koumasa. From these tombs in the course of the next twenty years Xanthoudides recovered a wonderful array of pottery, stone vases, sealstones, and metal objects. His excavations were well conducted and his records were, for their time, informative. In all he excavated more than a dozen tholoi, although some had been almost completely looted in antiquity, or more recently as Xanthoudides himself describes in his *Vaulted Tombs of the Mesara*.[1]

Whilst Xanthoudides and the Italians were excavating in the Mesara and Evans was digging at Knossos, the Americans had completed several excavations in the east of the island. The islands of Mochlos and Pseira and the mainland sites of Vasiliki, Gournia, Sphoungaras, Avgo, Agios Andoni, Vrokastro, Pachyammos, and Priniatiko Pyrgos had all been examined by Seager, Hall or Boyd-Hawes.[2] Most of these sites produced some Early Minoan finds but of particular importance were the sites of Vasiliki, Mochlos and Gournia. They were, and still are, the basis of Early Minoan chronology in the east of the island, and indeed to some extent in the north and south as well. In addition to the American explorations around the Gulf of Mirabello the British School at Athens had begun work on the east coast in 1902 and were finding Early Minoan ossuaries around Palaikastro and some small Early Minoan deposits within the settlement itself.[3]

Between 1920 and the Second World War there was not a great deal of Early Minoan material brought to light. Marinatos excavated several sites but few producing much Early Minoan material although the tomb at Krasi contained a sizeable collection and the settlement at Ellenes Amariou is one of the earliest Early Minoan settlements excavated.[4] In Lasithi Pendlebury's survey discovered the cave at Trapeza which produced both sub-Neolithic and Early Minoan pottery and small finds.[5] During the war the Germans themselves carried out some excavations including those at Koumarospelio (? sub-Neolithic) and Apesokari.[6] The small tholos tomb

[1] Xanthoudides *1918*, *1924*.
[2] Seager *1912* (Mochlos); *1912a* (Pseira); *1905*, *1907* (Vasiliki); Hawes *1908* (Gournia); Hall *1912* (Sphoungaras); *1914* (Vrokastro and Agios Andoni); Seager *1916* (Pachyammos).
[3] Bosanquet *1923*; Dawkins *1904* and *1905*.
[4] Marinatos *1929* and *1932*.
[5] Pendlebury *1936*.
[6] Matz *1942*.

found at the latter site is important for the understanding of what these structures originally looked like.

Since the war Dr. Platon and Dr. Alexiou have conducted excavations on several important sites. Platon's excavations at Viannos, Myrsini, and Gonies Maleviziou have been unfortunate in that on none of them was Platon able to detect any stratification in the deposits.[1] Our knowledge about these excavations is limited at the moment as they have not yet been published. Alexiou has excavated and published a cave ossuary at Kanli Kastelli which produced a very fine range of EM I pottery.[2] By far the biggest corpus of material however has come from the small tholoi excavated at Lebena by Alexiou.[3] The pottery is rich and varied, and is accompanied by small numbers of metal objects, sealstones and figurines. Most important of all, these finds were made in clearly stratified deposits which increase their archaeological value ten-fold. Preliminary reports of this excavation have appeared and the final publication is eagerly awaited.

Meanwhile, in addition to these excavations the work on many of those sites first excavated at the start of the century has been continued. Sinclair Hood has found further stratified deposits of EM I, II, and III at Knossos, Professor Levi has found Early Minoan houses at Phaistos and an important, if late, tholos tomb at Kamilari. At Mallia the French have discovered EM II and extensive EM III deposits beneath the palace and two important built ossuaries of EM III–MM I. In the east of the island Popham's excavations at Palaikastro found further small pockets of Early Minoan material and Platon has excavated some EM II tombs near Zakro.[4]

In spite of all this activity the only Early Minoan house to have been excavated on an extensive scale was that at Vasiliki, excavated in 1904–1906. In 1968 this situation was improved when Dr. Peter Warren completed the excavations at Fournou Korifi near Myrtos, just west of Ierapetra on the south coast. Here he found a large building complex, apparently of EM II date.[5]

Discoveries made over the last decade or so have thus given us a great deal of new material and a certain amount of new information. Nevertheless it is true to say that we now have a very large body of

[1] Platon *1957* 420; Daux *1960*; Hood *1955* 30.
[2] Alexiou *1951*.   [3] Alexiou *1958* and *1960*.
[4] Popham *1965*; Platon *1964*.   [5] Warren 1968.

Early Bronze Age material about which we do not know a great deal. This is because we still lack a really solid chronological framework into which the material can be fitted. In the case of prehistoric cultures such as that with which we are concerned the construction of such a framework is dependent on a study of pottery. Thus before we can begin to talk about the Early Minoans and their society, economy, religion, and other aspects of their lives we must concern ourselves with building some sort of framework in which these various topics can be seen in perspective. In the study of the past, be it prehistoric or otherwise, time is the most important element of all.

2 A framework for the period

The problems which surround any discussion of Early Minoan chronology are all basically centred on the absence of sufficient stratified material. This situation is the product of three unfortunate circumstances.

As we have just seen, a large proportion of the Early Minoan material known to us was discovered in excavations between 1900 and 1920. At this time the science of archaeology was still very much in its infancy, and the application of sound stratigraphical principles was virtually unknown. Where the principles of stratigraphy were understood and applied, then we find that the all important evidence has been rendered all but useless by totally inadequate recording and publication. Such is the state of affairs at Knossos and Vasiliki.

Although the palace sites suffered from these omissions at the beginning of the century, they have proved vast enough to leave ample work for more recent excavators. These have exercised great care in the excavation and recording of their sites, and we might expect the much needed stratified evidence to be produced from these excavations; but here a second circumstance intervenes. The evidence from Knossos and Phaistos indicates all too clearly that in building the palaces the Minoans removed considerable deposits belonging to the pre-palatial eras. It is not always easy to see where this has happened, and of course where it has been done it is impossible for us to gain any knowledge of what material was removed, unless it is found elsewhere on the site as a dump or spread. In this case however the material is of little or no value. Where there has been no levelling or terracing at a later date the Early Minoan strata have still often been badly disturbed by the foundations of the palace walls. These foundations were constructed, abandoned, repaired, re-used or torn out over a period of many centuries and the effect on the pre-palatial stratification was quite

Plate 1   A view of the plain of Mesara from Phaistos

Plate 2   The harbour site at Khrisoskalitissa

catastrophic. The palace sites are therefore very sparing in the evidence they offer for the period preceding the erection of the palaces themselves.

The other major type of site producing Early Minoan material is the burial chamber. This may be either a tholos or a rectangular ossuary, and at the start of the period perhaps a cave. The shape of the tomb matters little – all three were used for communal burial. Collective tombs inevitably result in the disturbance and confusion of the earliest burials in the tomb. Objects of two widely differing dates might end up alongside one another, and the situation is even worse when tombs have been re-used in a different era from that in which they were first employed. Some of the Mesara tombs for example had Roman burials immediately over or around them. The Mesara tombs are also good examples of the problem which often accompanies tomb deposits, namely looting.[1]

With these considerations in mind we should not be surprised to find that the chronology of the Early Minoan period is still very much a matter of controversy. The basis of the orthodox framework is that laid down by Evans which divided the Early Bronze Age into three periods called Early Minoan I, II, and III. The name Minoan was taken from the name of the legendary king of Knossos, Minos, and the Early Minoan period was itself part of a tripartite framework for the Cretan Bronze Age, being followed by the Middle and Late Minoan periods. Today these terms are often replaced by Prepalatial, Protopalatial, and Neopalatial respectively but Evans's basic system is widely accepted. There are two principal opponents of this system. The first serious objections were raised in 1933 by Nils Aaberg.[2] He argued that the Minoan culture arrived ready-made in Crete in MM II and that what we designate Early Minoan and MM I material is really the varying product of the differing Neolithic population of southern, eastern and northern Crete. In other words Aaberg absorbed EM I – III and MM Ia into the Neolithic, took that period down to the eighteenth century B.C., and utterly divorced the material which we label Early Minoan and Middle Minoan Ia from what emerged in MM II. Twenty years later Professor Levi published his own rejection of the Evans scheme.[3] His arguments are based on the evidence which he has found during his excavations at Phaistos. He argues that the

[1] Branigan *1968a*.   [2] Aaberg *1933*.
[3] Levi *1952*, *1953*, *1960* and *1963*.

Neolithic pottery shows close links with the Middle Minoan ceramics and that the 'Early Minoan' fabrics are always mixed in with Neolithic pottery. Levi therefore regards the 'Early Minoan' pottery types as short-lived transitional fabrics. The final result of Levi's theory is therefore not far removed from Aaberg's. There are certain pottery fabrics which we may, if we wish, call 'Early Minoan' but they do not represent any distinct or substantial period in Minoan history.

Caskey and Hutchinson however have both recently pointed out that Levi's interpretation of the evidence at Phaistos does not explain the abundance of Early Minoan material from other sites in Crete, and in particular it does not explain the large deposits of 'Early Minoan' material – found without any Neolithic associations – in the tholos tombs of the Mesara.[1] Many of these tombs are within an hour's walk of Phaistos. Furthermore Levi's interpretation of the evidence positively ignores the testimony of stratified deposits, scarce as such deposits may be. There are several sites of the Early Minoan period where stratification has been found and recorded, even though it may not be as simple or clear as we might wish. Before we discuss the pottery of the Early Minoan period and try to establish a chronological framework from it, it is best if we familiarize ourselves with the evidence from these sites.

The logical place to start is at Knossos, the site which produced the evidence on which Evans based his Early Minoan chronology. Evans's most impressive evidence in support of his scheme was published in 1904. In that year he published a drawing and a description of the stratification he had found beneath the west court[2] (fig. 2). Beneath deposits of MM II and MM III material Evans found four levels superimposed one above another. The uppermost contained pottery of the type he designated EM III, the next level contained dark-on-light pottery and other EM II fabrics, and the third included pottery closely akin to Neolithic fabrics and identified as EM I sherds. The lowest level was a thick stratum of Neolithic material. This stratification and the section which was drawn of it would appear to solve the problem at Knossos. Unfortunately however doubts have been voiced as to the accuracy of this report,[3] and certainly one cannot deny that the drawing published by Evans is little more than a schematic rendering of what he found.

---

[1] Caskey *1964* 31, 35; Hutchinson *1962* 137.
[2] Evans *1904* 18, fig. 7.   [3] Palmer *1963* xii.

In my opinion the probability that this section was drawn from memory some months after it was excavated does not invalidate the basic information it supplies. However, even if one sets aside this

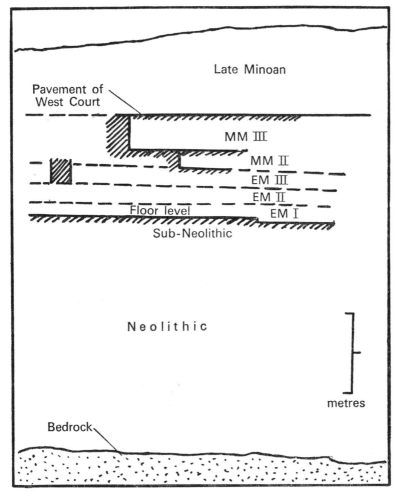

Figure 2 Sir Arthur Evans's section beneath the west court, Knossos

vital section, there were numerous other locations on the site at Knossos where Evans found a clear stratigraphical distinction between two of his Early Minoan sub-phases. This is not the place to quote these locations but they are all to be found in Pendlebury's *Guide to the Stratigraphical Museum at Knossos*, and I have personally had the opportunity to inspect the relevant material and can confirm the veracity of Pendlebury's guide in these instances.[1] From the correlation of these various deposits there emerges a picture which is in agreement with the scheme outlined by Evans, and with the section which he drew in the west court.

If we turn to other sites in Crete we find that in its broad outlines Evans's framework is confirmed. Eastern Crete has produced a number of stratified Early Minoan deposits. At Vasiliki Seager noted strata of EM II, EM III and MM Ia, and in fact found an important sub-division of EM II revealed very clearly indeed in the stratification. Mochlos produced evidence to prove the differentiation of EM I from EM II, whilst Pseira and Palaikastro yielded valuable stratification illustrating the distinction between EM II and EM III.[2] It should also be noted that the homogeneous deposits in some of the Mochlos tombs and an ossuary at Ta Ellenika are no less effective in their testimony to the reality of Evans's Early Minoan II and III.

In southern Crete stratified deposits of Early Minoan pottery are scarce, but Alexiou's excavations at Lebena have added considerably both to the corpus of complete vases of the period and to our list of stratified deposits.[3] The tholos designated Yerakambos IIa produced two clear strata. The lower contained EM II pottery and the level overlying it contained MM Ia fabrics. Another of the tombs had an EM I deposit overlain by one of EM II which in turn was covered by an EM II – MM Ia deposit. Many of the tholoi in the Mesara may once have contained stratified deposits, for Xanthoudides found two clear strata in tholos A at Platanos, the lower apparently containing material up to the beginning of EM III and the upper containing EM III and MM I pottery.[4]

It would seem therefore that in addition to the large amount of material which can be identified as Early Minoan, there are several sites where the Early Minoan period in one or more of its phases

---

[1] Pendlebury *1937*. The Managing Committee of the British School at Athens kindly gave permission to study this material.
[2] Seager *1912* tombs V and VI; Seager *1905* 211ff.; Seager *1912a* 17; Dawkins *1905* 272ff.
[3] Alexiou *1958, 1960*.
[4] Xanthoudides *1924* 89.

can be stratigraphically recognized. Furthermore the stratification from these sites when brought together and considered as a whole confirms that Evans's chronological scheme is basically correct. I say basically because there can be no doubt that in some of its details it is in error. In particular the various phases of the Early Minoan period seem to differ in duration in different parts of the island. It is for this reason that we must now examine in detail the various pottery fabrics of the Early Bronze Age and see how they relate to one another chronologically and geographically.

It is a great pity, I always think, that prehistoric pottery should be so completely involved with chronology, with the result that much of its beauty and originality escapes our notice. Yet the situation is inevitable and here we must be primarily concerned with using our Early Minoan pottery to construct a chronological framework. In a later chapter dealing with Early Minoan Art we shall return to the pottery and discuss its artistic merits.

There has been much confusion as to what pottery was being used in the Early Minoan I period, and this is not surprising for the change-over from a sub-Neolithic phase to an Early Bronze Age one was very often an irregular process. In Crete it seems likely that some parts of the island, particularly in the west, may have continued to use pottery fabrics which were essentially sub-Neolithic in character even though other areas had already moved into an Early Bronze Age ceramic phase. The situation at Knossos is not clear but some of the fabrics appearing in EM I deposits show continuity from the Neolithic period. We have already mentioned in the introductory chapter that at Phaistos Professor Levi has found a smooth transition from sub-Neolithic to Early Minoan. Nevertheless the beginning of the Cretan Early Bronze Age can be recognized by the appearance of three distinctive pottery fabrics. The pattern-burnished fabrics, called Pyrgos ware, would seem to be a further development of Neolithic ceramics, though not necessarily Minoan ones, whilst the dark-on-light and white-on-red pottery are clearly in a tradition new to the Aegean. Alongside these three new fabrics we find the Neolithic simple burnished pottery and domestic coarse wares continuing in use.

The pattern-burnished ware is called after the site of Pyrgos where an excellent group of vessels in this fabric was discovered by Xanthoudides.[1] The pattern takes the form of burnished lines either

[1] Xanthoudides *1918a*.

down or around the side of the vessel, with the horizontal burnishing most often found on the inside surface of chalices (pl. 3). The chalices are certainly the most striking form associated with this fabric and perhaps the most popular as well. They fall into two broad groups, the point of distinction being that one group has a short neck between the bowl and the pedestal. But this distinction would seem to have no chronological value, nor can we even suggest that the two types represent the work of different potteries. Within each group there are considerable variations of form, the bowl being usually convex-sided but occasionally straight or even concave-sided. Whether the bowl is high and narrow or broad and shallow, the effect is always pleasant.

In Crete the type predominates in the north of the island and certainly the finest specimens have come from that region. It occurs sporadically in the south however and Professor Levi believes that at Phaistos at least, this ware developed out of the sub-Neolithic fabrics, a belief shared by Hutchinson.[1] Unfortunately the deposits on which this view is based do not seem to be sealed deposits of the sub-Neolithic period and the theory, though attractive, cannot be proved. It must be admitted that there is some reason to relate this pattern-burnished pottery, and the chalice with which it is so closely associated, to contemporary pottery in western Anatolia and the Dodecanese. Pattern burnish appears in the Chalcolithic levels at Emporio in Chios and the chalice is known from several sites, the most recently excavated of which is Poliochni where the chalices turn up in the 'Blue' and 'Green' levels.[2] But attempts to draw precise parallels, and from them equally precise conclusions as to the origin of Pyrgos ware, are I feel rather pointless. It was long ago suggested that the pattern-burnish on many of the chalices is intended to imitate wood grain and that the chalices made of clay were therefore imitations of wooden forms.[3] The angular shapes of some of the short necks on the necked chalices would seem to confirm the wooden origin of the type. This being so we must face the fact that the originals from which our Pyrgos chalices were developed have long ago disappeared wherever they may have been. It does seem quite possible however that Professor Levi is right and that the Pyrgos ware is a native Cretan development, based on a series of wooden vessels of which we know nothing.

[1] Levi *1965*; Hutchinson *1962* 138.   [2] Bernabo-Brea *1964*.
[3] Hazzidakis *1913*.

Alongside the pattern-burnished chalices in the Pyrgos deposit were a large group of incised vessels, mainly bottles, which are called after the Cycladic site Pelos where similar pottery was found at the close of the nineteenth century.[1] This pottery varies considerably in fabric from one site to another and may be red, brown or grey in colour. The characteristic bottles are an interesting shape with a good globular body, and a long, narrow neck which is often quite angular. Low, flat pyxides are the other popular shape in this fabric. The decoration of these vessels is quite varied although it is confined to incisions. The bottles are often decorated all over the body with a herring-bone pattern, although some have long curving incised lines which run from neck to base. The pyxides are also subjected to the herring-bone pattern but are more often decorated with straight lines and zig-zags. Most of the bottles are fitted with suspension lugs.

This type of pottery predominates in northern Crete and would seem to be closely associated with the pattern-burnished Pyrgos ware. It occurs widely in the Aegean area and good examples of it have been found at Agios Kosmas on the mainland of Greece and just recently on Iasos.[2] There can be little doubt that Crete received this pottery from the Cyclades, and this may well explain why the fabric is so common in the north of the island. In the east and south of the island however it is found sporadically and in the south at least its popularity would seem to be usurped by two painted fabrics, the one dark on light, and the other light on dark.

The dark-on-light fabrics do not possess the same uniformity of fabrics and decoration that we have found in the pattern-burnished wares. The differences in the colour of the paint used, and the variety of fabrics were first noticed long ago, and Schachermeyr has recently suggested that two classes exist.[3] The earlier of these he calls 'Lebena' ware, after the vessels found at that site by Dr. Alexiou. These are painted with a reddish pigment. A secondary phase recognized by its brownish paint and rather plainer appearance retains the old 'label' of 'Agios Onouphrios' ware. But these subdivisions of the style are not easily supported by the archaeological evidence, and in fact there seem to be many more varieties of paint and fabric than just two. Paint occurs in red, pale brown, deep brown and black, and in two textures, thick flat and thin slightly

---

[1] Xanthoudides *1918a* (Pyrgos); Edgar *1897* (Pelos).
[2] Mylonas *1959*; Levi *1967a*.   [3] Schachermeyr *1962* 105.

glossy. The black paint appears mainly on coarse buff wares and occasionally on a somewhat finer fabric which is pale buff in colour The two brown paints occur mainly on hard buff fabrics but at Phaistos they are also found on fabric which is grey-brown in colour. The red paint is commonest on buff fabrics but occurs in several areas on a poorly-fired red fabric which is given a white or buff slip.

The decorative motifs employed by the manufacturers of these fabrics are completely linear with the exception of the black painted on coarse buff fabric which has broad festoons and sometimes solid circles. Variety of decor is restricted to vertical, horizontal, diagonal and diagonally cross-hatched lines (pl. 4). As far as we can tell, extensive use of cross-hatching is a later development. There seems to have been a period of simple decoration, apparently designed to emphasize the shape and form of the jugs and round-bottomed bowls, followed by a less pleasing tradition which uses cross-hatching and which largely divorces the painted motifs from the forms on which they appear. There appears to be some connection between this type of decoration and the introduction of a range of flat-bottomed vessels. Pendlebury first suggested that the round-bottomed vessels were the earlier, and although this criterion is certainly fallible in individual cases, it would seem to possess a general validity.

The round-bottomed vessels on which the geometric decoration occurs are very pleasing both in form and in their close affinity with the decoration itself. Jugs with high spouts and broad bases are amongst the best known and most pleasant shapes. Pyrgos, Kanli Kastelli and Lebena all produced these jugs along with two-handled cups, bowls, and narrow-necked jars with flaring rims.[1] At Phaistos some much larger vessels were recovered and although incomplete these almost certainly must have had flat bottoms despite being decorated in the earlier style. Apart from these practical shapes, the rich tombs at Lebena also provided us with some unusual vessels decorated in this Agios Onouphrios I style, including examples shaped like a bird and a gourd.

The flat-bottomed jugs which appear to have developed from the earliest of the 'schnabelkannen' are predominantly decorated with festoons of paint or a few diagonals and areas of cross-hatching. The latter often forms a double-axe or butterfly pattern on the front of

[1] Xanthoudides *1918a*; Alexiou *1951* and *1958*, *1960*.

the jug just on the waist. Small jugs with tripod feet are decorated with triangles of cross-hatching in a dark paint which fades to a washy red. 'Teapots' and two-handled open bowls are also subjected to the Agios Onouphrios II style of decoration.

In the east of the island there are several deposits which indicate the history of Agios Onouphrios ware in that region.[1] At Vasiliki it appeared in the stratum containing grey-ware, and was mainly of the black-painted variety, on flat-bottomed vessels. It was absent in the EM I rock shelter deposit at Gournia, but in shelter 1 at Agia Photia it was found alongside grey-incised ware and Vasiliki ware. The vessel from this deposit was a high-necked jar on a pedestal which looks very much like an adaptation of the 'Pelos' bottle. The only decoration was a large cross-hatched triangle in black/red on each side of the handles. A rather similar vessel turned up at Zakro. On Mochlos the Agios Onouphrios ware appears after grey-incised makes its debut but then co-exists with that ware. The conclusion to be drawn from the evidence of these eastern sites is that dark-on-light geometric was introduced to that region at a later date than elsewhere in the island. Indeed Agios Onouphrios I style does not appear in eastern Crete, and even Agios Onouphrios II never becomes popular.

Some of the finest Agios Onouphrios jugs and bowls come from the deposits of Pyrgos and Kanli Kastelli in northern Crete. Both deposits dated mainly to EM I. At Knossos however the Agios Onouphrios II style is the commonest and representative vessels were found in the 'Room of the Vats' deposit and one other of EM II date.[2] The earlier type does occur however and Sinclair Hood recently found an EM I well which contained typical Agios Onouphrios I jugs. Thus in northern Crete the Agios Onouphrios style appears from the start of EM I and continues into EM II. It also re-appears, in a form rather similar to some of the Agios Onouphrios II decoration, in MM I.

But northern Crete does not seem to be the first region to produce Agios Onouphrios ware. This honour must probably be accorded to the region of Mesara in the south. In many of the Mesara tholoi it must be confessed that only Agios Onouphrios II ware appears, although the two tholoi at Siva both contained the earlier style as

---

[1] Seager *1905* 213 (Vasiliki); Boyd-Hawes *1905* 183ff. (Agia Photia); Seager *1909* 278 (Mochlos).

[2] Evans *1903* 80, *1921* 71ff.

well.[1] At Lebena however the first style was found in a level alongside Pyrgos ware. This level overlay 'sub-Neolithic' vessels, whilst
it was itself overlaid by a mixed EM II/MM Ia stratum.[2] There
can thus be no doubt that the style was adopted in the Mesara in
EM I. This is clear also from discoveries at Phaistos. On this site
good deposits of fine Agios Onouphrios I ware have been found,
along with Pyrgos ware.[3] Very little of the Agios Onouphrios
pottery from Phaistos would seem to belong to the second style and
it looks very much as if style II was never popular there and that
style I continued in use for a long time. The appearance of white-on-
red and Vasiliki fabrics in some of these Agios Onouphrios I
deposits would seem to imply a long life for the style. Professor
Levi believes that at Phaistos there may actually have been the
development of the ware, by the sub-Neolithic inhabitants.[4] He
has found black-burnished pottery with red-ochre decoration and
other dark wares with incised linear decoration which he thinks
might have been the inspiration for the geometric dark-on-light
pottery. Neither examples are very convincing for the style of the
red-ochre decoration is a mixture of the curvilinear and rectilinear
such as we find on the mainland in the Late Neolithic and the
incised designs are distinguished by their tendency to cross-
hatching, which is not found in Agios Onouphrios I ware and which
is not particularly common on the Agios Onouphrios ware at Phaistos.
But Levi has also found sherds of buff ware with a burnished surface
on one side, and some of these even have decoration in Agios
Onouphrios I style. These sherds certainly suggest that Agios
Onouphrios ware at Phaistos has a close relationship with the sub-
Neolithic tradition.

It has always been argued that Agios Onouphrios ware was introduced from Anatolia and that it was just one of many signs of
Anatolian influxes in EM I. Pyrgos ware was another such sign,
but we have seen that there is some reason for doubting the validity
of its evidence and this would seem to be the case too with Agios
Onouphrios pottery. The main point of evidence is the shape of the
characteristic jug, which is a form widespread in western Anatolia.
But a good red/brown on buff tradition is absent in that area, and in
the Cyclades red-on-buff only appears in EC II. That the Cycladic
ware is in fact introduced later than Agios Onouphrios is also

[1] Parabeni *1913* 13ff.   [2] Hood *1960* 19.
[3] Pernier *1935* 130ff.; Levi *1963*.   [4] Levi *1965*.

suggested by the presence of a small, squat juglet of Cycladic manufacture alongside Agios Onouphrios II vessels at Marathokephalo.[1] The only plausible external source for the red-on-buff tradition is Syria-Palestine where a very similar style was in being at the end of the fourth millennium B.C. The spirit of the decoration is very similar to that of the Minoan ware and several of the shapes are too. Furthermore some of the preceding Chalcolithic pottery has affinities in Crete, particularly the so-called bird-vases. The author is inclined to see the development of Agios Onouphrios wares as taking place in Mesara, possibly under eastern influence, for which other evidence also exists.[2]

The 'white-on-red' ware has no site-name and having found that Schachermeyr's use of the term 'Lebena ware' is not really applicable to some of the Agios Onouphrios style vases, it would seem to be an ideal one to use in future for white-on-red ware. By far the most impressive group of vases in this fabric comes from the tombs of Lebena. These vases, and those discovered elsewhere, suggest that the Minoans regarded this style as an alternative to the Agios Onouphrios ware. This is not to say that it appears on all the same vase shapes. In fact very few shapes are found in both styles, and notably absent from the 'Lebena' range are the round-bottomed jugs so typical of Agios Onouphrios. But the shapes are predominantly round-bottomed and the type of decoration is identical with Agios Onouphrios ware (pl. 4). It is tempting to think of the 'Lebena' ware as being produced by different potteries to the Agios Onouphrios ware, but the almost complete lack of shapes common to both wares would suggest rather that they were produced by the same potters as two complementary wares. Strangely, the attractive Lebena ware seems never to have attained the great popularity achieved by Agios Onouphrios pottery.

Neither does it appear in such a large variety of fabrics. Its earliest manifestation is on a buff fabric with red slip on which the designs are finely painted in a slightly washy, yellow-white paint. In EM III and MM I a rather washy red slipped ware appears with designs painted on it in a thick cream coloured paint. This fabric is often used to produce low dishes and flat plates. A third variety, also used in EM III and MM I is a coarse red ware with the design painted direct on to the fabric in a chalky white paint. Only the earliest of these three varieties need concern us here and it is for that variety

[1] Zervos *1956* pl. 128.   [2] See p. 199.

alone that I propose the term 'Lebena ware'. Indeed there is no reason to suspect that the later varieties owe anything to the earlier ware, and this may well be the case with the early and late varieties of dark-on-light, only the former of which should perhaps be called Agios Onouphrios ware (I and II).

Lebena ware is unknown in the east of the island, where only the later varieties of white-on-red are found. This is what we found to be true of Agios Onouphrios I ware and this confirms our suspicions that Lebena ware is complementary to, and contemporary with, the early dark-on-light pottery. At Knossos small quantities of Lebena ware appeared in the deposit below the west court, in the level containing burnished, grey incised, and Agios Onouphrios wares.[1] Overlying this stratum was the EM III light-on-dark deposit. In the Room of the Vats the associations were similar. In the south of the island, at Phaistos, Lebena ware was found by Pernier in a deposit which contained Agios Onouphrios I ware but none of the burnished pottery. Similar associations were noticed in the southern tholos at the nearby site of Siva. On the other hand Lebena ware was also found at Marathokephalo with Agios Onouphrios II pottery.[2] These deposits would therefore suggest that in southern Crete Lebena pottery appears in EM I, at a time more or less contemporary with Agios Onouphrios I, but that it continues in use on some sites after the introduction of Agios Onouphrios II, at the start of EM II. The early introduction of the style, implied by its close ties with Agios Onouphrios I ware and the archaeological associations mentioned above, is confirmed absolutely by the stratification at Lebena where it occurs with Agios Onouphrios I ware above the 'sub-Neolithic' pottery and below the 'EM II MM Ia' level.[3]

The distinction between EM I and EM II is obviously not a particularly clear one, at least in terms of pottery. Lebena ware continues into EM II, and although the Agios Onouphrios I style would seem to be superseded in EM II by style II, the change from one style to another was presumably gradual and did not occur everywhere simultaneously. In particular some of the sites in the south of the island seem to have produced pottery of style I well into the EM II period. However, Pyrgos ware does not seem to

[1] Evans *1904* 18, 96.
[2] Pernier *1935* 130; Parabeni *1913* 13ff.; Xanthoudides *1918* 20.
[3] Hood *1960* 19.

last into EM II and in addition there are two new fabrics introduced
at the start of the period, fine grey ware and Vasiliki ware.

There has been a great deal of confusion over the date of fine grey
ware and it has often been regarded an EM I fabric. This is mainly
the result of confusion as to what constitutes fine grey ware. During
the EM I period there were grey fabrics – coarse grey ware with
incised decoration, part of the so-called 'Pelos' group of fabrics,
and burnished grey fabrics amongst the 'Pyrgos' wares. But the
fine grey ware of EM II is an altogether finer fabric with carefully
executed incised decoration and a slipped and often polished surface.
The common decorative elements are rows of diagonal incisions,
semi-circles, rings and dots. A large range of shapes occur in this
new fabric, of which the most characteristic is the pyxide. Many of
the spherical pyxides are quite dainty vessels which can nestle in the
palm of the hand. They feature short, straight necks and vertically
pierced suspension lugs. Usually only the area above the waist is
decorated. A number of examples found at Koumasa stood on three
legs. In shape some of the spherical pyxides are related to vessels
which appear in the painted fabrics, but the type of decoration is
surely derived from EM I incised ware. Other pyxides are cylindrical in form with circular lids. Amongst the other shapes which
appear in fine grey ware is a 'kernos' looking very much like a
condiment set.[1]

In eastern Crete the fine grey ware occurs at both Mochlos and
Vasiliki in association with burnished pottery, and a similar situation
is noted in shelters I and VI on the east promontory at Gournia.[2]
But these are mixed deposits and all three of the sites mentioned
have produced fine grey ware in association with Agios Onouphrios
II ware as well. At Pyrgos and Krasi in the north of the island grey
ware was found in deposits containing both pattern-burnished and
dark-on-light wares of styles I and II.[3] The Krasi deposit in
particular was very mixed, and the material from Pyrgos included a
little of EM IIa and EM III date as well as a great deal of EM I
pottery. In the south of the island, at Lebena, the fabric was again
found in an EM II level. Of particular significance perhaps is the
absence of the fine grey ware from a level at Phaistos which was

---

[1] Xanthoudides *1924* pl. I, p. 34.
[2] Seager *1909* 279ff. (Mochlos); Seager *1905* 211 (Vasiliki); Boyd-Hawes *1905*
181.
[3] Xanthoudides *1918a* 136ff.; Marinatos *1929* 102ff.

overlaid by a stratum containing Vasiliki and dark-on-light ware. The evidence from Lebena and Phaistos seems to indicate quite clearly that in the Mesara and the south at least, fine grey ware is an EM II fabric. Elsewhere the evidence is not so clear, but there is no reason to suppose that the fabric is introduced to the north and east of the island any earlier than to the south. Further evidence will no doubt become available, particularly with the publication of the EM II deposits from Knossos and Fornou Korifi, but the amount of fine grey ware found in deposits of any period is likely to be small for it never seems to have been produced in large quantities.

Considering the problems which still surround the chronological identity of grey ware the importance of Vasiliki ware as the determining ceramic characteristic of EM II is difficult to overestimate. The type-site, in eastern Crete, produced pottery of the Vasiliki style over a long period and in all the varieties of the fabric yet recognized.[1] Vasiliki ware is a mottled fabric produced by differential firing of the vessels, aided in its developed stages by painting the slip on, to form deliberate patterns. The characteristic shapes associated with Vasiliki ware are rather slim, flat-bottomed jugs, flat open dishes, spouted bowls, cups, goblets and teapots (pls 4 and 5). Both the jugs and the teapots often have a small pellet of clay either side of the spout, looking very much like eyes (pl. 4b).

Three different strata were found at Vasiliki, each of which showed a different stage of development in mottled ware. The earliest level contained sherds of grey ware and small quantities of Agios Onouphrios II pottery. In this level the pottery of Vasiliki type showed very simple mottling effects most of which were produced haphazardly. Some sherds however show signs of a deliberate attempt to control the pattern of the mottling. Among the pottery shapes represented was the 'teapot', which appears in the Mesara associated with the EM II variety of Agios Onouphrios ware. In the middle stratum at Vasiliki the deliberately patterned sherds were more numerous and the quality of patterns produced was much improved. Two new varieties of Vasiliki ware appeared in this level. One of them was not mottled at all but simply had the normal red slip which was highly polished. This is an attractive ware which appears elsewhere in the island during the course of EM. II The other new variety was not very numerous but of considerable

[1] Seager *1905* 211-18.

interest. It was characterized by white painted designs on the mottled wash, and would seem to foreshadow the white-on-dark EM III pottery which appears in the third stratum. In this stratum Vasiliki ware appears only in small quantities.

At Palaikastro, Gournia, and Pseira the Vasiliki ware would seem to have died out before EM III.[1] Fragments found in the EM III rubbish dump at Gournia are almost certainly residual. At Palaikastro a pure Vasiliki level was found beneath an EM III deposit in which mottled ware did not appear. An EM III level similarly overlay Vasiliki and Agios Onouphrios II sherds on Pseira. On Mochlos the Vasiliki ware was sandwiched between EM I pottery and an EM II white-on-dark deposit.[2] The sites which provide stratification would therefore all seem to tell the same story for the eastern region of the island. Vasiliki ware is widely adopted in EM IIa and on some sites is the only fine ware used during the latter half of EM II (EM IIb). But only at Vasiliki itself does the style survive until EM III.

Several vessels of Vasiliki ware were found in the Mesara tholoi but they were of course unstratified.[3] The shapes however are indicative of an EM. II date for these pieces and the association of Vasiliki pottery with Agios Onouphrios II ware at Marathokephalo would also suggest that, in the Mesara, Vasiliki ware is an EM II fabric. One deposit from Phaistos produced Vasiliki sherds in association with Agios Onouphrios II pottery. Levi recently reported a deposit in which Vasiliki ware was found alongside Pyrgos sherds and 'others of proto-cycladic type'. This seems to be a mixed or disturbed deposit and therefore of little chronological value.

The history of Vasiliki ware in the north of the island is not very clear, mainly because the fabric is not very common there. It was found however in the EM II level beneath the west court at Knossos, where it was accompanied by incised grey ware and Agios Onouphrios pottery of both styles I and II. As the deposit over this level was an EM III (white-on-dark) one it would seem that Vasiliki ware at Knossos was used in EM IIa and that an EM IIb period might not exist there. A few fragments of Vasiliki ware from Knossos carry a single band of white paint and these must be equated with the similar sherds and vessels already mentioned, found at

[1] Dawkins *1905* 272ff.; Boyd-Hawes *1908* 54; Seager *1912a* 17.
[2] Seager *1909* 278.
[3] Xanthoudides *1918* 20 (Marathokephalo); Pernier *1935* 130; Levi *1963*.

Vasiliki itself. The same late variety of Vasiliki ware occurs also on Pseira and at Agia Photia.[1] It would seem therefore that attempts at white-on-dark decoration were being made on several sites in the island, but it is difficult to decide which of these sites was the first to produce the true white-on-dark style which we call EM III. It was probably one of the eastern sites, for not only is the white-painted Vasiliki ware more common in the east, but EM III pottery is much favoured there and has a long and flourishing history in that region. Indeed until Hood's excavations, there was still much controversy as to whether or not a distinct EM III phase was experienced at Knossos.

The recognition of an EM III pottery style which was common to at least most of the island would seem to be beyond our capabilities at the moment though Zoes plausibly argues the existence of such a style. In particular we are faced with the problem of distinguishing what is EM III from what is MM Ia. Seager, Evans and Hall all believed that the pottery of these two phases could be told apart by the differing colour and texture of the paint which was used on each.[2] Evans describes the EM III paint at Knossos as 'dingy cream' and contrasts it to the 'new white' of the MM Ia ware. This is similar to Seager's conclusions regarding the paint used at Mochlos in EM III, which he describes as being 'yellowish white' with a smooth and hard finish. The MM Ia paint is said to be 'soft chalky' white. But this is the opposite of Hall's findings at Gournia. Here, the EM III paint was said to be white and chalky. It is important to note that the white paint on the Vasiliki sherds at Knossos is also rather chalky, and we must assume the white paint on the Vasiliki pottery to be ancestral to the white paint of the EM III white-on-dark style. The evidence of the paint is therefore confused and does not allow one to distinguish between pottery of the EM III and MM Ia phases.

The fabric of the EM III vessels at Gournia was buff in colour and well fired. This is true too of some of the sherds from Knossos which we might describe as EM III. The slip on these EM III sherds is brown/black and is not metallic in appearance. This is perhaps one of the distinctions between MM Ia and EM III

---

[1] Evans *1904* 18 (Knossos); Knossos white-painted Vasiliki sherds unpublished, seen by me in the Stratigraphical Museum; Seager *1905* 215 (Vasiliki); Seager *1912a* 17 (Pseira); Boyd-Hawes *1905* 183ff. (Agia Photia).

[2] Evans *1921* 111; Seager *1909* 278ff.; Hall in Boyd-Hawes *1908* 54.

Plate 3

a A chalice of 'Pyrgos' ware, EM I

b An EM III jug with polychrome decoration from Palaikastro

Plate 4

a An Agios Onouphrios jug (from the type site) and a 'Lebena' Ware bowl. EM I

b Vasiliki Ware bowl and teapot. EM II

pottery, for MM Ia sherds are usually covered with a rather washy and metallic-looking slip.

Further distinctions may be made according to the shapes of certain vessels. At Gournia in EM III most of the cups were of a conical type with round handles. Hole-mouthed jars, teapots, and lids were all quite numerous. The same shapes appear in the levels designated EM III at Vasiliki, Mochlos and Knossos.[1] In the MM Ia levels on these sites we find several differences. Flat handles are much more popular, narrow based cups with flaring sides appear, *Schnabelkannen* reappear in a rather 'heavier' form, and dipper cups develop rather angular profiles.

Finally distinctions between EM III and MM Ia pottery can be made on the basis of decorative motifs. Miss Hall examined and analysed the pottery from the EM III dumps and MM I deposits at Gournia very carefully.[2] Zoes has carried the study of EM III and MM Ia pottery much further and emphasized that its repertoire includes both rectilinear and curvilinear motifs. This pattern of development is what we should expect. The EM III pottery clearly owes something to the Agios Onouphrios ware which preceded it, but is developed into a very distinctive style which is given over to the curvilinear and the naturalistic.

On the basis of Zoes's work it seems that a close examination of sherds and vessels will often enable EM III pottery to be distinguished from MM Ia. But there would appear to be no one criterion on which such distinctions can be made, and it is quite clear that many sherds will defy classification. This is probably because they belong to a true transitional phase. Seager recorded evidence of such a phase on Pseira, and the links between EM III and MM Ia pottery are so close that we can hardly doubt that it existed. Nevertheless we should not think in terms of a single EM III/MM Ia period as Schachermeyr would have us do.[3] We shall see as we read through this book that the EM III period is not only a phase in its own right but quite an important one in many ways.

Nowhere is the distinction between EM III and MM Ia more clearly marked than at Gournia, facing out on to the Gulf of Mirabello. The pottery from the 'North Trench' is rarely paralleled

---

[1] Hall in Boyd-Hawes *1908* 57 (Gournia); Seager *1905* 218 (Vasiliki); Evans *1903* 94 (Knossos); Seager *1909* 278ff. (Mochlos).
[2] Hall *1907*, *1905*. [3] Schachermeyr *1964* Chapter 4.

in the deposits found beneath the floors of the houses in the town. The pottery from the former area also has very good analogies with the pottery found at Vasiliki overlying the EM IIb deposit. At Palaikastro Dawkins found an EM III level over a deposit of EM II date, and the existence of a clear EM III phase here was recently confirmed by Popham's discovery of another EM III deposit.[1]

As we said at the start of our discussion of EM III pottery, the existence of an EM III phase at Knossos has been a subject for controversy. Evans found several areas in which he, and later Pendlebury, were prepared to distinguish EM III pottery. But Sinclair Hood found that what Evans described as EM III pottery did not seem to exist at Knossos. In fact it looked as if Evans described EM III pottery in terms of eastern discoveries of the ware, and used rather different criteria to distinguish an EM III phase at Knossos. However, towards the end of his excavations at Knossos Hood found a deposit which was quite clearly EM III in date, representing a distinct phase of pottery development.[2] It is clear however that EM III at Knossos was a very short phase.

It is still not clear whether the south of the island ever underwent an EM III phase of pottery development. There is little evidence of such a phase at Phaistos for example, and Dr. Alexiou suggests that this phase was not experienced at all at Lebena. In tomb II at Lebena an undisturbed level was found to contain EM II and MM Ia pottery. In the adjoining chamber (IIa) a level of sand separated EM II and MM Ia levels. In none of the Lebena tombs did the excavator recognize any EM III pottery.[3] Certainly one suspects that in the Mesara and the surrounding areas some of the pottery styles were in use for very long periods of time. In particular a crude form of dark-on-light ware was probably in use continuously from EM II to MM Ia. Furthermore there are many sealstones, stone bowls, and pieces of metalwork which on typological or stylistic grounds one may ascribe to EM III. The almost complete absence of the light-on-dark pottery style of EM III in the Mesara should not necessarily be taken to indicate that the Mesara passed from an EM II phase of culture directly into the MM Ia phase. The EM III pottery style is principally associated with

---

[1] Hall *1907* (Gournia); Seager *1907* 111ff. (Vasiliki); Dawkins *1905* 273; Popham *1965*, 250 (Palaikastro).

[2] Hood *1962a* 295; also reported verbally at the Cretological Congress 1966.

[3] Alexiou *1960*.

eastern Crete. It appears in the north but not in large quantities and its scarcity in the south, where the people of the Mesara had developed a distinctive culture of their own, is therefore hardly surprising.

Before leaving our discussion of the 'skeleton' of the Early Minoan period and concerning ourselves with the 'flesh and blood', we might briefly try to give our relative chronology some absolute values. There are no published C. 14 dates for Early Minoan Crete at present so we are dependent on relating our various sub-divisions of the Early Minoan period to cultures elsewhere for which C. 14 dates are available. In addition there are also the historical dates which can be obtained by relating Egyptian and Minoan chronology.[1]

There is reason to think that EM I began earlier than the Early Helladic I period. Two C. 14 samples found in an early (but not the earliest) EH I level at Eutresis provided dates of 2,670 and 2,673 B.C. This being so, it seems entirely reasonable to suggest that EM I began some time during the period 2,900–2,800 B.C. It is difficult to date the start of EM II although again it seems likely that it began earlier than Early Helladic II. The earliest EH II floor at Eutresis went out of use c. 2,431 B.C. according to a C. 14 sample. In this case I would be inclined to date the beginning of EM II between 2,600–2,500 B.C. Late EH II levels at Lerna provided two C. 14 samples which gave dates of 2,283 B.C. and 2,102 B.C., whilst the destruction debris which marked the end of the period on this site produced an archaeomagnetic date of 2,200 B.C. This is probably contemporary with the end of EM II in Crete. Egyptian material found in Early Minoan deposits suggests that EM III begins about the time of the First Intermediate period, that is c. 2,170 B.C. Evidence of the same sort suggests that in general MM Ia may be taken to begin at the same time as the XIIth Dynasty, c. 1991. I say 'in general', as the duration of EM III seems to vary considerably in different parts of Crete. At Knossos MM Ia may have begun a little earlier than this, whilst in eastern Crete it may have begun considerably later. The dates I have suggested are intended as a broad guide, and I have made no attempt to justify them in detail; that would take up much time and space and involve a great many complicated issues. Our concern is with broader horizons.

[1] For the C. 14 dates see Kohler and Ralph *1961*; for discussions of relative chronology see Ehrich *1965*, Hutchinson *1948*, *1954*, Weinberg *1947*.

3   Domestic architecture and settlements

It seems likely that many of the inhabitants of Crete continued to live in caves throughout the Neolithic period, especially in the most mountainous regions of the island. At the close of the period there were certainly cave dwellers at Miamou in the Kophinos range south of the Mesara, at Trapeza in the plain of Lasithi, and at Koumaro in the far west of the island.[1] Other caves which may have been used for occupation are those at Zakro, Sphoungaras, and Agia Photia, all in the east of the island. The caves were in many ways not unsuited to the climatic conditions of the island. Cool in summer, they were quite capable of becoming warm and dry in the wet and sometimes bitterly cold winter. They afforded some degree of protection not only from the elements but also from the more troublesome members of society.

They were however a serious bar to any real progress towards civilization. They allowed no sense of society outside of the immediate family circle inhabiting the cave. Indeed, the usually remote situation of the caves encouraged their inhabitants to remain socially isolated and highly possessive of their individual freedom. The isolation and difficulty of access which the position of most of the caves presented also opposed the progress of crop cultivation. Crops would grow best in the areas of low, reasonably flat ground well away from the caves on the upper slopes of the hills. A good yield of grain was achieved only by long hours of close care and attention lavished on the plants. The cultivator needed to be close at hand both to care for and protect his crops. His only sure method of enforcing his claim to a plot in one of the all too small and all too few lowland areas was to be resident on it. He could confirm his ownership of the plot by building a permanent home there.

[1] Matz *1942* iff. (but there may have been *only* burials); Taramelli *1897*; Pendlebury *1936*.

There were too the benefits of social contact, and especially the benefits of commercial contacts, on a scale hitherto unknown. 'Commercial' may perhaps be a rather grand adjective to apply to the bartering activities in which Cretan sub-Neolithic men indulged. But the effects of this commerce were to be of considerable importance. Social progress and commercial progress were closely linked; where society existed and flourished, trade prospered likewise. And trade in turn led to wider contacts bringing not only immediate material benefits but new ideas, which bred new aspirations. The sudden flowering of village life which seems to take place at the start of the Early Bronze Age in Crete cannot be easily explained. The abandonment of a cave and the building of a house by an individual can be explained in terms of the greater flexibility and comfort which a house could offer. But the sudden emergence of village communities cannot. This can only be explained in terms of a growing social and commercial awareness, to which the sub-Neolithic population of Crete responded.

At Knossos there had been a village, of considerable size, ever since the Early Neolithic, but this seems to be the only such village in Crete until we reach the end of the Late Neolithic period when we find a Neolithic village at Phaistos. Elsewhere in the island we have only the odd remains of single farmsteads like those at Katsambas and Magasa.[1] The walls of the latter, at least in their lower courses, were built of large undressed limestone blocks. In plan the building is uninspiring, but nevertheless interesting as it seems that this type of house was common during the Early Bronze Age. The house is L-shaped (fig. 3) and this feature is utilized to offer some shelter to the doorway, which is tucked away in the corner of the right-angle. It leads into a small oblong room which presumably acted both as a vestibule and a store-room. In the far corner of this room, well away from the entrance, was the door into the main room. This we may safely assume to have served as living-room, dining-room, and bedroom. The room measures some thirty feet in length and is half as wide. Such a room could have housed a large family.

Large families would also seem to be indicated by the remains of the Late Neolithic village at Knossos[2] (fig. 3). Only one house plan was recovered completely, but the indications are that the

---

[1] Alexiou *1954* (Katsambas; Dawkins *1905* 260–8 (Magasa).
[2] Evans *1928* 1–21.

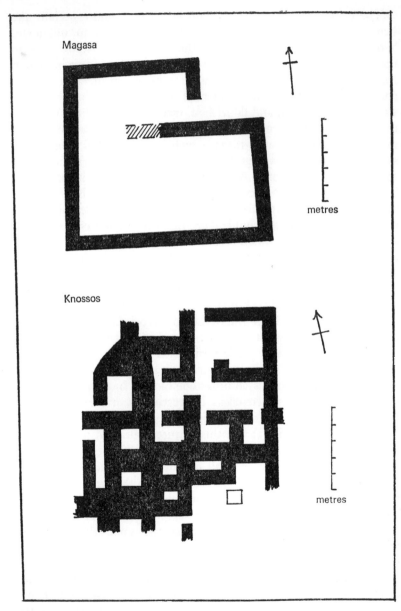

Magasa

metres

Knossos

metres

Figure 3 Late Neolithic houses

plans of the houses may have been quite standardized. In the plan made by Evans there seem to be the fragments of two other houses as well. All three houses are joined together to form a block, a system adopted in some areas of the mainland of Greece in the Early Bronze Age. House A, which is complete, features a living-room with a fixed hearth, a small area which might have been open to the sky in order to provide light, and an L-shaped arrangement of five small, almost square rooms along two sides of the 'courtyard'. The fragments of house B and the third house (which we label C) both reveal small rooms of a similar nature to those in house A and we may surmise that the plans of the three houses were basically the same. The social awareness of which we spoke earlier is clearly manifested in this architecture of the Late Neolithic at Knossos, and the emergence of a standard house plan testifies to the total acceptance of the idea of community life.

The technique of construction at Knossos differs little from that employed on the less sophisticated building at Magasa. Undressed limestone blocks again form the surviving lower courses of the walls, though in this case they rest on a bed of clay and pebbles. The upper part of the walls was almost certainly of packed clay, a method favoured throughout the Neolithic period at Knossos.

This discussion of Late Neolithic architecture is necessitated by the paucity of architectural remains dated to the first phase of the Early Bronze Age. There are only two sites which have produced remains of this period, Mochlos in the east, and Ellenais Amariou in the west.[1] The traces of buildings which Seager found at Mochlos belonged to rectangular houses, but more than this simple fact we do not know. At Ellenes Amariou there was clearly a small village of several houses, and here again as at Knossos in the Late Neolithic, the houses form blocks. A free standing building was also found. Details of this excavation have never been fully published, but we know that amongst the pottery the occupants were using was that pattern-burnished variety which we call 'Pyrgos' ware and which dates to the EM I period.

Many of the islanders may still have lived in caves, for the caves we mentioned earlier all contained some pottery which would seem to belong to the start of the Early Minoan period. The cave at Miamou was reasonably undisturbed in later times, and here there was a thick occupation deposit which clearly represented a

[1] Seager *1912* (Mochlos); Marinatos *1932* 177 (Ellenes).

prolonged use of the cave as a dwelling place. It seems possible that in the more mountainous areas small round huts may have been built. A clay vessel found by Alexiou at Lebena in the far south of

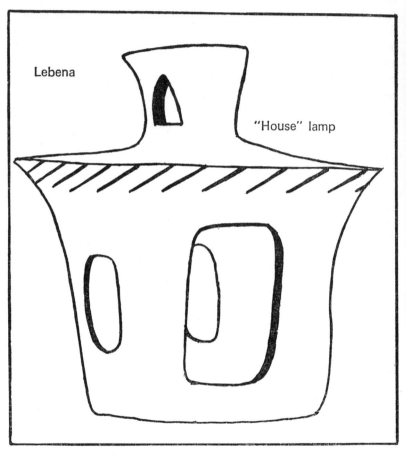

Figure 4 Lebena 'house' lamp

the island appears to represent such a dwelling (fig. 4). Windows and doorways are indicated by rectangular holes in the walls, and the knob in the centre of the roof we might interpret as the tied ends of thatching material. But huts such as this would probably leave very few traces for the archaeologist to find, and certainly none have yet been discovered.

The early houses found by Levi at Phaistos may perhaps belong to the Early Minoan I period.[1] The two vessels found actually on the floor both seem to be of the first Agios Onouphrios style, and the only sherds from the level over the floor which are not clearly of EM I date are a few of the Agios Onouphrios II style. Although the small area excavated has allowed us to uncover only a fragment of these houses the fragment is a revealing one. The walls are well built, with a facing of roughly worked stones (fig. 5). The core of the wall is of small stones and packing. A doorway less than 2′ wide leads from the outside, perhaps a courtyard, into a rectangular room. Inside, the floor is covered with red stucco. This is the earliest appearance of this form of decoration in Crete, and later we find it used on walls of the EM II period, at Vasiliki and Fournou Korifi. It is clear that another house was built on to this one, but it does not share one wall, such as is the practice at Knossos and at Agios Kosmas on the mainland. Instead there are two walls built flush with one another. To the same period as these houses, the fragment of a house discovered by Pernier would also seem to belong[2] (fig. 5). The construction however is not identical, but rather poorer in quality. The stones are again only roughly dressed and in this case the courses are not always bonded. The construction of corners would also seem to have presented the builder with problems, and we find that the corners of the building betray the use of a butt joint very clearly. Although the fragment of the plan is very small, it does reveal that this building probably consisted of at least three rooms. As the plan is shown by the excavators, we might postulate that it was slightly L-shaped, like some of the EH II houses at Zygouries.[3] However the writer has inspected these remains very closely (they are still exposed) and there appear to be traces of another wall to the west of them. This alters our whole conception of this building, for it would appear to indicate that there was a corridor in the building, not unlike those found in the mansion at Vasiliki. The poorer quality of building here, compared to the houses found by Levi, might well deter us from suggesting that this fragment is part of a sizeable mansion. However we should remember that in this case we have only the bottom one or two courses of the foundations, resting immediately on clay, and that we cannot make a fair assessment of the quality of the construction above floor

[1] Levi *1958* fig. 348, 167ff.   [2] Pernier *1935* pl. VI.
[3] Blegen *1928* figs 18, 19.

level. The house does stand on the highest point of the rocky hill of Phaistos and its position is therefore comparable to that of the mansions at Vasiliki and Fournou Korifi. Like these buildings this one would appear to have its corners orientated to the four cardinal points of the compass.

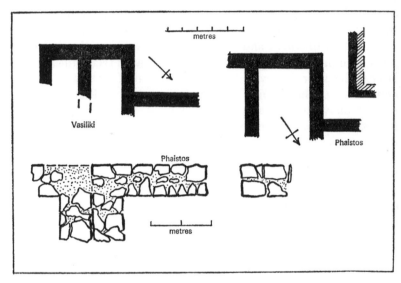

Figure 5 Early Minoan I/II houses

This building and the fragments found by Levi indicate that from the summit on which the former building stood, the settlement at Phaistos spread down the steep slope to the south-west for almost two hundred feet at least. It presumably spread over the area covered by the central court as well. We might therefore estimate that the EM I – II village of Phaistos covered about an acre, and that already it may have been grouped round the house of the village dignitary standing on the highest point of the hill.

Elsewhere in the island similar towns were probably growing up. At Knossos we know nothing of the houses which immediately succeeded the Late Neolithic block which we looked at earlier, although Sinclair Hood recently found and excavated a deep well which had been cut during the EM I period.[1] But in EM II, houses were certainly erected on the eastern slope of the site, looking out

[1] Hood *1960* 25.

over the stream. The fragments of these buildings which survive show them to have been quite well built rectangular houses of stone. Higher up the hill, any houses which stood there – and common sense tells us that there must have been some – were swept away when the palace was built in Middle Minoan I. Professor John Evans's excavation of the Neolithic remains beneath the central court has shown quite clearly just how much deposit must have been removed during the construction of the palace.

In the east of the island Priniatiko Pyrgos, Vasiliki and Palaikastro have yielded fragments of houses which would seem to have been constructed at the beginning of the Early Minoan II phase. Only short stretches of wall could be traced at Palaikastro where the EM II remains were overlaid by extensive remains of the Late Minoan town.[1] Even from such small fragments, it is apparent that there was at least one house of considerable size in early EM II. The walls are stone built, and seldom less than six feet thick. They thus compare favourably in size to the walls of the houses at Phaistos and Knossos. Walls of this thickness could easily have supported an upper storey, and we might at least expect them to belong to a building of substantial size and impressive plan. As far as the plan can be traced it meets our expectations (fig. 6). The building was at least 65 feet long and about 90 feet broad. As far as we can tell, the rooms were oblong. Whether in fact the northern 'room' on the plan was a single large room, or even part of the same building, we cannot be certain, but even the two rooms to the south of it measure about 13' and 16' wide, which is certainly large enough to suggest that the plan of the building was as substantial as its walls.

The fragment of an EM IIa building at Vasiliki can add nothing to what we know of the buildings of this period.[2] Like the Palaikastro house, its walls are well built of small stones, but in this case they are much narrower. The building itself would seem to be L shaped, with at least three rooms (fig. 5). Its main interest is that like the house found by Pernier at Phaistos, and the house we have just discussed at Palaikastro, this house has its corners orientated to the four cardinal points of the compass. This would therefore seem to be a regular practice by the EM II period. One might be tempted to see some deep ritual significance in this, but it is probably to be explained in terms of climate, and especially of sun and shade.

[1] Dawkins *1905* pl. X.   [2] Seager *1905* 209, fig. 1.

The importance of the house at Palaikastro and perhaps those on the hill-tops at Vasiliki and Phaistos, is that they provide us with evidence of some sort of substantial architecture in Crete in the early EM II period. But for these scattered traces we might well be overwhelmed by the late EM II building which succeeds the one we have already mentioned at Vasiliki, and we might arrive at some mistaken and misleading conclusions as to its significance.

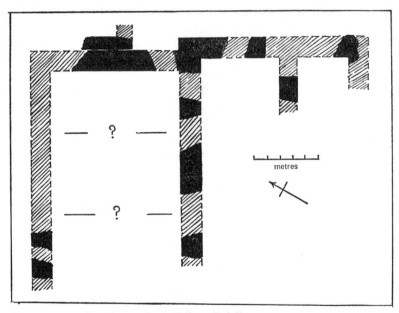

Figure 6 Early Minoan II building, Palaikastro

The EM IIb house at Vasiliki cannot be regarded as anything less than a mansion (fig. 7).[1] We still cannot be sure if in fact it is a single house, but the design would seem to hang together well enough. The building was never completely excavated and we have the plan of what appears to be two wings. Whether or not there were two further wings, thus forming a hollow square, we do not know. But Seager did find traces of paving in the space between the south-east and south-west wings and it does seem likely that this area was taken up with a courtyard. This being so it is certainly tempting to imagine another two wings, which would then completely surround the

[1] Seager *1905, 1907*; Boyd-Hawes *1908*.

court. The existing wings are very impressive. The south-western is about 100′ long and consists of a suite of oblong rooms fronting onto the court, and behind this suite two long narrow rooms, each with 3 or 4 small rooms attached. These rooms we might reasonably identify as storage rooms. The suite of rooms before them are presumably personal quarters, although two of the small chambers

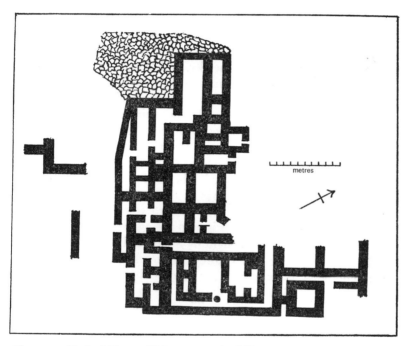

Figure 7   Early Minoan II house-on-the-hilltop at Vasiliki

at the northern end of the suite open directly on to the court and have no other means of exit or entrance. To the west of this wing is a paved courtyard of undetermined extent. The south-east wing of the building has been excavated to its total length perhaps, and this is a little over 100′. Unfortunately, its north-western limits were not found and so we have no idea of its precise relationship to the south-west wing. In this wing are the two largest rooms yet found in the building, at the extreme east end of the suite. It seems likely that these two rooms were originally shut off from the rooms immediately to the east of them (39–42), as the wall between 42 and

44 is a rather thick one, similar in size to that which separates the stores from the suite of quarters in the other wing. The size of rooms 44 and 45 would certainly suggest that they were part of the principal quarters, and their separation from the rooms 39–42 is perhaps best understood if we regard the latter as being used for the domestic services. The only evidence which might confirm this conjecture is the presence in 'room' 39 of a well.

It was a rock-cut well, with small notches cut into the side to enable a man to descend it, presumably to clean it out when necessary. Unfortunately Seager did not record the depth of it. The well most probably was open to the sky, and 'room' 39 is perhaps best seen as a small courtyard. In fact, light-well might be a better term, for it seems that there were almost certainly two storeys on this side of the building at least. In the main rooms of both wings, Seager found very deep deposits of clay and brick, as well as occupation material. In places this was up to seven feet deep. The clay had clearly come from the ceiling, and from the impressions in the clay and the remains of wooden beams found beneath it, we can be quite certain that the ceilings of the rooms were made of clay laid on a cane framework which in turn rested on large wooden beams. The depth of this debris, and the appearance of occupation material amongst it were thought by Seager to be evidence that both of the main wings had upper storeys. There is every reason to accept this hypothesis, especially in the case of the south-east wing, for the rooms of which we have the plan are in effect basement rooms to those in the south-west wing. The slope of the hill is responsible for this. Thus, if the court was to be bordered by rooms on its south-eastern side, then rooms 39–45 must have had upper storeys. No stairs have been found, but these would probably have been of wood. Wooden stairs might well have been erected in the long, narrow corridor 42.

Wood was certainly used for constructional purposes at Vasiliki. We have just mentioned the ceiling timbers and we find other timbers used in the construction of the walls. The techniques of construction are of considerable interest. The basic structure was of small stones held together by earth plaster bonded with straw. Bricks made of similarly bonded clay were used in the upper structure. Vertical, square-section timbers were placed in the walls and smaller, circular ones were built-in transversely. The walls were then covered with plaster which dried very hard and gave strength to walls which were otherwise hardly worthy of the plan of the building. The plaster was painted red to give a more finished appearance to the walls.

To the west of the south-west wing, and attached to it, were a series of small irregular rooms. These lay down the slope of the hill from the main suite of rooms. No clay ceiling material was found in these rooms and certainly they could never have supported an upper storey. If these rooms belong with the mansion they can only be regarded as store-rooms, and in fact some of them apparently contained broken storage jars. Alternatively we might see them as poor dwellings. Our understanding of them is in any case rather difficult to achieve for it seems clear that the walls are not all contemporary.

The House-on-the-Hill at Vasiliki is clearly of great importance. Apart from the newly excavated and as yet unpublished house (or houses?) at Fournou Korifi it is the only Early Minoan house of which there is a plan showing at least a large portion of the building. It does enable us to visualize the quality of Minoan building techniques at this time, and also perhaps to get some idea what the fragmentary EM II buildings at Phaistos and Palaikastro might have looked like in their entirety. Certainly the excavations and discoveries at Fournou Korifi have shown that the building at Vasiliki should not be regarded as a unique phenomenon – a fate which has befallen the House-of-the-Tiles discovered at Lerna by Caskey.

From the details so far published, it seems Dr. Warren has discovered a building which is in some ways similar to Seager's mansion at Vasiliki.[1] The architectural complex at Fournou Korifi contained over eighty rooms although some of these are presumably small corridors, cupboards, light wells and perhaps even industrial structures. In two places kitchens and adjacent magazines packed with pithoi were found. Most of the rooms seem to be small – about ten feet square – but their walls are well constructed of unworked blocks of stone, at least to a height of approximately five feet in places. Parts of the superstructure however were built of mud-brick, and the wall surfaces were plastered over and the plaster then painted in either red or brown. Surviving pieces of roofing plaster provided clear evidence that the plaster had been laid on to reeds, presumably supported on wooden beams. There are thus several

[1] Warren *1968*.

constructional similarities between this building and that at Vasiliki. Mud-brick superstructure, reed or cane supported roofing plaster, plastered and painted walls – these are features common to both buildings. On the other hand the use of quite large blocks of stone for wall building is in contrast to the small stones and mud which were used at Vasiliki. At Fournou Korifi there are also preserved staircases built of large flat slabs of stone, and, at the northern end of the site, a series of rooms arranged down the slope of the hill which there is reason to think were used for industrial purposes. There was too, a room used as a potter's workshop. At Vasiliki no such rooms were identified by Seager, and there is perhaps a real difference in the nature of the two buildings. Nevertheless I would rather see these industrial activities as a secondary feature of the building, not in chronological but in architectural terms. The building would seem to represent yet another wealthy man's mansion, and in this case we have some clue as to the source of his wealth. It would be a mistake to see Fournou Korifi as a primarily industrial settlement. The final publication of this important series of excavations should provide us with a great deal of information about the EM II period, and should allow us to arrive at a clear picture of what the building was meant to be.

The building at Fournou Korifi may perhaps be earlier in construction than the mansion at Vasiliki, at present we do not know. Even if it is no earlier, however, enough of the earlier buildings from Palaikastro and Phaistos survive to indicate that these two mansions were not without their Minoan precedents, even though those precedents may have been on a less lavish scale. Nevertheless the importance of the House-on-the-Hill at Vasiliki and the mansion at Fournou Korifi is not purely in their relationship to the earlier dwellings – or the scraps of them that remain. They are important because they link those scraps to the great palaces of the Middle Minoan period. In the two mansions we find many features which are incorporated into the palaces – the light-well, wall timbers, narrow corridors, long magazines, wall benches, off-set doorways, western and central courts, painted walls, wide, paved staircases, and inter-mural wells. Indeed the whole concept of these buildings is akin to that of the palaces. Not all of the features mentioned are found in both mansions, and certainly it would be wrong to claim that all of the features are necessarily direct ancestors of the details of palace architecture. But the concept of the palace is there and we can hardly doubt that important men occupied these houses. It is a pity we know nothing of the communities over which they exercised their authority.

We do know, however, that at Vasiliki the great house was burnt down in a savage fire, and that the subsequent occupation of the site belongs to a different phase of the Early Minoan culture. Something very similar happened to the impressive House-of-the-Tiles at Lerna in the Argolid. At the end of EH II it was burnt down, whilst still uncompleted it seems. The evidence at Lerna is repeated on several other sites in the Argolid[1] and we cannot doubt that the widespread destruction which brought EH II to a close in that part of the Greek mainland was the result of an influx of new peoples. But it does not seem possible to ascribe the destruction of the great mansion at Vasiliki to any such dramatic event. The destruction would seem to be entirely a local affair although the house at Fournou Korifi seems to have suffered a similar fate during EM II. The importance of the event to the well-being of the settlement at Vasiliki is clear however. Built up against the ruins of the mansion, Seager found a series of poorly built dwellings which he himself described as 'hovels'. The walls, built of small stones in clay, collapsed often and the remains found by Seager were a complicated mass of fragments, the residue of constant rebuildings. Amongst the decaying ruins of the mansion, only the well continued in use. Clearly the occupier of the mansion had in some way been the source of Vasiliki's well-being. We might surmise that he had been a merchant or perhaps the social and political leader of the whole district, thereby inevitably elevating the town in which he dwelt to the same position.

Pendlebury appears to have arrived at the conclusion that the 'hovels' at Vasiliki reflect a general lowering of architectural standards in EM III.[2] But he had very little evidence to go on, for very few remains of EM III buildings have been found. He suggested that some of the MM I buildings from Pseira, Mochlos and Tylissos may have been adaptations of earlier houses, and this would certainly seem to be the case at Tylissos.[3] The fragmentary nature of the remains at Tylissos do not enable us to say much about the architecture, but certain points do emerge from a study of them. In the south-western sector of the area excavated, fragments of two

---

[1] Caskey *1960*.   [2] Pendlebury *1939* 80.
[3] Pendlebury *1939* 80; Seager *1912a* 8 (Pseira); Hazzidakis*1921*, *1934* (Tylissos).

substantial buildings came to light, one apparently lying over the other (fig. 8). The smaller fragment has a corridor preserved with two well-constructed doorways at one end. It is not clear whether the other structure is a single building or two houses adjoining one another. I am inclined to favour the former solution. Both elements of this structure however would seem to have at least one long, narrow room. The houses are by no means small either. The

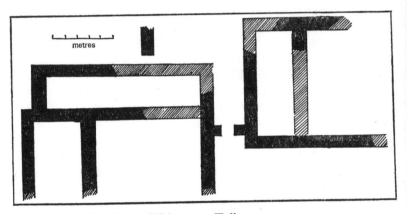

Figure 8   Early Minoan III house at Tylissos

western element is almost 60′ long, and the eastern survives to about 35′. If we have the full width of the latter, then it was about 35′ wide, and as far as we can tell, its long, narrow room was 30′ in length and some 10′ broad. It is hard to avoid the conclusion that here too we have buildings occupied by wealthy people, and if one sees the two elements as belonging to one building, as the writer does, then certainly the building assumes proportions comparable to that of the mansion at Vasiliki. The method of construction in no way invalidates these remarks. Whilst the core of the walls is made up of rubble, they are faced with dressed stones; they are fully worthy of the design.

Despite the lack of architectural remains of the EM III period, it would seem certain that there was not a decline in standards, nor any break in the general continuity of development. This is clear for two reasons. The fragmentary buildings at Tylissos suggest this not only in their construction and size but in the details of their plans. The off-set wall which we found on the Neolithic house at

Magasa, both the EM II buildings at Vasiliki, and the EM II house at Palaikastro, appears on the fragments of no less than four buildings at Tylissos. The narrow corridors, turning at right-angles, which we have seen in the EM II houses of Phaistos and Vasiliki, and the long, narrow rooms seen at Palaikastro as well, feature clearly in the Tylissos buildings. The continuity of the earlier tradition is there.

And we find these same simple features used again in what follows the architecture of EM III. In the houses of MM I the traditions are preserved, whilst in the palaces of the same period they are not only preserved but used freely. If evidence is needed for the continuity of a distinctive Minoan tradition of architecture during EM III it is surely provided by the palaces. We have already noted the remarkable similarities which exist between the palace architecture and that of the mansion at Vasiliki in EM IIb. It is inconceivable that between the two there is a period of architectural decline. The small, scrappy huts at Vasiliki must not be allowed to obscure the general continuity of development in EM III, to which the MM I palaces testify only too clearly.

If one accepts this continuity in architectural development as a fact, then the various theories which have been put forward in the past as to the origins of the Minoan palaces and their architecture become an irrelevance. The most favoured source of inspiration has always been western Asia, although Mellaart and Lloyd have suggested that close parallels exist between the Minoan palaces and the one which they have recently excavated at Beycesultan in western Anatolia.[1] But all the Asian and Anatolian parallels that can be considered provide only broad similarities of design. Closer similarities exist between Minoan and Near Eastern techniques, but this of course is what we might expect. We know that Crete was in constant contact with western Asia and that such techniques could easily be adopted from there, and we must not forget that Cretan architects were building houses and palaces for much the same sort of climate as those areas spread around the eastern end of the Mediterranean. Similarities of technique, and even of design, must therefore be expected. But the differences between Minoan and Near Eastern palaces are far more striking than the similarities.

We could point to many particular points of design which are characteristic of Minoan palaces and found but rarely in palace

[1] Lloyd and Mellaart *1955, 1956, 1957, 1960, 1962*.

architecture in western Asia. The alternation of pier and column, the lustral chamber, the light-well, the 'inverted' column, – these are features of Minoan architecture for which it is very hard to find parallels, and there are many others.[1] But above all the whole conception of a Minoan palace is totally different from that of palatial architecture anywhere else in the Bronze Age. A Minoan palace had as its focal point the central court; the palace was laid out around this court and grew from the centre outwards. Thus we find that the architect was not obliged to fit his scheme into a predetermined space or shape. He was free to let his imagination and his building wander at will.

This is what happened, within the limits of certain broad principles which would seem to have applied to palace architecture. These principles are not at once apparent, and for this reason several authorities have come to the mistaken conclusion that the palaces are the rambling, illogical end result of a slow and unplanned process of development.[2] But such conclusions are both understandable and excusable, for the surviving remains of the palaces are very misleading in the impression which they create. Professor Graham has only recently reminded us that what survives, particularly at Knossos, is for the most part the service quarters of the palaces.[3] What we see today is, in effect, the basement; the main living quarters and reception rooms were upstairs. When one remembers the complexity of the functions which any one Minoan palace had to fulfil, – as palace, stores, workshops, offices and shrines – then the maze of rooms which we find in the 'basement' should not surprise us nor should it be allowed to obscure our understanding of the way in which the Minoan architects worked.

Here of course we are only concerned with the first palace buildings, which were erected in MM I, and it must be admitted that a discussion of MM I palace architecture has severe limitations imposed on it. The palaces were of course occupied for a period of 500 years and during this time suffered at least one major destruction and several minor ones. The remains which survive are therefore mainly much later than MM I in date and we can produce no plan of an MM I palace. Fortunately the palace at Mallia has a well preserved ground plan which as far as we can tell preserves much of the original layout of the MM I palace and from this plan we can

[1] Graham *1962*, 233.   [2] e.g. Zervos *1956* 497; Lawrence *1900*, 34, 41, 291.
[3] Graham *1962* 235.

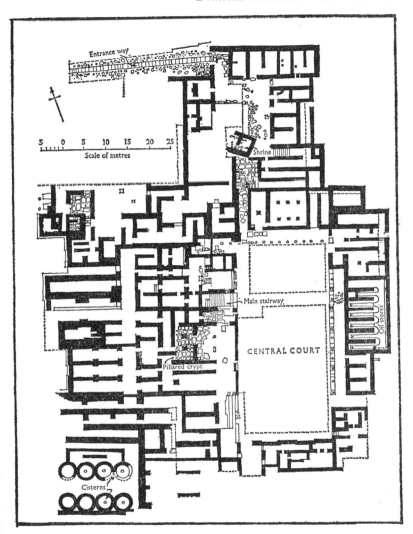

Figure 9 The palace at Mallia. *From R. W. Hutchinson, 'Historic Crete',* *1962*

perhaps obtain some understanding of the first Minoan palaces (fig. 9).[1]

The dominating feature of Mallia, as with the other palaces, is of

[1] On this see Hutchinson *1962* 187.

course the central court, and if we are to understand the design of the palace it is from here that we must start, as almost certainly did the architect and builders responsible for the palace's construction. It measures 80′ x 170′, a measurement repeated almost exactly at Knossos and Phaistos. All three of the palaces have their central courts orientated north-south. There can be no doubt that these courts were the focus point of everyday life in the palaces as well as the situation of the various rituals observed at the appropriate times in the year. Despite a long-standing controversy on the question, there seems to be no alternative situation for the bull-games either. Professor Graham has put forward some positive arguments which point to the same conclusion.[1]

To the west of the court at Mallia we find a series of rooms including a 'pillar crypt' which would also seem to be associated with ritual practices. Behind these, and separated from them by a long corridor, are a series of store-rooms, mostly of the long, narrow type which is best seen at Knossos. In the south-west corner of the palace are the eight circular towers, which may be cisterns or granaries. Next to them are three suites of rooms, one of which Graham suggests might be for the use of visitors. But they are rather small rooms and they might perhaps be best interpreted as offices concerned with the everyday running of the palace. Across a broad paved passageway from the rooms just mentioned, and immediately south of the court, is a suite of rooms which would appear much better fitted to fulfil the function of guest rooms. A vestibule, one or two reception rooms, and two small chambers which might be bedrooms, make this a suite not unsuited to the purposes of hospitality. However, it does seem unlikely that the guests would be expected to occupy the rooms on the ground floor, whilst the hosts remained in their lighter, more airy and almost certainly more luxurious rooms on the upper floors.

East of the court, behind a colonnade, were two groups of magazines, one of which is again composed entirely of identical long, narrow rooms. On the immediate north of the central court we find a hall with six piers, entered through a vestibule (pl. 7). It seems reasonable to associate this group of rooms with ritual usage as well, but Graham is probably correct in suggesting that a large hall, probably for banquets, was situated over these rooms and reached by the stairs to the right and those to the rear of the rooms

[1] Graham *1962* 73–83.

in question.[1] A banquet hall here would certainly be well situated not only for its fine view over the central court but because it is close to the service rooms which lie just to the north. More stores and some workshops are also situated at this northern extreme of the palace.

There remains just the small suite of rooms in the north-west corner. These have been identified, by Platon,[2] as a royal residential suite. Two small halls, a bathroom, and a pillared portico are the features which enable this identification to be made. This is clearly only a minor suite and the major private suites were undoubtedly upstairs.

The foregoing is only a very brief outline of the palace of Mallia, but it is of course an outline which we need here. As we have said, so little survives of the first palaces that to describe any of the palace plans in detail would be misleading. From this outline we may perhaps gather some understanding of Minoan palace architecture and architects. There would indeed seem to be few principles to palace architecture. The central court was clearly the focus of life within the palace and the palace would seem to have been built up around it. Usually, the main entrance to the palace is to be found on the west side. But having said this much we have exhausted the list of possible architectural principles employed by the palace builders.

Yet these two broad rules are quite insufficient to explain the remarkable similarity which exists between the three great palaces. It used to be thought that this was due to adherence to another principle, that of building each palace as a complex of separate insulae, but it is clear from the palaces of Phaistos and Mallia that there was no such principle and that the palaces were, from the first, coherent units.[3] We must therefore look elsewhere for an explanation of the similarities between the palaces, and the author believes we should look in the direction of Minoan attitudes rather than architectural principles. We have tried, and failed, to find a substantial set of rules (or principles) in accordance with which the palaces were constructed. I suggest that it is from this negative point that we might begin to look in our new direction.

The absence of a set of principles implies that the palace architects possessed considerable freedom of design. They would have been limited only by the attitudes of their clients and themselves.

[1] Graham *1962* 126.   [2] Platon *1947* 635–6.
[3] Graham *1962* 230; Hutchinson *1962* 164, 184.

Indeed we have already noted that the one principle of palace construction that was recognized, that the palace should be built around a central court (which was laid out first), gave the Minoan architect almost unlimited scope in the size and shape of his building. Thus we find that the common appearance of an indented surface on the outer walls of the palaces is not the result of the application of a certain principle, but rather the result of an attitude. The Minoan, building from the central court outwards, regarded the outside walls of the palace as essentially rear walls to each particular group of rooms or magazines. He did not conceive of a single outside wall which confined his building within a certain size and shape. Similarly the Minoans were lovers of light, colour and luxury, and so we find the palaces are constructed with light-wells and baths in abundance, the walls are decorated with fine frescoes and a variety of colourful building materials is used. The natural Minoan inclination towards spacious buildings is evident in the spreading quarters of the palaces, but is surely also to be seen in the plentiful use of pier and column within the buildings to replace the solid wall. Even in the (mainly) service quarters of the ground floor we find an air of spaciousness created by the use of pier and column.

Contrary to the opinions of some scholars, the Minoans did not allow either their freedom from architectural rules or their various predilections – for space, light, luxury – to become the predominant considerations in the design of the palaces. As we have said earlier, the palaces had to fulfil a multiplicity of roles and for this reason we find that the palaces are, above all else, functional. Professor Graham has argued this point at length in his book on palace architecture and we need not repeat his arguments here.[1] He has convincingly shown that the various quarters of the palace were planned, both in detail and in their relationship to each other. It is indeed for this reason that the service quarters, which are mainly what we see on our plans of the palaces, present such a complicated and not particularly pleasant impression of the palaces. It would seem true to say that the Minoan palaces which appear in MM I are functional in design but aesthetic in constructional detail.

The main walls of the palaces were constructed on very sturdy foundations, usually of huge blocks of stone. Above the foundations the rubble core was faced with ashlar masonry and given further strength – and resilience – by the insertion of wooden beams at

[1] Graham *1962* 235.

regular intervals. The minor walls however were of little better construction than those found in the private houses, being built of semi-dressed stones bonded with clay. But the lavish use of plaster hid their lack of finish and also provided spacious surfaces on which both colour and decoration could be brought into the rooms and corridors of the building.

The attraction of the palace interiors however is not entirely due to the painted wall plaster, indeed we know nothing of the wall decoration when the palaces were first constructed. Just as attractive as the frescoes are the several architectural elements which appear in the palaces, though here again we cannot be certain that all of them were introduced in the palaces of MM I. The light-well of course we have already found, in basic form, in the House-on-the-Hill at Vasiliki, but in the palaces it is used in a much more sophisticated and even subtle manner. In particular it is used in conjunction with columns and even columned flights of stairs. The resulting variations of light and shade must in themselves have provided an attractive 'decoration' of the walls and floors.

Such light-wells must also have contributed to the atmosphere of spaciousness which pervades the palaces. So too do several other features of the palace architecture, and in particular the recurrent use of the column and the pillar, sometimes in alternation, in place of the solid wall. In the upper floors both verandahs and large open windows added considerably to the illumination and ventilation of the private and official suites which were found there. Neither were the upper floors reached by means of narrow, darkened staircases but by broad flights of well-paved stairs whose walls were just as brightly decorated as those of the living-rooms, and as we have noted earlier, these broad stairways were not infrequently associated with the light-wells. Some of these palatial features we find repeated in the best of the private houses of the period, and there are perhaps traces of palatial influence to be noted even amongst the contemporary architecture in the villages.

Beneath the west court in the Palace of Knossos Pendlebury excavated some interesting private houses of the MM I period, although he could not recover their complete plan as they were overlaid by later storage pits.[1] It was clear however that he had found the basements of the houses concerned, for not only did he find steps leading down into them, but in the house beneath kouloura 3

[1] Pendlebury *1932* 53ff.

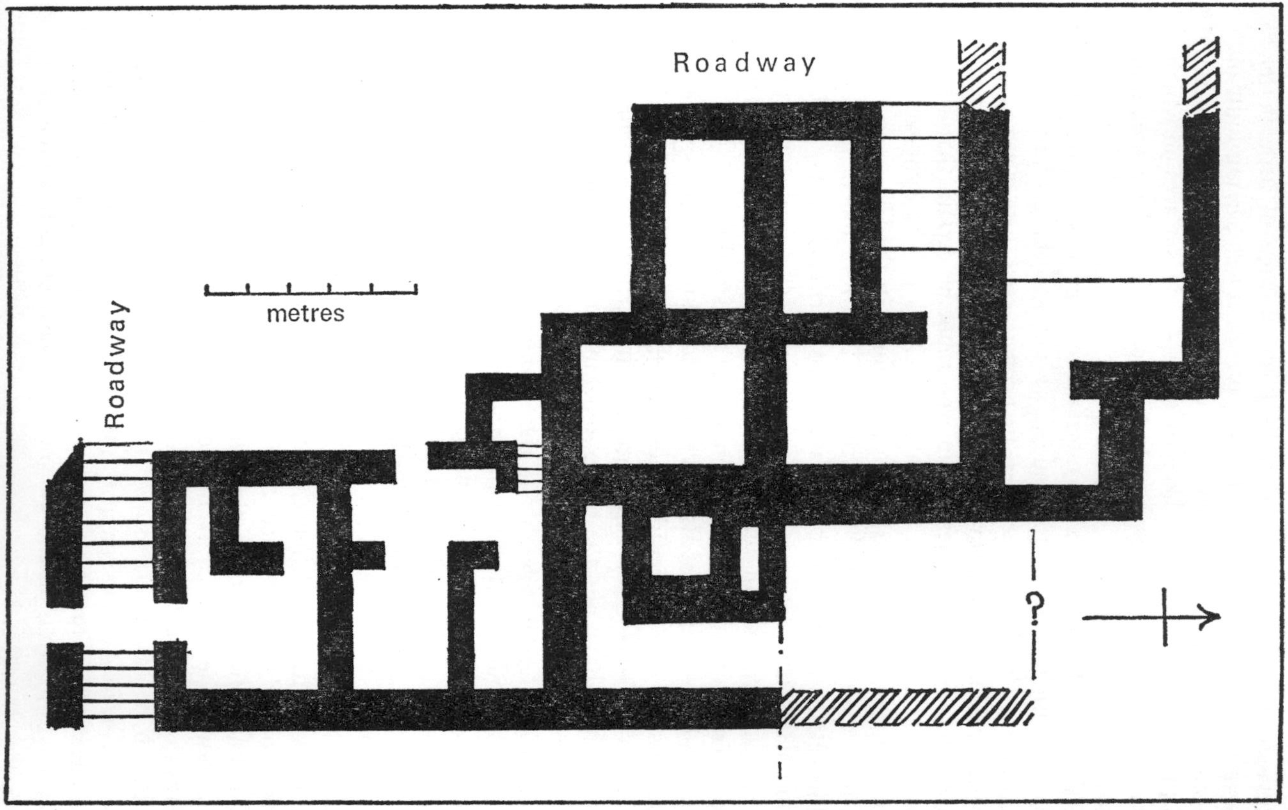

Figure 10 House 'A' (MM Ia), Vasiliki

he actually found part of the ground floor level (rooms 5–8). The basements were clearly used as storage rooms. Both houses had red plastered floors and red and white plaster on the walls. Plastered walls and floors were not new to Minoan domestic architecture, they appear in EM II at Vasiliki, Fournou Korifi and Phaistos. Similarly the low benches built against the wall and plastered curbs forming corner bins are two features previously incorporated in houses of the EM II–III period (although the idea of corner bins appeared at Knossos in Early Neolithic II!). There is one notable innovation however; the houses found in the west court have drains which run outside the walls. The construction of such drains is a useful pointer to the further emergence of an acceptance of urban life and its communal obligations.

Urban life was by now of course well established in Crete. Apart from the palace sites, places such as Vasiliki and Pseira were now flourishing towns rather than villages. At Vasiliki we find houses which would seem to be direct descendants of the EM II 'House-on-the-Hill', although they cannot match that building for size. Only one of the houses was excavated completely enough to allow an understanding of its design, this being house 'A' (fig. 10).[1]

This house was situated it seems on the corner between two streets, one running along the side of the hill and the other down the slope in a series of steps. The north-east and south-west corners of the building had unfortunately been destroyed and the plan we have is thus unbalanced and represents only about half of the original building. House 'A' faced east and was built into the slope. It had one narrow doorway giving on to the stepped street and one suspects another may have given on to the other street. Fragments of pithoi discovered in the area of the south doorway perhaps suggest that the store-rooms were situated in this part of the house. The situation of the private chambers is difficult to assess, although the missing north-east corner would seem to be an ideal situation with a pleasant view across the valley towards Monasterakiou. It is likely that the living quarters were on an upper floor, for a mass of fallen clay plaster found in room 16 contained pots and lamps which must surely have fallen from above. These particular vessels are said to be very numerous and all the examples to be of the same shape and design. For this reason the excavator (Seager) very reasonably suggested that this building may have been a shop as well as a

[1] Seager *1907* 124ff.

house. Room 12 produced similar evidence – masses of small red and black cups. The interest of this building is in its basic similarity to the EM II House-on-the-Hill. Not only does it take advantage of the slope in the same way, but we find the stores similarly situated and the design of the rooms on the upper part of the slope almost repeated (cf. fig. 7). The most marked difference is the improvement in the regularity of design and construction, improvements which vitally affected the development of palatial architecture.

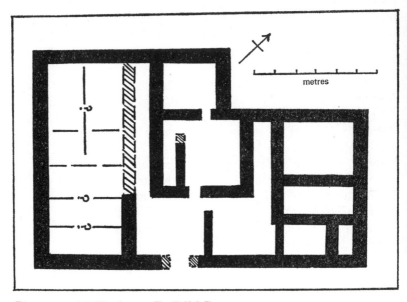

Figure 11   Mallia, house Zc (MM I)

In size, house 'A' at Vasiliki was comparable to some of the contemporary houses at Mallia. The plans of these buildings during MM I are unfortunately not certain, due to later alterations and repairs. But from what we know of houses such as Mallia Zc,[1] it is clear that these residences must have been erected for people of a similar status to those at Vasiliki (fig. 11). One feature which does not appear at Vasiliki however is the small open courtyard inside the main entrance, and one wonders whether the appearance of this feature in the private houses at Mallia is in fact an indication of the influence of palace architecture on that of the private residence.

[1] Deshayes *1959* pl. IV.

The small court inside the entrance to house Zc appears to fulfil a similar function and occupy a similar place to that of the west courts in the palaces. The preserved parts of house Zc apparently represent the living quarters of the building and feature three large rooms and three or four smaller ones, divided into two suites by a corridor which leads from a large vestibule to the north of the courtyard. To the south of the courtyard another corridor separates the central suite of living-rooms from a third block of rooms which are all but destroyed. We may postulate that this block included the magazines or store-rooms, perhaps in the south-east corner as in the contemporary house at Vasiliki. In this case the kitchen and other domestic rooms were probably to be found in this block, near to the magazines.

At Phaistos too the private houses show signs of palatial influence in their design. The block of magazines recently found to the west of the west court and separated from it by a roadway, are much nearer in design to the palatial magazines than those of the EM II and III periods (fig. 12). The single entrance giving on to a row of magazines is particularly reminiscent of the minor magazines in the palaces, like those in the north-east quarter at Knossos, the eastern block at Mallia, and at Phaistos itself in the north-east quarter. Presumably the spacious arrangement of the principal magazines in the palaces, provided with their own corridor off of which each store-room opened, was neither a practical proposition nor a functional necessity in the ordinary town house of MM I.

It is tempting to see the influence of palatial architecture in a detail of the village houses at Kalathiana.[1] Here we find that the walls have indented surfaces, such as are common features of the outside walls of the palaces. In the palaces this pecularity is explained by the principle of designing the palace outwards from the central court, but this principle does not apply of course to the houses in the MM I village at Kalathiana where the indented walls have no apparent explanation either in terms of function or design. They can only be explained it seems, as imitations of palatial walls and in particular those at the nearby palace of Phaistos.

Xanthoudides excavated some ten houses in the village at Kalathiana but never seems to have published a plan of them. All we know is that all the buildings were square in plan, and divided into several rooms of differing size. Like the tholos tomb nearby, the

[1] Xanthoudides *1924* 49.

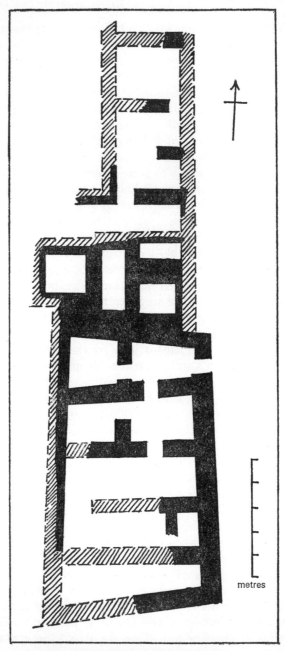

Figure 12 MM I houses at Phaistos

appearance of the buildings is perhaps rather deceptive, for they are not built of well-dressed stones, as they appear to be, but of the local stone which fortunately breaks up into regularly shaped blocks. The normal house wall construction of this period was in fact little better than that of the EM II and III periods, as the walls of houses at Vasiliki and on Pseira indicate all too clearly. Even the houses at Mallia had walls built with very small stones in a rather crude manner. Thus the tremendous advances in design, represented particularly by the palaces, were not really paralleled by advances in construction techniques, except perhaps within certain parts of the palaces themselves.

Apart from the houses at Kalathiana, Xanthoudides noted the traces of MM I–II villages at both Koumasa and Christos. In the east of the island Seager excavated sections of the MM I towns at Vasiliki and on Pseira.[1] The almost continuous excavations on each of the three main palace sites have also produced some evidence for the towns which surrounded the great palaces. Yet despite this we know virtually nothing of what an MM I village or town looked like, or how it was arranged. One is perhaps tempted to think in terms of the palace standing on the highest point of the site and being surrounded by a collection of private houses which were built with no thought of a coherent and practical over-all plan for the settlement as a whole. Even at Phaistos, however, where the palace overlooks a sheer drop on two sides, it does not occupy the highest point on the hill. Similarly the palace of Knossos was surrounded it seems by houses which not only lay around the foot of the 'tell' but also on the slope of the hill above the palace. Mallia of course is on a low-lying stretch of land close to the sea. On the other hand it cannot be denied that, as far as we can tell from the fragmentary remains recovered, there was no town planning. The private houses just seem to cluster around the palaces on whatever land was available and practical for building. Nevertheless signs of communal planning are to be seen at Knossos. We have already mentioned the drains built outside the houses beneath the west court, and east of the palace a viaduct was constructed across the stream of the Vychia. At Phaistos Professor Levi has recently found a well-metalled road which winds up the southern slope of the hill, probably coming from the houses he excavated at the very bottom of the slope.[2] This too hints at some measure of

[1] Seager *1907* 124ff. (Vasiliki); *1912a* 8ff.   [2] Levi *1967* fig. 31.

communal effort, other than that involved in the construction of the palace.

On one side, the road at Phaistos was bounded by a wall of modest proportions. This might be construed as a defensive barrier, though it could never have been an effective one. With this possible exception, the Minoan palaces and the towns around them were never, it seems, surrounded by defensive walls. The settlements of Bronze Age Crete seem, from the first, to be entirely at their ease and thriving on a sense of security not noted elsewhere in the Aegean world. Sinclair Hood believes there may have been a general move to the higher hills during the Early Bronze Age, and in this context he cites two examples of Early Minoan settlements he discovered in the region of Rethymno, both of which are situated on high hills.[1] One of them, Melidhoni, is especially interesting as it seems to replace a Late Neolithic site on lower ground and then, in turn, to be replaced by a Middle Bronze Age re-occupation of the lower site. But it seems wiser to explain examples such as this in terms of local circumstances rather than trends which affected whole regions of the island. No such large scale and widespread trends can be traced, although the distribution maps of sites for each of the main sub-divisions of the Early Bronze Age period do show one or two interesting developments in the pattern of settlement (fig. 13).

The maps are based on material discovered both in field surveys and in excavation and are divided into the three most easily defined chronological sub-divisions of the Early Bronze Age in Crete. Thus it is hoped that sites known only from surface finds have still been placed on the correct maps, for characteristic pottery fabrics enable each of these three main sub-divisions to be recognized with a reasonable degree of accuracy. The map of sub-Neolithic/EM I sites may perhaps obscure one important point – namely the relative scarcity of sub-Neolithic sites in the Mesara and the south. Whilst other regions of the island seem to have seen a slow transition from the Neolithic to the Early Bronze Age, in the Mesara and south the change-over seems to have been much more rapid. This might be indicative of a limited immigration into southern Crete by peoples who already knew the secrets of metallurgy. Certainly the Mesara produces a very distinctive culture of its own, even though it is clearly related to the cultures of the north and east.

The apparent 'depopulation' of the western end of the island

[1] Hood et al. *1964* 51.

Plate 5

a Vasiliki Ware jugs with 'seams' marked by incisions. EM II

b EM III jug and teapot

Plate 6

a Barbotine jugs with polychrome decoration, MM I

b MM Ia cups from Palaikastro

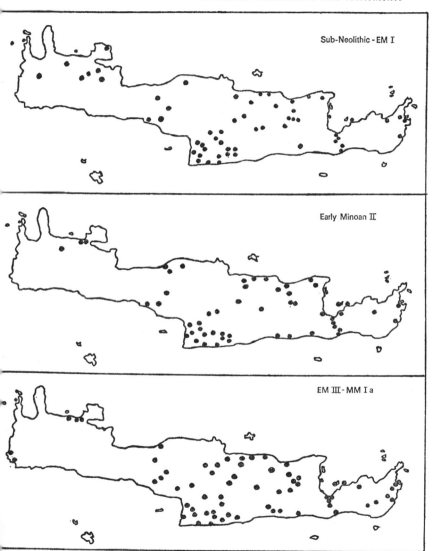

Distribution of Early Bronze Age sites

during EM II (three sites compared to seven previously) may perhaps be explained by assuming a slow ceramic development in the west, although the Vasiliki ware from Khania clearly indicates that typical EM II pottery was used in this region. Nowhere is there any indication of a startling increase in population or a major population drift during the prosperous second phase of the Early Bronze Age. The EM III/MM Ia distribution map however does reveal an increase in the number of sites, and it is a large enough increase (something in the region of 40 per cent) to suggest that this is not merely the result of chance in exploration. The prosperity of EM II may thus have had some long term effect in that an increasing population eventually led to the establishment of new settlements, apparently further inland in central Crete and in the east of the island. In particular we might relate the growth of settlement in the foothills around Iraklion to the sudden emergence of a great palatial centre at Knossos, and the marked increase in settlements in the east of the island to the increasing prosperity of this region, itself a result (one imagines) of the new trading contacts being established in the eastern Mediterranean. However it must be stressed that the known pattern of settlement may vary considerably from that which actually existed in Minoan times. The recent surveys of Hood and his associates and of Faure have shown all too clearly how a concentrated search, even within a small area, can totally alter our knowledge and our ideas about the settlement of specific regions.

4 The economy

The Neolithic inhabitants of Crete found that whilst the island was moderately endowed with fauna and flora it lacked several species in both categories which were essential elements of a balanced and regular diet. For example deer, agrimi, pigeons and partridge were all available for hunting, but sheep, pigs and cattle were not to be found in their wild forms in Crete and thus they had to be brought to the island. Similarly whilst wild forms of celery, asparagus and lettuce, and plentiful supplies of herbs like sesame, mint, and thyme could be found, the edible grass crops had to be introduced to the island. Only in its supply of sea-food was Crete rich. Apart from the common fish – tunny, mullet and mackerel – there were delicacies like octopus, lobster and crab and a variety of shell fish.

The people of the Early Bronze Age however were not beset with the problems presented by the deficiencies in Crete's natural food resources, for during the long Neolithic period all of the essential crops and domestic food animals had been introduced to the island. This does not mean that there were no longer any problems in the acquisition of food. Indeed whilst the gathering of wild vegetables and nuts and the catching of sea-food probably continued much as before, the hunting of the deer and agrimi may have become more difficult by the time of the Early Bronze Age because these animals were slowly being driven to extinction. The frequent appearance of the agrimi in the art and religion of the Bronze Age is probably indicative not of its proliferation but rather of its increasing scarcity. There were too the same problems facing agriculture and animal husbandry as are met with in Crete today. Permanent rivers and streams are rare, and water is normally available only from the more numerous springs. The prehistoric farmers of Crete, though they dug wells, did not have mechanized pumps to bring the water up in sufficient quantities to irrigate their land. Cultivable land is itself scarce and even today represents only about ten per cent of Crete's surface, concentrated mainly in the fertile coastal plains and valleys. About the same percentage of land is given over to the production of olives and various fruits, and rather less to permanent pasture. A fifth of the land is useless for any sort of food production, and there can be no doubt that this has been so throughout the ages.[1] Most of the remaining land – about half of the total amount – is today given over to irregular grazing. This is one feature of the land usage which has changed dramatically since ancient times. We know that in antiquity Crete had very large forests which today are almost completely gone.[2] Much of the land now used for nomadic grazing would have been under forest in the Early Bronze Age, very probably more than half of it. Thus the number of sheep and goats which could be grazed in the Early Bronze Age was almost certainly far less than are grazed now. On the other hand the additional forests were probably utilized for the rearing of swine.

Animal husbandry is attested in the Early Bronze Age by several deposits of bones, and by a variety of representations in contemporary art. Some of our best information about the range of animals available to the Early Minoans comes in fact from deposits which date to the period immediately preceding the Early Bronze Age.[3] The bones of sheep were found in Late Neolithic deposits at Miamou, Magasa, and Phaistos, and in an Early Bronze Age tomb at Krasi. Short-horned cattle were represented in the deposits from Miamou and Phaistos, and also in a group of bones found at Knossos. The same deposit at Knossos yielded bones of goats and pigs, whilst the Miamou bones included some of goats and the Krasi group a selection of pig bones. How far we can regard the Late Bronze Age deposit at Tylissos, where sheep were twice as common as pigs and goats and cattle were in a minority, as being typical of the Early Bronze Age preference is difficult to estimate. At Fournou Korifi, however, where a woollen industry was practised, it is significant that ninety per cent of the animal bones were those of sheep or goats. The popularity of the major food animals is confirmed by the range of zoomorphic vessels, figurines and seal-stones. In addition to the

[1] Allbough *1953*; Hutchinson *1962* 40–2.
[2] Willetts *1965* 37.
[3] Vickery *1936* 69–73; Taramelli *1897* 297; Dawkins *1905* 368; Evans *1928* 10; Hazzidakis *1912* 231.

Lebena pig vessel, swine are represented on a seal-stone from Platanos (No. 1086), (fig. 30) an amulet from Sphoungaras (fig. 22) and several small figurines found in the peak sanctuaries.[1] Sheep and rams are also found amongst these figurine deposits and at Koumasa several vessels in the form of a ram were found.[2] There is no need to enumerate the many representations of the bull in Early Minoan art, but it is worthy of note that amongst them we find evidence that the long-horned species was also known in Early Bronze Age Crete, in addition to the short-horned cattle to which the bone remains attest (pl. 11).

There is rather less evidence for the agricultural activity of the villagers. In particular we have no direct evidence at present as to which grain crops were grown. We know that wheat, barley and millet were introduced to the Greek mainland at the very start of the Neolithic period, in the seventh millennium B.C.[3] It is certain that, isolated as it was during the Early and Middle Neolithic periods, Crete must have adopted the growing of at least one of these crops, and barley is attested in the EM II settlement at Fournou Korifi. The climate is well suited to wheat growing in particular, but the earliest evidence we have for grain production is a group of three millstones from the Late Neolithic house at Magasa.[4] It is not until MM I that wheat grains are attested archaeologically in deposits at Mallia. Nevertheless it seems certain that, by the start of the Bronze Age, wheat and barley would have become an important part of the economy, and both of these crops were presumably ground on the dozens of saddle querns found in the Early Bronze Age settlement at Fournou Korifi.[5]

Vegetable crops are equally difficult to prove during the Early Bronze Age, although lentils were found in an MM I deposit at Mallia.[6] Beans and peas occurred in Late Minoan deposits at Knossos and Agia Triadha and were almost certainly grown during the Early Bronze Age, since they too were produced in the Neolithic period on the mainland of Greece.[7] In addition to these vegetables,

---

[1] Alexiou *1960*; Xanthoudides *1924* pl. XIII, 1086; Hall *1914* fig. 107; Faure *1967*; Platon 1951; Myres *1903*.

[2] Myres *1903*; Faure *1967*; Xanthoudides *1924* pl. XXVIII.

[3] Vickery *1936* 55–6; Rodden *1964*, *1964a*; Weinberg *1965* 13.

[4] Dawkins *1905* 268.

[5] Warren *1968*, also refers to grain impressions on a sherd of pottery.

[6] Hutchinson *1962* 244.

[7] Vickery *1936* 56; Weinberg *1965* 31.

the carob and olive tree provided beans and olives respectively during the Late Bronze Age. The olive was certainly grown during the Early Bronze Age, as oil separators testify,[1] and the carob may well have been introduced at this time. There were of course the wild vegetables – asparagus, celery and lettuce – which could be gathered. Similarly grapes and pears, both of which were probably introduced during the third millennium if not before, could be supplemented by the gathering of almonds and quince.

For the remainder of their food supply the early Minoans relied upon hunting and gathering activities.[2] At Miamou the bones of stags, rabbits and hares attested to the success of the hunters of the Mesara in the Late Neolithic. Middle Minoan bone deposits at Tylissos indicated that agrimi were also considered a worthy prey, and a rectangular sealstone of MM I from Mallia shows a man carrying two dead agrimi on a pole over his shoulder[3] (fig. 14). The various models of agrimi found in Mesara tholoi and in peak sanctuaries may thus be related to the hunting of the animal.[4] Fish and sea-creatures occur less often in Early Minoan art, but they were certainly caught and eaten in large quantities by the Cretans of the third millennium B.C.[5] Fish bones of an unspecified sort were found in the tomb at Krasi, those of crab and lobster in the Late Neolithic deposit at Miamou, and limpets, cockles and whelks in the Late Neolithic levels at Knossos. A copper two-pronged harpoon from Agios Onouphrios and a net-mending implement of copper from Platanos give some clue as to how the fish were caught. It is possible that copper spearheads from Mallia, Chamaizi, Porti, Mochlos, and Amariou were also used to spear fish (fig. 14).

The way in which all these various food sources were combined and utilized is not easily assessed. It is most unlikely that anyone specialized as either a stock-breeder or agriculturalist. As in modern Cretan villages each man would probably own a goat or two, a few sheep perhaps or a few cattle, and in addition work a small area of the precious agricultural land. Some Middle Minoan I bowls from Palaikastro and Porti which appear to show large flocks of

---

[1] Warren *1968*; Olive seeds were also found at Lebena in the tholoi.
[2] Vickery *1936* 76–9, 82–5; Taramelli *1897* 297.
[3] Hazzidakis *1912* 231; Kenna *1960* 92 (Ash. Mus. *1938–763*; Kenna Cat. 36).
[4] Xanthoudides *1924* pl. VII, 5114; Myres *1903* pl. XIII, 58; Faure *1967* fig. 10.
[5] Vickery *1936* 76.

sheep or cattle[1] (pl. 8) might perhaps suggest that at the time of the emergence of the palaces some men at least had accumulated considerable wealth in livestock. Apart from sheep and cattle, it

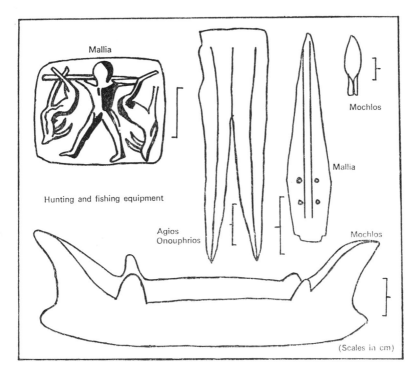

Figure 14 Hunting and fishing equipment

seems likely that the biggest source of wealth from food production was olives and olive oil. Tall pithoi and squat lakarnes attest to the production and storage of large quantities of olive oil[2] (fig. 15). The washed and crushed olives were put into the lakarnes to allow the water to settle and the oil to float. Water and waste material was drawn off through a large spout at the base of the vessel, and the remaining oil was then put into the huge pithoi for storage (pl. 8). Whether or not there was any great demand for wine at this time is uncertain, though the Vasiliki 'teapots' were clearly intended for

[1] Marinatos *1960* pl. 18; Xanthoudides *1924* pl. VI, 5054.
[2] Warren *1968*, larkarnes, pithoi, and an olive stone.

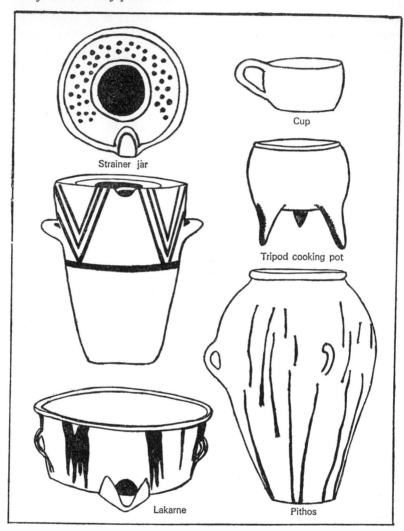

Figure 15 Early Bronze Age domestic pottery

holding liquor as were the Agios Onouphrios and Vasiliki jugs. It has been suggested however that a sort of beer was probably consumed during the Early Bronze Age.[1] Whilst milk was also drunk, small vessels thought to be churns suggest that it was made into

[1] Hutchinson *1962* 244.

cheese as well.[1] Important as grain was, it seems that grain production very probably played a secondary role in the food producing economy. Cultivating the ground with the simple one-piece plough must have been difficult, and there is a marked shortage of agricultural implements in the Early Bronze Age. Stone-axes, for clearing ground, are rare and no sickles seem to have existed, although a few of the obsidian blades found on sites could have been hafted in a wooden sickle handle. Some idea of how the Early Minoan housewife cooked these various foods is perhaps suggested by contemporary kitchenware – large, open baking plates and sturdy tripod vessels (fig. 15).

The production of domestic pottery was one of the essential industries in the Early Bronze Age economy. The majority of the vessels which we find in the tomb deposits were intended for use in everyday life and they are found in those few Early Bronze Age settlements which have been excavated. Having already discussed the various types of fabrics at length we need not concern ourselves again with this question, neither need we discuss the artistic merits of the Early Minoan ceramics for these are examined in a later chapter. Our concern here is with the methods and organization of the pottery-making industry. The industry catered for three 'markets' – ritual and funerary occasions, domestic purposes, and industrial purposes. The vessels produced for religious ceremonies and burials were very varied in type and ranged from the zoomorphic and anthropomorphic jugs to the votive 'trousers' from Koumasa. In addition to these, many vessels initially produced for everyday use eventually found their way into tomb deposits. Domestic vessels were produced in a remarkably wide range which varied in content at various times. Jugs, cups or goblets, storage jars, mixing bowls, baking plates and cooking pots were in constant demand throughout the period. Pyxides on the other hand were more popular in the early part of the period, whilst teapots were not introduced until EM II. Pottery production for industrial purposes was confined to vessels such as pithoi and lakarnes which were used in the process of making and storing olive oil.

To what extent the start of the Bronze Age saw a change in the traditional organization of the pottery industry is not known. In the Neolithic period it is thought that pottery was made by the women as part of their domestic chores. This view has long been held, but

[1] e.g. Dawkins *1903* fig. 2b (comparable to 'churns' from Ghassul, Palestine).

there is really very little evidence to uphold it. Certainly from the start of EM I the painted Agios Onouphrios ware is of such superb quality and is, relatively, so uniform in style and type that one must admit the possibility that pottery manufacture had become a specialized industry. It is widely agreed that, with the introduction of the wheel, this became the case, and that at the same time men became the potters. Wherever wheel-made vessels appear they show few signs of having been made by novices in the craft of pottery making and one is led to conclude that the change over from women potters to men must have taken place before the adoption of the wheel. This being so, it seems reasonable to associate the change with the many other changes which took place during the early stages of the Early Bronze Age. At Troy the wheel appears early in the history of the second settlement, which we must surely equate – approximately – with early EM II. It is difficult to believe that the wheel did not arrive in Crete for another seven centuries, particularly as the fast wheel appears in EH III at Lerna in the Argolid.[1] The small potter's workshop with eight slow wheels still on the floor, found in the complex at Fournou Korifi, has, however, demonstrated that specialist potters were at work in Crete in EM II, apparently before the fast wheel made its appearance.

Many Minoan prism beads illustrate pottery, but the interpretation of the scenes associated with the vessels is controversial.[2] It seems to me that these scenes can be correlated with the various stages of pottery production which can still be witnessed at Thrapsynon in central Crete. The potters prepare their clay and to this day add filler material which they have previously pulverized with a flattened branch cut from a tree. This action is seen on a prism in the Ashmolean collection (fig. 16a). The other sides of this seal show a man attaching a handle to the pot, and the actual firing of the vessels. Many prisms appear to illustrate the spinning of pots, and in particular the production of pithoi. At Thrapsynon, whilst the

---

[1] It is interesting to note that two sherds found by Hood, Warren and Cadogan at Fournou Korifi were thought to be made on the fast wheel, and that excavations on the site show the site to be exclusively EM II in date. Hood, Warren, Cadogan *1964* 95; Warren *1968*.

[2] A good selection of them are illustrated by Kenna *1960* between p. 163 and pl. I; Matz. *1928*. The late Professor Grumach did not accept the interpretation of these prisms which I offer here. His own interpretation is partially explained in his lecture to the 2nd Cretological Congress, published in the *Proceedings*.

small jugs and other vessels are produced individually on a single wheel, the pithoi are produced by a three man team and several vessels are made at one time on a row of wheels. Each wheel is in its own small pit but the individual wheels are joined together by a long, straight trench. Up to six wheels may be connected in this way, and there may be either one or two rows of wheels. While one man sits and spins the wheel the second man builds up the pithos body.

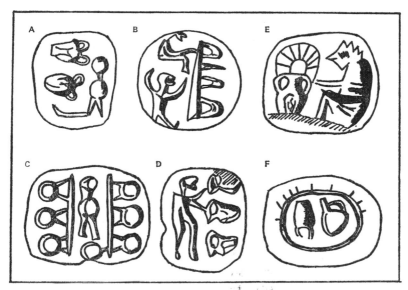

Figure 16   Potters on Early Minoan III/Middle Minoan I prism beads

The third man meanwhile prepares the next vessel in the row for spinning. About a dozen of the early prism beads show rows of circles joined together by a line, in association with scenes which are clearly connected with pottery manufacture. It seems reasonable to identify these rows of circles, which sometimes appear in pairs, with the rows of potter's wheels (fig. 16c). On another prism in the Ashmolean collection one can actually see a man seated and apparently turning the wheel with his hand, whilst another member of the team strides towards him (fig. 16b). Handles are of course attached after the body of the vessel has been spun and in Early Minoan Crete this was usually done by simply applying the strip of clay to the outside of the vessel, although in the first half of the period the handles were sometimes pushed right through the wall of the pot. This part of the operation is to be seen on four of the beads in the Ashmolean collection. After the vessels are spun and their handles attached, they are laid out to dry in the sun, usually lying on their sides. Several prisms show pots lying on their side – an unusual position in which to portray vessels – and a prism from Kastelli Pediada apparently illustrates a man about to give the vessels one of their periodic turns (fig. 16d). The circular kilns with ash-pit and perforated floor which are used at Thrapsynon for firing the pots are perhaps represented on further seals in the Ashmolean collection (fig. 16e and f). If our interpretation of these prisms is correct, then it becomes clear that by EM III Early Minoan potters were using the wheel and that they were a specialized group of workers producing on a relatively large scale. Furthermore it is clear that most of the work was done by the men, although a woman is seen engaged in applying a handle or turning a pot over on one prism.

It would be interesting to know to what extent the Early Minoan lapidaries competed with the potters, or indeed whether the potters and lapidaries were not one and the same as Schachermeyr has suggested was the case during the palatial era.[1] Certainly the art of making stone vases developed rapidly during the Early Bronze Age, although it may not have begun before EM II. Dr. Warren has studied the development of the stone working industry in great detail and his book on the subject should give us a clear picture of the origins and progress of the craft in the Early Bronze Age. The earliest stone vases seem to have been made of green chlorite, a soft and attractive stone, and include small rectangular boxes, circular pyxides and broad ladles, all of which are decorated with incised hatched triangles (fig. 19) and in some cases with friezes of running spirals (pl. 14a). The three lids with handles in the form of a dog belong to this early group of stone vases, and indicate that already the lapidaries were displaying a great deal of artistry in their work[2] (pl. 12). The introduction of the tubular drill is difficult to date from the archaeological evidence, for so few stone vases have been found in stratified deposits. Warren believes it was introduced in EM III, but it is perhaps worth noting that Seager records fragments of 'splendid stone vases' amongst the material in the

[1] Schachermeyr *1964* 230.
[2] Zervos *1956* pl. 146; Platon *1964*; Higgins *1967* 38.

EM II well at Vasiliki and comments that fragments found in the EM III levels on the same site 'show that the art of stone-cutting has already reached a high level'.[1]

This fits well with the evidence from Mochlos. In the tombs of the Mochlos cemetery Seager found large numbers of stone vases of many varieties[2] (pl. 9a and c). Several of the tombs contained deposits which date to EM II–III, and one tomb (XIX) contained material which the present writer regards as exclusively EM II. In this tomb there were some fine stone vases – a slender pedestalled jar of grey steatite, two bowls of grey and white marble, a footed vase of green steatite, and a cup of yellow alabaster. Similar shapes and stones are used for vessels found in some of the other EM II–III tombs on the island, and we may recognize amongst them shapes which are common in contemporary ceramics – egg-cups, teapots, and bridge-spouted jars. This need not imply any sort of competition between the potters and lapidaries however. The commonest shape in EM III is the 'bird's-nest' bowl and this is represented more often amongst the Mesara tomb deposits than those of Mochlos (pl. 9b and d). Some of these bowls have incised decoration on their exterior which is perhaps derived from the early, green chlorite tradition, being based on the hatched triangle. At their best however the 'bird's-nest' bowls and other vases rely on the natural decoration of the stone from which they are made.

Crete is blessed with an abundance and variety of interesting stone. Apart from many varieties of limestone there is breccia, banded tufa, calcite, marble, schist, steatite and many varieties of serpentine. From MM I onwards the last named – serpentine – was commonly used for the production of stone vases, the supply very probably being drawn largely from the deposits near Gonies.[3] Before MM Ia however a wide variety of colourful and variegated stones were utilized, and nowhere is this better illustrated than in the vases from Mochlos. A spouted bowl from tomb I (I. j) is a good example of the many vases made of marble. The lapidary has used his stone in such a way that the natural veins of grey, white and yellow run in horizontal stripes around the body. A very fine teapot executed in similar stone achieves a fine balance of grey and white bands around its circumference (VI. 1). A small pedestal vase

---

[1] Seager *1907* 123.
[2] Seager *1912* Tombs I, II, VI, XIX, XXI, in particular.
[3] Warren *1965* 155.

from the same tomb (VI. 13) has the grain of the marble tilted at thirty degrees, so that the veins produce a spiral effect and lighten the 'solidity' of the shape. Polychrome effects were achieved by the use of alabaster, veined limestone and, above all, breccia. A bridge-spouted vessel found in tomb V for example (V. i) is made of a wavy lined alabaster which runs through many shades from white to yellow to orange and finally to a rich red-brown. A bright and simple scheme is seen on a small goblet (M7) which utilizes a red and yellow veined limestone to produce a red goblet with a yellow band around it. Breccia was used for a variety of shapes both on Mochlos and in the Mesara, and its sharp contrasts of colour – black, red and white – brought polychrome vessels to Crete at the same time as the Vasiliki ceramics were endeavouring to do the same.

Surprisingly few stone vases are found in settlements and many indeed were clearly never intended for practical use. In particular the bird's-nest vases normally have only a small hole bored in their centre. The manufacturers of stone vases were therefore catering very largely for a demand for funerary vessels. Thus their major 'market' was different from that of the potters and both trades flourished accordingly. The amount of labour required in the discovery and quarrying of the right stones and in the drilling and carving of the vessels themselves was almost certainly so great that there was in fact no question of a man being both a potter and a lapidary. In addition to vases, the stone-worker was involved in the production of stone-axes, which persisted from the Neolithic period throughout the Early Bronze Age, and very probably in the initial cutting of seal-stones, even though the designs and the finishing of the stone may have been done by a specialist in that particular art. The tradition of skilled and artistic workmanship established by the lapidaries of the Early Minoan era was maintained during the palatial epoch up until the time of the destruction of Knossos.

Another industrial activity which first appeared in Crete during the Early Bronze Age was, of course, metallurgy. Indeed the introduction of metal-working is taken to be the feature which divides the Neolithic era from the Bronze Age, although the first metal worked was unalloyed copper. Crete was not as well endowed with natural resources of copper, tin and silver as it was with workable stones, but it was nevertheless capable of producing some of the minerals required by the early metallurgists. Both Professor Faure and myself have published accounts of Minoan copper sources and these are summarized on the map in figure 17.[1] It will be seen that they are concentrated in the area to the south of the Mesara and in the extreme west of Crete. We do not know enough about the Early Bronze Age in the west of Crete to say whether or not the relatively high quality ores found in this region were ever exploited by Early Minoan metallurgists, but it seems very likely that the sources in the mountains south of the Mesara were tapped during the third millennium. It is in the Mesara that the arts of metallurgy seem to have developed the most quickly, and it is reasonable to think that this was largely due to the proximity of the copper sources. It must be admitted that there is no evidence that directly confirms the hypothesis, except a possible copper mine at Lebena of unknown date.[2] But the ores found in this region are all to be collected on the surface, they do not need to be mined and only a minimum of quarrying is required. None of the ores is of high quality and few have a metallic copper content higher than two or three per cent. In the Early Bronze Age, however, when copper sources had not been fully explored and discovered and when mining techniques and equipment were lacking, supplies of low grade ore would have been widely used, particularly if they were easily obtained like those in southern Crete. Furthermore there is the probability that in the Early Bronze Age there were surface enrichments to be obtained on many of these sites where now we find only the two and three per cent ores.

It is perhaps significant that we find many of the ore sources in close proximity to Early Minoan settlements. This is particularly true of Lebena and Fournou Korifi, and very probably of Chrysostomos (Andiskari) where the author found two small Early Minoan tholoi about a kilometre distant from the copper source.[3] Almost all of the known Early Bronze Age settlements in the Mesara are within ten kilometres of a copper source. In the tombs associated with these villages we find clear evidence of a flourishing metallurgical industry. No metal objects which we may confidently ascribe to EM I have been found, because not only must metal have been scarce in that initial stage of the period but pure EM I deposits are very hard to find. A deposit which contained mostly EM I material

[1] Faure *1966*; Branigan *1968*, 49–53.
[2] Discovered by M. Diallinas. Faure *1966* 51.
[3] Unpublished, but see fig. 38.

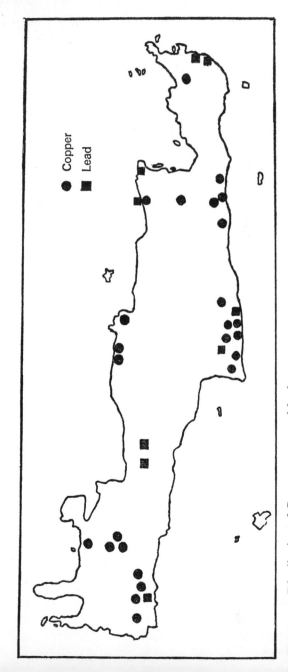

Figure 17 Distribution of Cretan copper and lead sources

a The EM II–MM I promontory site at Galatas (middle distance), in Western Crete

b Pillared room and north end of central court, Mallia

Plate 7

Plate 8

a Oil press arrangement at Vatheypetro. (Late Bronze Age.)

b A shepherd and sheep in a bowl from Palaikastro. MM I

but some EM IIa pottery was found in northern Crete at Kanli Kastelli.[1] In this deposit were three simple knives and some pins and awls. It is clear from metal objects found in EM II deposits that the north was retarded in the craft of metallurgy until EM III–MM Ia. The early appearance of these items at Kanli Kastelli is thus a good, if indirect argument, for an EM I metalworking industry in the Mesara. This is confirmed by metal objects found in early EM II deposits in the Mesara itself, for amongst the objects we find several simple types of daggers, tweezers, and scrapers (fig. 18, 1, 2, 7, 8, 10, 11) which show little or no affinity with weapons and implements from elsewhere in the Mediterranean.[2] The 'triangular' dagger (fig. 18, 5 and 6) and the small scrapers in particular appear to be entirely Minoan and their ancestry must therefore go back to EM I if we are to see the varieties evolving from original basic types. During EM II and EM III the Mesara metalworkers produced a fine range of daggers, spearheads, chisels, awls, tweezers, scrapers, razors and items of jewellery (fig. 18). Copper was being alloyed with arsenic – a dangerous process which died out in EM III – but already the first tin bronzes were appearing, often with only four or five per cent tin. Two piece moulds had been introduced in the production of some daggers and double-axes, and of these moulds an EM II example from Vasiliki and several from Mallia of MM II or possibly MM I date survive. Beating and hammering were still a common method of working however, and it was by such means that metal vessels were made. The only example of a copper vessel that we have from Early Bronze Age Crete is a cup of EM III–MM Ia date from Mochlos. There must have been many more however for it is quite clear that many of the pottery shapes are imitating metal vessels, and the Vasiliki fabric may itself be an imitation of copper. Apart from pellets suggesting rivets on the teapots and tall jugs of EM II, there are a few vessels which have the rivets carefully marked out on their surface. Such is the small jug from Sphoungaras and the spouted jar from Mochlos[3] (pl. 5).

In EM III metallurgy was considerably influenced by types and techniques used in Syria and Cilicia and in this and the following period there are some actual imports of Syrian daggers (fig. 42, 6 and 9). At the same time some Minoan daggers were traded into

[1] Alexiou *1951*.   [2] Branigan *1968* 55–6.
[3] Zervos *1956* pl. 134 left, pl. 135 right.

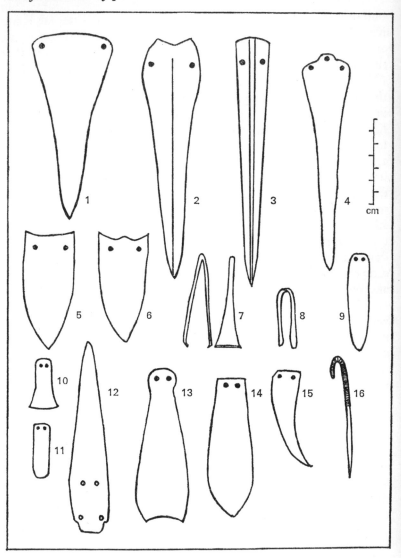

Figure 18 The metalworkers' repertoire

Cyprus[1] (fig. 43, 1, 2, and 5). This contact with the east was probably in the interests of trade as a whole, but contacts with the

[1] Catling and Karageorghis *1960* (but see also Branigan *1966*); Branigan *1968* 60–1; Branigan *1967*.

western Mediterranean were aimed principally at ensuring an adequate supply of tin and perhaps silver. Tin was now needed for alloying, and silver of course was required for producing jewellery. This was particularly true in EM III, for the great gold-working crafts of EM II seem to be less practised during EM III and MM Ia, although the quality of the work is as good as ever. Silver had never been very common in Early Minoan Crete, and what few pieces there are, are in the main jewellery of one sort or another – rings, bangles, pendants, and pins. Lead is scarcer still in Early Minoan Crete, and silver and lead artifacts together number only thirty – about 6 per cent of the total for copper and bronze objects![1] Small quantities of lead and silver such as these could have been obtained in the Cyclades, but tin could not, and Minoan influences on Italian metallurgy in the late third millennium B.C. suggest that the Minoans turned to the west for their supplies.[2]

Despite the eastern influences on metallurgy in EM III, Early Minoan metalworking was for the most part distinctive and inventive. We have mentioned earlier the scrapers and triangular daggers which are exclusive to Crete, and in addition to these items we may draw attention to the leaf-shaped razors and organic-handled tweezers which were first produced in Early Minoan Crete. This inventive ability inevitably produced the distinction to which we have just referred, and it also led to the emergence of regional and even local schools of metallurgy. The metalwork from Agia Triadha, Koumasa, and Platanos reveals that the metallurgists of each village had their own types and even their own techniques.[3] Platanos, for example, is noted for its peculiar variety of the 'scalloped' triangular dagger, and its apparent lack of interest in the use of arsenical bronze. In contrast the metalworkers of Agia Triadha made three-quarters of their artifacts of copper alloyed with arsenic![4]

In a sense the metallurgists catered mainly for a different 'market' from either the potters or lapidaries. The potters mainly supplied the women with domestic containers, eating vessels, and kitchen wares whilst the lapidaries produced a large percentage of their vases for funerary use. The main product of the metallurgist, on the other hand, was the dagger blade and this of course was worn and used by the men, whether for warfare or for everyday use in the fields

---

[1] Xanthoudides *1924* p. 67, No. 239; pl LVI, 497; Seager *1912* fig. 25, VI, 25a, b; Hall *1914* 107; Branigan *1968c*.   [2] Branigan *1966b*.
[3] Branigan *1968* 20, 25, 49, 56.   [4] Branigan *1968* 56.

and pasture. There were other 'markets', however, and in particular the metallurgist produced tools for other craftsmen to use, just as he probably used the lapidaries' stone hammers for breaking up his ore and the potters' jars for storing the water he needed during his working of the metal.

One of the village crafts which must have undergone many changes with the coming of copper and bronze was carpentry. Before the introduction of metal, the Neolithic carpenter was confined to using stone axes and small obsidian blades. This situation was changed in the Early Bronze Age because of copper's malleability and fusibility. A variety of tools could be, and was produced which were made according to the dictates of the carpenters and their needs, rather than the limitations of working stone and obsidian. Several of these new copper and bronze tools have been found in Crete. The initial task of cutting down selected trees may still have been done with stone axes, which were very efficient for this purpose. Metal double-axes are known in the Early Bronze Age – from Chamaizi and Vasiliki – but the evidence suggests that they were probably used for ritual purposes rather than practical ones.[1] A single-axe from Agia Photia on the other hand is large enough to have been used for felling trees and shows signs of having been used in some such task. The trimming and preliminary working of the wood may well have been done with either small single-axes, like the ones found at Palaikastro, or axe-adzes like those from Chamaizi and Palaikastro. Shaping the wood and all the more detailed work was done with saws and chisels. A chisel was found in the predominantly EM I deposit at Pyrgos, and others of later date were found at Chamaizi and Koumasa. We cannot be sure whether or not saws were produced early in the period, but the fragment from Priniatiko Pyrgos may date to EM II and the complete example from Koumasa could be as early.[2]

In contrast to this small but representative selection of tools, we have no direct evidence of the sort of things which the carpenters made. Wood only survives under exceptional circumstances, and in the case of the Minoan Early Bronze Age we are entirely dependent on contemporary representations in art for an impression of the carpenter's products. Much of his time must have been taken up with making furniture, but we know little about it. Four-legged stools are represented with the seated Cycladic musician

[1] Branigan *1966a*.   [2] For all these tools see Branigan *1968* 29–32.

figurine from Tekes and a seated clay figure found at Petsopha.[1]
A similar stool is probably represented on a prism bead from
Kastelli Pediada, which also appears to show a table.[2] One of a
group of clay models found in the tholos tomb at Kamilari shows a
woman at work at a table, probably preparing food.[3] Tables and
chairs – or stools – may have formed the only wooden furniture
required and used by the Early Minoans, but there were many small
household articles which were probably made, in whole or in part,
of wood. Many of the products of the metalworkers would need
wooden handles. Axes would have to be hafted, knives would need
handles, spears would require shafts and so on. Equally the products
of the potteries probably failed to satisfy all of the storage require-
ments of the Early Minoans. The clay sealings found at Lerna on
the mainland of Greece carried on their backs the impressions of
the wooden chests and boxes from which they had come, and we
cannot doubt that similar boxes would have been made in Crete.[4]
On a smaller scale we may conjecture that some of the contemporary
pottery shapes are imitations of wooden vessels which have not
survived. The most obvious candidates are the 'Pyrgos' chalices,
many of which have pattern burnish decoration which appears to
imitate wood grain. Some of these chalices also have sharply cut necks
which suggest a derivation in woodworking techniques. Small,
flat, circular pyxides with zig-zag incised decoration would be very
easy to produce in wood, whilst the small green-stone boxes with
their notched ends and long flat lids look very much as if they were
copies of wooden boxes (fig. 19). We might indeed carry this line
of thought further and wonder if the green-stone pyxides with
handles in the form of a dog were also first produced in wood – a
material far better suited to the delicate workmanship required. It
may be that we have lost some of the finest works of art produced
in Early Bronze Age Crete.

The carpenters had at their disposal a wide range of woods, and
as we mentioned earlier in this chapter, far more wood was available
in Crete during the third millennium B.C. than there is now. Willow,
oak, plane, and maple all grew on the hillsides and mountain slopes,
and in particular there were very extensive cypress forests.[5] No

[1] Zervos *1956* pls 113, 234.
[2] Kenna *1960* (Ash. Mus. 1938. 745 and Kenna Cat. 38).
[3] Levi *1962* pl. 177.   [4] Heath *1958*.
[5] Hutchinson *1962* 42–4.

doubt it was these forests that produced the timber required for architectural and constructional purposes. In the palatial era timber was used in great quantities in the palaces and villas, as roofing

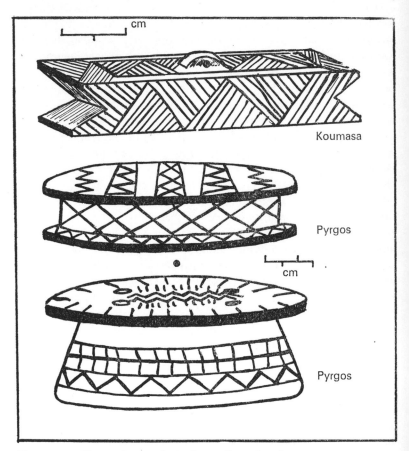

Figure 19　Clay and stone imitations of wooden boxes

beams, wall timbers, and columns. At Vasiliki in the EM IIb building, Seager found evidence that wall timbers were already being used, and similarly we can be sure that the ceilings of the larger rooms must have been supported on large timbers. Besides being used in the construction of houses, timber was used for the construction of carts and wagons, and above all in the building of ships. Both of these tasks were crafts which called for skill and training beyond that of the normal village carpenter and we shall return to ship-building and the wider question of communications in a later chapter.

Another of the village crafts using tools produced by the metal-workers was leather-working. Some of the earliest copper tools produced in Crete (and elsewhere) were awls and punches which were probably used in leatherworking. In addition copper needles and leather cutters were utilized, although only one example of each has so far been found in Early Minoan deposits.[1] On Egyptian tomb paintings of the XVIIIth dynasty we see the leather cutters being used for cutting leather thongs which were then twisted together to form halyards for sailing vessels. The rigging which we see on depictions of Early Minoan ships was probably made in the same way. Other products of the leather-worker's shop are rarely represented in contemporary art, and like objects of wood they do not themselves survive. However, several of the bull vessels found in the tombs of the Mesara and Mochlos show that these animals wore a harness, painted on the vessels in brown paint and presumably imitating leather. The fine bull vessel from Mochlos reveals the complexity of these harnesses.[2] Probably the most common items made of leather were bags of various kinds, and clothes and foot-wear. Our only evidence for this however are the brown leather? boots worn by the male figurines from Petsopha and other peak sanctuaries.

Many of the clothes worn by the Early Minoans, however, would have been made from wool, and weaving was certainly one of the old established village industries. Several settlement sites of the period have produced the tell-tale loomweights of stone or clay – Knossos, Palaikastro, Fournou Korifi – and the small spindlewhorls indicative of spinning have been found at Viran Episkopi, Melidhoni, and Fournou Korifi (fig. 20). These sites are well distributed throughout the island, as one might expect this basic industry to be. The site at Fournou Korifi however is of particular interest as here part of the mansion seems to have been given over to wool working.[3] A group of 'rooms' excavated on the northern edge of the summit were apparently joined to one another by a series of channels which utilized the slope of the hill and finally gave out into a steep and very narrow 'corridor' running off down the hill. In each of the 'rooms' a hard, white deposit was found, its purity suggesting that

[1] Branigan *1968* 32.   [2] Seager *1912* 60, fig. 29.   [3] Warren *1968*.

it was a sediment of some sort – possibly dissolved plaster from the sides of the 'rooms'. None of the 'rooms' were as large as the normal rooms at Fournou, and none had recognizable doors. This complex may therefore perhaps be interpreted as a series of tanks for the washing and dyeing of wool.

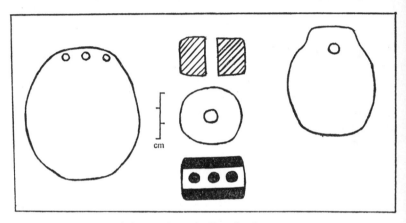

Figure 20   Loomweights and a spindle whorl

Certainly the position of the house, on a prominent hill, ensured that there was ample wind for drying the wool after it was washed, and equally this position would put water supplies at a premium. Hence there would be every reason to build a series of tanks whereby water might be used several times over. Apart from several loomweights and spindlewhorls there are other artifacts which might well have been used during the wool working processes – pierced stones in large number (to hold down cloth put out to dry ?), spouted tubs suitable for the preparation of dyes from vegetable matter, rubbers and grindstones (some of which could have been used for similar purposes), and great pithoi which may have fulfilled the important function of water butts! Further excavations here may well reveal more details about Early Minoan methods of wool working.

Of the quality of the wool, the type of loom, and the various weaves we know nothing. The only clue as to the dyes used are the shells of *murex trunculus* found at Palaikastro. On the other hand contemporary figurines have preserved for us some of the garments

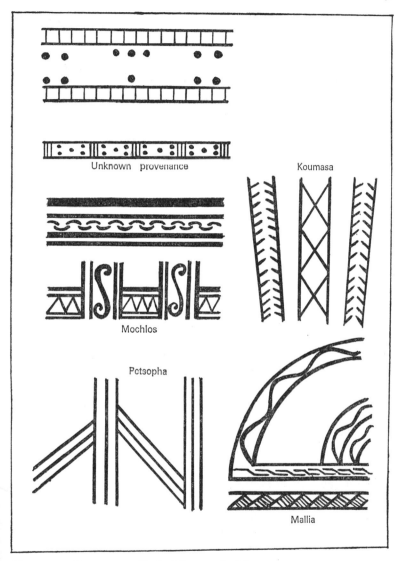

Figure 21 Patterns on Early Minoan clothing

which were manufactured and some idea of the wide variety of patterns produced by the village weavers.[1] The most characteristic

[1] See especially Myres *1903*, and also Zervos *1956*.

dresses are the belled skirts with low necks and high backs. These are seen on some of the three-sided prism beads as well as on the female figurines from the peak sanctuaries. A rather different dress is worn by a female figure found at Chamaizi. Like the other dresses, it is full length, but it hangs loosely from the waist and has no high back. On a vessel made in the form of a woman and found at Mallia, the painted decoration suggests that she is wearing a woven jacket, not unlike those that can still be bought in Heraklion. Of men's clothing we know little. Male figurines from the peak sanctuaries are clothed only in belts and boots, whilst male figures on prism beads and sealstones are drawn only in outline. Whether or not the curious clay 'trousers' found in the Mesara tholoi actually represent garments worn by men during the Early Bronze Age we cannot ascertain. If they were intended as models of trousers, then the trousers were decorated with simple linear designs which are painted on the models in white paint. Women's woollen clothes were certainly woven with a variety of designs, judging by the painted decoration seen on the female figurines (fig. 21). The elegance and good taste of the Minoan ladies and their wardrobe during the palatial era is already evident amongst these early figurines. It seems that a Minoan tradition of colourful woven goods was established early in the Bronze Age, and it has been suggested that the Early Minoans exported wool or woollen items to the mainland of Greece.[1]

The question of 'exports' is a topic which is fully discussed in a later chapter, but the use of the term tends to conjure up visions of large scale, well organized industrial production of goods – be they woollens, stone vases, or metal objects – for the purpose of overseas trade. There is no evidence of the Minoans ever producing specifically for the 'export market' and certainly this was not the case in the Early Bronze Age. With the rise of the palaces overseas trade may have become well organized and the commodities involved may well have come under the control of a central authority, but in the Early Bronze Age the various crafts were practised as village industries and were all inter-connected as part of the village economy. Production was principally for consumption within the village and its environs, and this may well explain the remarkable variety and individuality which pervades so much of the Early Minoan material which remains to us. The social and political developments which

[1] Frodin and Persson *1938* 236.

took place during the latter half of the period may have resulted in new demands on some elements of the economy during the succeeding era, but as far as we can tell the village economy remained much the same, and worked in much the same way, throughout the duration of Minoan civilization.

5   Religion and ritual

One of the most difficult tasks facing the archaeologist is the reconstruction and interpretation of prehistoric religion. The evidence is often abundant but almost always ambiguous. This is certainly so in the case of Crete during the Early Bronze Age, for by far the greatest proportion of Early Minoan material has been found in tombs and is therefore implicitly connected with religion. Amongst this material some groups of objects will inevitably be more closely linked with religious beliefs than others. Figurines, amulets, and specially made vessels for specific ritual purposes are all groups of this kind which appear in Minoan tomb deposits. But religion is not concerned solely with death and of course we find some evidence for rituals which were practised perhaps monthly, or seasonally. In particular we find the places where these rituals were performed. The evidence, rich as it may be however, will inevitably produce a very sketchy picture and in the sense of it being incomplete, an inaccurate picture too. There have been many attempts to compensate for the paucity of archaeological evidence bearing on religion, and the lack of information which such evidence can provide, by referring to the evidence for ritual and worship during the archaic and classical periods. The religion of these eras is of course much better understood because there is a large amount of written evidence which directly refers to myth and ritual in these periods. Using evidence such as this Nilsson, Persson, Willetts and others have carefully reconstructed the broad outlines of Aegean religion during the Late Bronze Age. However, in view of the disruption of civilization at the end of the Aegean Bronze Age, the outlines of Aegean religion drawn by these scholars must remain for the most part tentative, in spite of the scrupulous care with which they have been traced. For this reason, if for no other, the student of the Early Bronze Age cannot confidently use these contributions as the basis of his own studies of the religion of a full millennium earlier. Furthermore it must be recognized that during that millennium there must have been a great many changes in Minoan religion, conservative as religions may be. A remarkable social and political evolution took place during the middle centuries of the millennium and this must have had its effects upon religion, as we shall see. In particular it would seem to have diminished the importance of a 'personal' religion and promoted the adoption of communal worship and ritual. Thus the nature of Minoan religion in 1,500 B.C. must have been very different indeed from that in 2,500 B.C., and little can be safely deduced from the former about the latter. Even the controversial evidence of the Linear B tablets is therefore of little assistance to us, and we are thrown back almost entirely upon the evidence of the artifacts and architecture discovered by the archaeologist.

As we have said, by far the most prolific evidence of Early Minoan life as a whole and religion in particular is to be found in the tomb deposits of the period. In a later chapter we shall examine funerary architecture and ritual in detail, but we must briefly mention here the more obvious implications of the tombs and their contents. The communal tombs of Early Minoan Crete and the great richness of pottery and metal objects found in them clearly attest to a belief in the survival of either the body or the personality after death. They may attest to a belief in both. The rather careless treatment afforded to the human remains within the chamber tombs of both the south and east of the island might perhaps imply that the body was not considered to be immortal and that it was the soul or personality which endured. Certainly any man who had been involved in the burial of a relative within a chamber tomb must have been aware of the perishable nature of the body. This being so, the offerings and libations which may have been made in the cemetery area at a time subsequent to the funeral are perhaps to be interpreted as being intended for some deity to whom the souls of the dead were responsible. The alternative explanation, that they were intended to placate the souls or spirits of ancestors is an unlikely one because there are no other manifestations of the veneration of ancestors in ancient Crete.[1]

---

[1] If one believes in links with the Levant then a tradition of ancestor veneration could be postulated in Early Minoan Crete, for in Palestine the tradition seems to be maintained from the pre-pottery Neolithic through to the Iron Age.

The funerals themselves were probably conducted with fitting ritual, the situation of which may have been in the small rectangular vestibules in front of the tombs. Some of the tholos tombs, such as those at Apesokari and Platanos, had rectangular structures built on to their front and these appear to be complexes of small rooms connected with either funerary or post-funerary rituals. The existence of two altars at Apesokari, one inside the complex and one outside, may imply that the rooms were for funerary use, and perhaps special festivals connected with the belief in an after-life, and that the outside altar was used for the occasional visits to the tomb by relatives or friends coming to make offerings. Paved areas surrounding tombs at Koumasa, Platanos, and Mochlos, and a clearly defined 'area' at Kamilari suggest that the cemeteries were regarded as sacred areas and were perhaps the scene of ritual performances such as dancing. Indeed the cemetery area would not be an inappropriate setting for rituals concerned with the fertility of the soil and the seasonal cycle, and in many primitive societies these rituals involved dancing. Death, life, fertility, and the seasonal cycle are so closely bound together in primitive cultures that for the majority of villages the cemetery area might well be the focus of religious life.

But even if this were the case, such areas would be used for periodic rituals and regular festivals; they would not be used daily. Until the emergence of the palaces we have no evidence of private household shrines and we must conclude that for the Early Minoan villager his everyday personal religion was manifested in small, moveable possessions. Several examples of these have been preserved to us. As a group, the most interesting and comprehensible objects are the amulets. These occur in bone, steatite, ivory and copper and in a much wider variety of shapes (fig. 22). The shapes can be broadly classified into five groups. Human figures are not particularly numerous and include both male and female (fig. 22a and d). Animal figures are rather more common and almost always delightfully carved. Apes, pigs, cows, birds and hedgehogs are all known and in each case the carving is fine enough to allow of no doubt in their identification (fig. 22b, h, and i). The copper amulets all belong to a small class of blades which look like miniature axes but in fact are close relatives of the toilet scrapers (fig. 22f). A numerous and intriguing group of amulets are those in the shape of a foot, usually human but sometimes animal (fig. 22g). Finally there are the simplest amulets of all, plain pebbles or smoothed and engraved stones (fig. 22j). It is very easy to look at all of these amulets, to marvel at their quality and spirit and to forget that the majority of them at least were worn for their talismanic qualities rather than their artistic merits. But it is by no means easy to comprehend the particular powers believed to be possessed by an amulet in the shape of, say, a cow or a hedgehog. The animals themselves were perhaps valued possessions or pets and the amulets were to ensure their well-being. An alternative explanation of the animal amulets is that we have completely misconstrued their purpose and that they are quite simply pendants with no magical qualities at all.

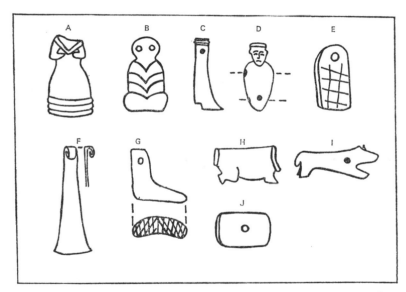

Figure 22   Early Bronze Age amulets

Certainly it is easier to explain the four other groups of amulets. Human figures may be regarded either as representing certain deities (as may the figurines) or more probably as a close relative for whom protection was sought. Some curious examples carved in ivory and found at Platanos are shaped like a human trunk.[1] One wonders if they were intended to cure or prevent an upset stomach! The foot amulets are, next to the simple pebbles, the most common amulet

[1] Xanthoudides *1924* pl. LVIII, 232, 233.

in use in Early Bronze Age Crete, and their use seems to have spread to the mainland where examples were found at Agios Kosmas and Zygouries[1] (fig. 43, 3 and 6). They would seem to have their origins in Egypt where they occur in Ist Dynasty tombs tied to the ankles of the dead.[2] This was apparently intended to strengthen the limb, and there is no reason to think that this magical support was only accorded to the limbs of the dead. Indeed the two examples found on the mainland both came from within the settlements, and one of the Minoan examples was found in the houses at Tylissos. The animal hooves, we may safely assume, fulfilled a similar function to the amulets in the shape of a human foot and were not worn by the animals but by their owners!

The scraper pendants are the last type of scraper to be developed, although suspension holes in the handles of the earlier scrapers suggest that most of the scrapers were intended to be worn. However, the scrapers in question were quite clearly intended primarily as amulets for not only do they have no handle, only a suspension loop, but they are also too thin to be used more than a few times. Some later examples of the scraper amulets are also decorated with simple designs in repoussè. The sacred nature of these pendant scrapers is finally established by their clear connection with sign 18 of the Minoan hieroglyphic script.[3] It looks very much as if the scrapers were first developed as a toilet implement, perhaps to be used in ritual painting of the face or body, and through this function eventually, by MM I, acquired a religious significance of their own. The pebble pendants probably underwent no such development from a practical to a ritual usage. Pebbles have been regarded as possessing amuletic values from the Old Stone Age onwards and their appearance in Early Bronze Age Crete need occasion no surprise.

Some small objects with suspension holes which we might regard as amulets are found to have designs carved on their bases and were clearly used as seal-stones (fig. 23). It seems not unlikely that some pieces at least served the purposes of both sealstone and amulet, and the two functions may well have been quite closely associated. Many later seal-stones carry ritual scenes and some of course are

---

[1] Mylonas *1959* pl. 166, 14; Blegen *1928* pl. XX, 3. Minoan examples are known from Tylissos, Krasi, Marathokephalo, Agia Triadha, Lebena, Koumasa, and other sites.

[2] Evans *1921* 125.   [3] Branigan *1965*.

Plate 9

a Stone vessels from Mochlos. Mainly EM II-III

b Stone vessels from Platanos. Mainly EM III-MM Ia

c Stone vessels from Mochlos. Mainly EM II-III

d Stone vessels from Koumasa. EM II

Plate 10

a Figurines from peak sanctuaries at Petsopha and Chamaizi. MM Ia

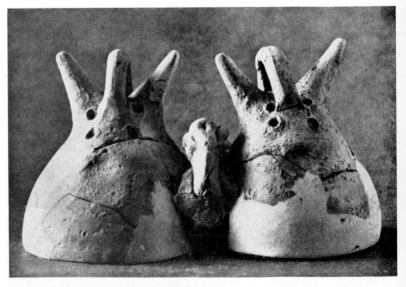

b 'Bell' idols from Tylissos. MM I

inscribed in the hieroglyphic script which has very clear religious connotations. In the Early Bronze Age the close link between seal-stones and religion is not so manifest, but the recurrence of some rather unusual shapes, especially that of a 'bottle' (fig. 3of and g), may be indicative of an amuletic use.[1] The designs of the seals themselves are open to widely differing interpretations and none of them can be ascribed with certainty to a religious motivation. We shall see later in the chapter however, that some motifs found on Early Bronze Age seals are best interpreted in terms of religion.

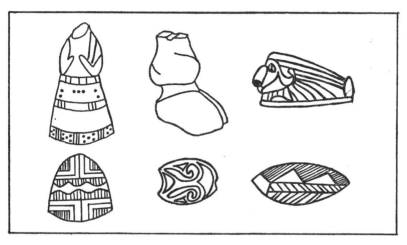

Figure 23   Amuletic seal-stones

Neither must we forget that the designs on the seal-stones were probably the equivalent of a man's signature, and that the seal-stone was in a way representative of its owner. This being so, the seal was probably identified with its owner and regarded as a part of him. Its ritual significance could thus be quite considerable.

The magic and the beliefs centred on a seal-stone or an amulet are of a very personal nature and in terms of popular religion in Early Minoan Crete these objects serve only to tell us that super-stition was commonplace. They tell us nothing of the beliefs of the

[1] This is the view of Kenna. The bottle shape seems to be a very convenient one for gripping in the fingers and may be common for that reason. Many examples are known e.g. from Trapeza, Mochlos, Krasi, Kalathiana, Mallia, Phaistos, Agia Triadha, Platanos.

community in general, except perhaps in the case of the foot amulets and the copper scrapers which are both common enough to suggest that they bear witness to a common belief found throughout the island. Into this same category fall the human figurines of the period.

The figurines themselves fall into three groups, one of which is the well-known 'Cycladic' type with very stylized head and usually with the arms folded across the waist and the legs placed together (pl. 13). A second group with quite clear affinities outside the island are the very schematic figurines with bodies which taper to a point. These are closely paralleled in Egypt. Finally there is a group of clay figurines in a realistic style which would seem to be a form entirely native to the island. This group provides us with useful evidence as to the clothes worn by the Early Minoans. The function, or functions, of all prehistoric figurines have been the subject of much discussion and they have been variously interpreted as deities, supplicants, the dead, and even toys. The Cycladic figurines, a remarkably homogeneous and distinct group, have naturally attracted a great deal of attention.[1] Picard thought that they represented the great Mother Goddess, and Mosso thought they must be regarded as something similar, perhaps a Mother Goddess of Nature. Mylonas saw them as deities in a somewhat more restricted role. He compared them with Mycenaean figurines which seem to be particularly connected with children, and arrived at the conclusion that the Cycladic examples represented either a 'divine nurse', or a Goddess of Blessing. A more humble role was assigned to them by both Dawkins and Nilsson who thought they were to be compared with the Egyptian ushabtis and were thus intended to perform services on behalf of the dead person with whom they were deposited. Evans had something similar in mind and suggested that they might represent wives or slaves. None of these explanations can be applied to all of the Cycladic figurines discovered, for some at least are male figures and a few have been found in settlements rather than cemeteries.[2] There are too the small group of figurines playing either the harp or the flute, and even an example of two identical figurines joined together.[3] Such variations,

---

[1] For a full discussion of these figurines and the many theories concerning their significance see Mylonas *1959* 138ff.

[2] e.g. Mylonas *1959*.

[3] For examples of these from Crete see those from Tekes, Marinatos *1933*.

though they account for only a small proportion of all the figurines, make it difficult to find any common interpretation of the group.

There are a few features of the figurines which perhaps give us some indication of the beliefs behind them. We can be sure that they were not manufactured specifically for use in the tombs because we find them repaired and also occurring occasionally in settlements.[1] Similarly we may be sure that they do not represent a single deity – for we find the variations which we have mentioned above. Neither are they accorded respect, for not only do we find repaired figurines but recent excavations in the Cyclades have shown that the figurines were thrown into the tombs and often buried beneath the other grave goods.[2] Most of the figurines represent females with the pubic triangle and stomach emphasized. The limbs are not of great importance and are sometimes omitted altogether on female figurines, but male figurines are invariably found with some additional feature – a helmet, a musical instrument or something similar. We may thus summarize the evidence of these features as indicating that the figures represent human beings, mainly pregnant women or men with a particular attribute, and that the figurines were made for use in life and were buried without ceremony at death. It seems likely that the figurines were buried with the people that they represented but this has never been archaeologically confirmed. Whether or no this be so, it looks very much as if the figurines were thought to be in some way a protection for either women in childbirth or for people with a certain status or talent which deserved to be preserved. Superstition would demand the burial of the figurines with the person whose spirit might otherwise inhabit them and haunt the living. Crete was of course only one of several areas where this Cycladic belief seems to have been adopted. Similar figurines occur in Greece, Sardinia and Malta, and their antecedents are found in Neolithic deposits throughout the Aegean and west coast of Anatolia.[3]

The Cycladic figurines are typical of the Keros-Syros culture in the Cyclades and have always been thought to be of EM II date in Crete. This was confirmed when two examples were found in

---

[1] Good examples of repaired figurines come from Agios Kosmas, which also yielded a fragmentary figurine in the settlement. Mylonas *1959*.
[2] Unpublished. Information kindly given by the excavator C. Doumas.
[3] For distribution of Greek finds see Renfrew 1967a pl. 12; for Sardinia see Guido *1963* pls 5, 6; for Malta see Trump *1961* fig. 10.

EM II deposits at Lebena.[1] A date cannot yet be established for the second group of figurines, although seven very crude examples were found with a Cycladic figurine in EM I–II associations at Pyrgos.

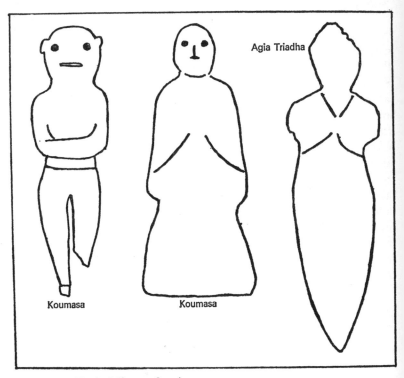

Figure 24 Early Minoan figurines

These examples from Pyrgos are little more than pointed stones, but others from Koumasa and Agia Triadha have clearly shaped heads and indications of arms[2] (fig. 24). Although the Minoan figurines are made of limestone, alabaster and marble, they are very similar to clay figurines of the Egyptian pre-dynastic period which also have pointed bases.[3] But unlike the Egyptian examples the Minoan give no indication as to the sex of the figure. What these figurines mean in terms of belief is not known. They occur exclus-

[1] Daux *1961* 890, fig. 8.
[2] Xanthoudides *1918a* fig. 14 (Pyrgos); Zervos *1956* pl. 92–3 (Agia Triadha etc.).
[3] Woldering *1963* pl. 1.

ively in tomb deposits, but it is possible that they were used in much the same way as the Cycladic figurines and it is perhaps of some significance that they have the same blank faces and the same basic proportions.

The third group of figurines is much less uniform than the other two and for that reason it is probable that they do not represent any single concept. A good group of the clay figurines was found at Petsopha in eastern Crete and very similar ones at Tylissos and Koumasa in the centre and south of the island[1] (pl. 10). These were figurines of women dressed in full dresses with high collars and others of men in loin-cloths and leather boots. In all of these the modelling is careful and realistic – a marked contrast to the Cycladic and other stone figurines. Other examples have been found at Siva and Vasiliki, each of a quite individual nature.[2] That at Siva, surviving only from the waist upwards, has arms folded across the waist and a rather large head with long nose, small mouth and two tiny ears. The Vasiliki figure is known only from Seager's description, and apparently only the head survived. The interest of this piece is in its painted decoration, which includes not only eyebrows but hair which 'falls from the top of the head to below the neck in a heavy triangular mat'. It must have been very similar indeed to the well known Mycenaean figurines of almost a millennium later. To this group of clay figurines we might add a small group of ivory ones carved in realistic manner. They represent both male and female and are perhaps the equivalent of figurines such as those from Tylissos and Petsopha, for they too show women in full dresses and men in loin-cloths[3] (fig. 24). One small figure of this type from Porti is remarkably like Sumerian statuettes in both the posture adopted and the facial features,[4] but this seems to be the result of chance.

The function of these figurines in the everyday religion of the Early Minoans very probably varied with their individual owners, although we shall see shortly that some at least were used in rituals performed in communal shrines. On the other hand the anthropomorphic and zoomorphic vessels with spouts and handles can safely be assumed to have fulfilled a single function despite their

[1] Myres *1903*; Hazzidakis *1912*.
[2] Parabeni *1913* fig. 17; Seager *1905* 219.
[3] e.g. Xanthoudides *1924* pl. XXXIXb, 171; Zervos *1956* pls. 188–90.
[4] Xanthoudides *1924* pl. XXXIXb, 171.

wide variety of type and date. Although they may have been used in a variety of rituals in each case they must surely have been used for the pouring of libations. Eight interesting anthropomorphic examples are known, each of them representing a woman. Those from Mochlos and Trapeza date to EM III, and the examples from Mallia and Koumasa perhaps to MM Ia[1] (pl. 11 and fig. 26). The breasts are marked on all the vessels, but in the case of the Mallia and Mochlos examples the breasts are perforated so that liquid could be poured from them. This would seem to indicate a ritual performed to obtain sustenance, and although the vessels from Koumasa and Trapeza have their spout at the shoulder they too may have been used in the same way. Whether or not we may associate with these vessels the strange 'double-bell' figurines found in MM Ia associations at Tylissos is difficult to decide[2] (pl. 10). They have perforated breasts, but could not have contained liquids for they have no bottom. The relationship of the zoomorphic vessels to the anthropomorphic ones is more assured, even though the significance of the libations poured from them escapes us. They are found, almost exclusively in southern Crete, in the form of bulls, rams, pigs and possibly birds (pl. 11). Examples from Lebena dated to EM I and II, whilst other vaulted tombs produced others of EM III–MM Ia.[3] We might perhaps associate the bulls, rams and pigs with the efforts of the farmers to preserve their animals, but equally the bull vessels may be associated with more communal rituals, for examples from Koumasa and Porti have men hanging on to the horns. Their significance, however, is not easily determined, for we find other small human figures clinging to the rims of small juglets where they have no apparent connection with bull-leaping.[4] In addition to these vessels there are also vessels shaped like gourds, again with spout and handle and presumably used for the pouring of libations also. In view of the later popularity of zoomorphic rhytons it is possible that some of the vessels mentioned were used in that way rather than as vessels for libations but the decoration and form of others is more in keeping with a ritual usage.

So far we have spoken only of the everyday, personal religion of

[1] Seager *1912* fig. 34 (Mochlos); Pendlebury *1936* pl. 13 (Trapeza); Marinatos *1960* pl. 10 (Mallia); Xanthoudides *1924* pl. II (Koumasa).

[2] Hazzidakis *1912*.

[3] Alexiou *1960*; Xanthoudides *1924* pl. XIX.

[4] Xanthoudides *1924* pls II and XIX.

the people of Early Minoan Crete but there are signs too that a
communal religion was emerging in Crete before the erection of
the great palaces. The clearest evidence of this is the appearance of
small peak sanctuaries, about two dozen of which are now known.[1]
It is true that they date, in the main, from MM I and are thus
contemporary with the erection of Knossos, but the sanctuary at
Petsopha may perhaps date to EM III, and a small domestic shrine
at Myrtos may have been followed, in EM III, by an arc-shaped
peak sanctuary erected over the ruins of the EM II settlement.
The peak sanctuaries certainly testify to a certain degree of uniformity in Minoan religion by MM Ia, for they occur in all three
regions of the island where survey work has been extensive. Some
dozen examples have been identified in the east of the island, of which
the best known are Petsopha, Traostalos, and Zakro. In the north
of the island there are some six peak sanctuaries, including those of
Iuktas, Prophet Elias (disputed by Faure) and Korphi, as well as
two in Lasithi. At present only three peak sanctuaries are known in
the south of the island, at Ailias, Kapetaniana, and Koumasa, for
Professor Faure has rightly drawn attention to the complete absence
of any ritual material in the building at Christos described by Evans
as a peak sanctuary. Even in the west of the island where survey
work has been much neglected until recently, MM I peak sanctuaries are known near Gonies and Rousospiti. Clearly the sanctuaries appearing in MM I were most common in the east of the island,
but they represent the first manifestations of a uniform, communal
religion for the people of Crete. This conclusion is supported not
only by their wide distribution but by what we know of their design,
situation, and accompanying ritual. The term 'peak sanctuary' is
sufficient explanation of their common situation, and one need go
no further than Knossos to see how impressive these situations could
be. From the central court one can look southwards to the great
black mass of Iuktas, on the peak of which stands the sanctuary
excavated by Evans. Of the buildings themselves we know little,
since few have been excavated and fewer still published (fig. 25).
Furthermore, the exposed situations of these sanctuaries have resulted in their extensive destruction. Nevertheless, it is clear that
many of the sanctuaries stood inside a 'temenos' area, usually
delineated by an enclosure wall. This was the case at Iuktas and Petsopha and surface traces of similar features can be seen at Zakro,

[1] Platon *1951*; Faure *1967*.

Zou, Katelionas and Skinokephalo. These 'temenos' areas were normally circular or oval, and could be up to thirty metres in length.

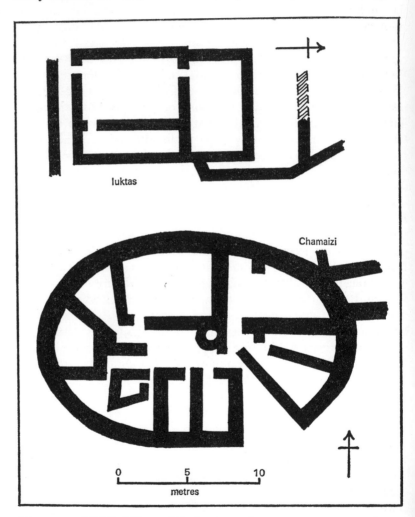

Figure 25   Middle Minoan I Peak sanctuaries

The structures erected inside the enclosures seem to have varied considerably from one sanctuary to another. At Zakro there is a small horseshoe shaped structure with a niche in the wall, which Faure suggests served as an offering table. A similar structure may have existed at Katelionas where four large stone blocks arranged in a semi-circle are apparently the remains of a substantial structure, to judge from the other large blocks of stone which have been spread over the site. At Mallia and Traostalos, and probably at Petsopha too, a two-roomed sanctuary was erected. One room presumably served as an ante-chamber to the other, and this arrangement was preserved at Iuktas although a third room was built to one side of the ante-chamber. Its long, narrow shape suggests that it served as a store-room itself. This basic two-room design led Evans (who also regarded the two-roomed building at Christos as a peak sanctuary) to associate the design of the sanctuaries with that of the 'butt and ben' houses.[1] From this association Evans moved to the conclusion that the peak sanctuaries were regarded as the houses of the deities worshipped in them. We have already seen, however, that the 'butt and ben' house was uncommon in Early Minoan Crete, and certainly by MM I had been succeeded by more sophisticated architecture. The plan of the peak sanctuaries is simply that commonly adopted for shrines – an ante-chamber and shrine room. Internal fittings seem to have been few, although at Mallia a bench was found to run around three walls of the inner room. Its purpose, one suspects, was not to provide seating for the worshippers, but rather to take small votive figurines brought to the shrine. The well known Late Bronze Age 'Fosse Temple' at Lachish in Palestine had rows of benches in the shrine room for such a purpose.[2]

Apart from the simple two-room designs already mentioned, two of the excavated sanctuaries proved to be rather more complex in plan. Of the sanctuary at Koumasa we know little except that it featured several rooms, but we have a complete plan of the sanctuary found at Chamaizi[3] (fig. 25). There has been much controversy as to the nature of this building, but there are several distinctive features of the building which suggest that Platon is right in describing it as a peak sanctuary. Its situation is certainly in keeping with this designation, and the discovery of an ash stratum and figurines inside the building also bring the building into close relationship with the peak sanctuaries. The multiplicity of rooms is indeed unusual, but the sanctuary at Koumasa shows it is not unique, whilst the oval shape of the building immediately recalls the oval

[1] Evans *1921* 158.   [2] Kenyon *1960* fig. 49.
[3] Hutchinson *1962* 169 fig. 31; Noack *1908*; Platon *1951*.

enclosures at Zou, Katelionas, Skinokephalo and probably Petsopha. Finally the strange little room in the south-west corner of the Chamaizi building, apparently breaking up the regular 'segmentation' of the structure, could perhaps be compared to the horseshoe structure at Zakro and the similar feature at Katelionas.

Figurines have been found in large numbers at almost all of the peak sanctuaries, even where there has been no excavation. Apart from complete human figures like those from Petsopha, the votive pieces also include individual arms and legs and examples of bisected human figures. The various limbs and the complete human figures presumably represent the votaries or their relatives for whom protection or cure was sought. Bisected figures may perhaps be interpreted in the same way for bisection would be one way of revealing to the deity the source of internal ailments. Equally it seems certain that the figurines of domestic animals – sheep, bulls, goats, dogs, pigs, oxen, and cows – were brought to the shrine for the same purposes. In the case of figurines of wild animals the question is a little more complex. Some of them, such as weasels and beetles, were pests and the votary was presumably seeking protection *from* them rather than *for* them. Others – the agrimi and birds – were not pests but probably food animals and in this case the votary who offered their figurines may have been seeking assistance in the hunting of these animals. The great majority of these figurines were of clay, but four bronze figures were found at Traostalos and a stone statuette of a woman is reported from Plagia. Only three of the sanctuaries have produced evidence for the existence of large clay figures, which might possibly have represented a deity. Three were found at Chamaizi and fragmentary remains of one at each of Petsopha and Katelionas. The sanctuary at Piskokephalo produced the remains of a large clay ox, however (possibly as much as 50 cms in length), which was presumably not regarded as a god but was simply a very fine votive piece.

The other material found in the peak sanctuaries is mainly sherds of pottery, but there are other items as well. Fragmentary stone vessels were found at Skinokephalo and Plagia, and a piece of black quartzite was found at Zou. Chamaizi produced a small group of bronze tools, but the bronze double-axe from Ailias and the six gold rings from Traostalos are probably of Late Minoan date. Finally the shrines at Koumasa, Chamaizi and Katelionas produced tall cylindrical vessels, some of which had a series of loops running down either side (fig. 26). All of these artifacts from the peak sanctuaries seem to occur in one of three situations.[1] Some of them seem to have been swept away over the edge of the summit, presumably during a periodical clearing of the site. Others are found tucked away in crevasses in the rock, in such number as to suggest that they may have been put there deliberately. Finally, in all of the excavated examples and in many of those known only from surface finds, a large number of figurines have been found in a thick deposit of cinders or ash. Sometimes the ash seems to be situated in the 'temenos' area and sometimes actually within the antechamber.

We are therefore able to draw some conclusions about the rituals practised in the peak sanctuaries. It is clear they involved the use of fire, although the amount of ash found has never been great enough to suggest that a fire was kept burning for long periods throughout the year. Rather it seems that the sanctuary was visited on specific occasions. The ash deposits at Petsopha, Iuktas and Chamaizi all appear to have been the debris from the last few occasions of use. At Petsopha, at least, it is certain that the figurines were thrown into the fire, and this immediately raises the question as to whether the figurines were intended as symbolic sacrifices. It is an attractive theory but it cannot explain the appearance of limbs, bisected human beings, or pests for it would be a brave man who would offer any of these to the god or goddess of the sanctuary. More probably the figurines were thrown into the fire so that the 'prayers' that they carried would be raised to the deity in the sacred smoke.

The nature of the deity or deities worshipped at these sanctuaries must have been quite complex to have encompassed these various aspects, but the identity of the deity remains a mystery.[2] Hutchinson suggested perhaps Britomartis was their patron deity, arguing that the distribution of these sanctuaries is mainly in the east, concentrated in that part of the island where her name was retained and revered for many centuries. Platon was less specific and suggested that they were dedicated to the 'Earth Mother', in which case the action of some worshippers in pushing their votive offerings into rock crevasses might perhaps be more easily understood. Faure, however, emphasizes the many differences which exist between the

[1] For details of all these finds and their find circumstances see Platon *1951*, and Faure *1967*.
[2] Hutchinson *1962* 221; Platon *1951*; Faure *1967* 132.

various sanctuaries and argues that they cannot be connected with any single myth or deity. Nevertheless, the similarities, I think, are more striking than the differences, and we must remember that these peak sanctuaries would seem to appear within a very short space of time throughout the island and without any recognizable predecessors. A considerable variation of design is therefore to be expected. It is difficult to argue against such a broad concept as Platon's 'Earth Mother', but the uniformity of ritual, figurines, situation and to some extent design, suggest that the sanctuaries were dedicated to a more 'specialized' deity whose attributes and powers were well defined and demanded certain specific rituals. The same considerations also suggest that, by MM Ia, there was an organized priesthood, however small, which was responsible for the sanctuaries and the rituals performed in them.

A possible clue as to the nature of the deity to whom the sanctuaries were dedicated may be found in the tall, cylindrical vessels previously mentioned. These vessels provide us with a point of contact between the Middle Minoan peak sanctuaries and the Late Minoan palace shrines. Vessels of this sort, and particularly those with the loops running down the sides, are found in the household shrines of MM III–LM III.[1] In these later shrines the loops are clearly representing snakes and are associated in some cases with figurines of the Snake Goddess. It is perhaps of some significance that the peak sanctuaries were most active during the period MM Ia–MM II, whilst the household shrines only become common in the period beginning in MM III. Could we perhaps postulate that the household shrines largely replaced the peak sanctuaries, at least in the vicinity of the palaces and larger villas, and that the two types of shrine therefore fulfilled much the same sort of role? In other words, is there any further evidence to suggest that the peak sanctuaries may have been dedicated to the Snake Goddess, or the Household Goddess as she was designated by Nilsson?

The snake, along with the double-axe and the bull, is one of the best known elements in Minoan religion of the palatial period, but it is not widely recognized that all three elements first appear in the Early Bronze Age religion practised in the villages of Crete. Of the snake there is admittedly little sign. Apart from the cylindrical vessels already mentioned there are only the seal-stones from Platonos and

---

[1] e.g. the shrine at Gournia (the shrine group is illustrated in Hutchinson *1962* fig. 43.)

Sphoungaras (and a third from Mochlos ?) and the anthropomorphic vessels from Koumasa discussed above (fig. 26). The best preserved of these, however, is a most important piece for here we have a woman dressed in garments decorated down the centre with a net pattern and with a snake entwined around her shoulders. She is thus a direct ancestor, one suspects, of the famous Snake Goddess of Knossos and the LM III Snake Goddess of Gournia.[1] Similarly the various bull figurines and vessels referred to earlier in this chapter may be considered the ancestors of the bulls portrayed in frescoes, on seals, on vessels, and in small statuettes during the palatial period. Bull figurines from the Neolithic deposits at Knossos suggest that the cult associations of the bull go back even beyond the Early Bronze Age.

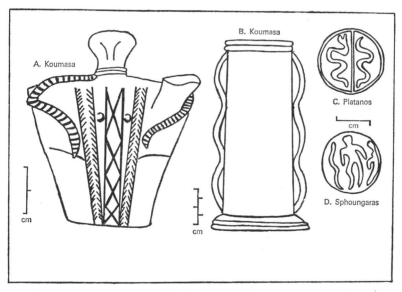

Figure 26 The Household (or Snake) Goddess

It is a pity that we do not know more about the importance of the bull in Early Minoan religion, for it would help us to understand better the planning of the palaces erected in MM I. Professor Graham has now assembled an impressive array of evidence in

[1] Hutchinson *1962* pl. 9.

support of the theory that the central courts were used in the cele-
bration of the bull sports.[1] If it could be established that the sports
were practised prior to MM I then the bull sports, and other rituals,
could be recognized as important factors in the planning of the
palaces. At the moment, however, the small amount of evidence we
have suggests that the role of the bull in Early Minoan ritual was
somewhat different from its role in the palatial era. The bull vessels
from Koumasa and Porti might seem to contradict this assessment,
for on these two bulls we see men hanging on to the horns.[2] Indeed
one of the three men on the horns of the Koumasa bull is lying
along the animal's head, a position which we might well associate
with the somersault over the bull's back as depicted in the famous
scene from Knossos (pl. 11). As we pointed out earlier however,
small human figures of the same sort can be found on ordinary
spouted jugs from the Mesara where they appear to have no
connection with bulls or rituals. In addition to this it is perhaps
significant that four of the six large model bulls of the Early Minoan
period have painted decoration which quite clearly represents
harness of some kind. This is nowhere more evident than on the
fine model bull from Mochlos.[3] Three model bulls of MM II date
found at Phaistos also show traces of harnesses in the painted decoration. Yet the bulls represented in the art of MM III and the Late
Minoan period – the bulls involved in the bull sports – do not wear
harness.[4] Thus it looks very much as if the bull sports may be contemporary only with the later palatial era and that in the early days
of the palaces the bulls were involved in some other form of ritual.
That they were involved in some way is indicated not only by the
group of libation vessels/rhytons already discussed but also by
the appearance in an EM I context at Mochlos of a clay model of
the 'horns of consecration'. These horns also appear on a Middle
Minoan model of dancers found in the tholos at Kamilari.[5] It is
very likely that before the bull sports were practised in the central
courts, the courts were used for ritual dances which the model from
Kamilari suggests were in some way connected with the bull. The
bull sports appear to be a late development from these earlier, less
strenuous activities.

The Early Bronze Age usage of the double-axe has already been

[1] Graham *1962* 73–83.   [2] Xanthoudides *1924* pl. II.
[3] Seager *1912* fig. 29.   [4] Cf. Zervos (*1956*) pls 284–9 with Zervos pls 487–8.
[5] Levi *1962* fig. 174.

examined by the author elsewhere.[1] The double-axe would seem to have had a ritual rather than a practical use in Early Minoan Crete, and examples were found in the peak sanctuary at Chamaizi as well as two axes apparently broken ritually which were discovered at Vasiliki. Hutchinson has emphasized the connection between the double-axe and the Household Goddess[2] and it is perhaps significant therefore that two double-axes should appear at Chamaizi where the cylindrical vessels associated with the Household Goddess (Snake Goddess) were found. Such an association would explain also how the broken Vasiliki axes were found in a house rather than in a sanctuary. Finally, association with the Goddess would also explain the value of wearing small double-axe pendants, three of which are known in Early Minoan Crete.

Also associated with the Household Goddess in the shrine groups of the palace period are models of birds, and it is not surprising perhaps to find that birds commonly occur in the art of the Early Minoan period.[3] A strange vessel of EM I date found at Lebena may perhaps carry representations of birds at either end, although the identification is not certain. There are several EM II 'birds', including a fine rock crystal pendant from Mochlos and a rather cheeky jug from Koumasa (pl. 12). In EM III and MM Ia the number of model birds increases. Several examples come from the peak sanctuaries, bird vessels occur at Platanos and Agia Triadha, and a prism seal from Mallia shows what appears to be a row of birds on one side and a bird in flight on another. Few of these birds are capable of detailed identification and not all need be associated with Early Bronze Age ritual. But vases like that from Lebena, and the bowl from Palaikastro in the centre of which is a column terminating in a flying bird are completely useless for any normal function, whilst the appearance of birds on prism seals implies their involvement in religion. Of particular interest is a vase in the Giamalakis collection which is in the form of three birds almost certainly to be identified as doves. Doves occur in ritual associations in the palace era, and in particular we might mention the trio perched on columns from a small shrine at Knossos, so that again it seems possible to trace back to the Early Bronze Age one of the elements in Minoan religion of the later Bronze Age.

The relationship between Minoan ritual and the agrimi is not at

[1] Branigan *1966a*.   [2] Hutchinson *1962* 224.
[3] e.g. Marinatos *1960* pls 9, 18; Zervos *1956* pls 184, 201, 210.

all clear. It appears often in art, both of the Early Bronze Age and palatial period, but its significance there is difficult to establish.[1] Earlier in this chapter we have suggested that the agrimi models from Petsopha were votive offerings to secure the help of the deity in hunting the animal. Small bronze models of agrimi horns from Palaikastro and Platanos perhaps confirm this impression. On the other hand these horns were all found in tomb deposits, as were several seals depicting the agrimi in their designs. A very fine clay model of the animal was found close to the tholos at Porti and two smaller models of less merit were found at Koumasa. Votive offerings seem unlikely in these contexts and again the appearance of agrimi on prism seals suggests that they had a more important role to play in ritual than that of a hunted animal whose capture was sought. This is perhaps confirmed by our discussion of the bird models and vessels, for in the deposits from the peak sanctuaries the birds and the agrimi were the two groups of figurines which did not fall into the category of protective votives. The birds we have already seen to be involved in contemporary religion and it is reasonable to think that the agrimi was similarly involved, even though the role of the animal cannot be ascertained. The strength and the virility of the animal were qualities which the Early Minoans undoubtedly envied and the models and depictions of the animal may well have been intended to secure for those who deposited or wore them the same vital characteristics.

In the palace period several of the animals and deities we have mentioned were closely involved with one another. The connection between the Household (Snake) Goddess and the double-axe has already been mentioned and its origins in the Early Bronze Age have been suggested. But the double-axe is also associated with the bull, and the horns-of-consecration are in turn associated with both the Household Goddess and Dove shrines. The birds are found in association with both the Household Goddess and with the sacred pillars. This complexity in the religion of the palatial era is of the greatest interest and one is anxious to know whether the intricate relationships between these various elements were established during the Early Bronze Age. One might expect that the various elements were originally distinct from one another and that they became more and more entangled as religion and ritual became increasingly

---

[1] e.g. Xanthoudides *1924* pl. VII, 5114; Myres *1903* pl. XIII, 58; Kenna *1960* K2, K13, K14, K18, K36, K40, K44, K46 etc.; Branigan *1965a*.

Plate 11

a Bull vessel from Koumasa. MM 1a

b Vessel in the form of
a woman, from
Mochlos. EM III

Plate 12

a Stone pyxide lid with handle in the form of a dog, from Mochlos. EM II

b A juglet in the form of a bird, from Koumasa. EM II?

focused on the palaces and increasingly organized. There is little evidence to either confirm or contradict this hypothesis but it is perhaps significant that it is not until the appearance of the peak sanctuaries at the end of the period that we find any suggestion of a close connection between any of the elements. Then, we find that the snake-cylinders, double-axes, birds, agrimi, and bulls (including individual horns) all appear together in the peak sanctuaries. The assemblage of material in the peak sanctuaries is really very similar indeed to that of the material found in the later household shrines, the one significant difference being the vast quantity of small clay figurines found in the former. The scarcity of votive figures in the household shrines may imply that the ritual associated with the Snake Goddess changed its form when its situation was changed, but the continuity seen in the cult furniture suggests that the deity worshipped in the household shrines was very probably identical to that worshipped in the peak sanctuaries. Thus it appears that several elements in the religion of the palatial era have their origins in the Early Bronze Age, and in particular it is possible to recognize the initial appearance of the Household Goddess towards the end of the period.[1]

[1] Branigan *1969*.

6 Society and social organization

The reconstruction of ancient society, its government, organization, laws and customs, is one of the most difficult tasks facing the prehistorian. His sources of evidence are not law codes and letters, but pots and pans, skeletons and cemeteries, house plans, jewellery, weapons and all the other variety of material objects which have survived in the soil. Unlike law codes and letters, this sort of evidence is not intended to convey information. Indeed it was not intended to be 'evidence' at all; archaeological evidence is by nature unconscious evidence. This being so, the prehistorian has no direct sources of information whatsoever, he must draw his conclusions about ancient society from secondary sources of evidence which present the effects of government, laws and custom, rather than those determining factors themselves. To try and arrive at some understanding of the causative factors, the prehistorian must therefore work backwards from the effects and in doing so he must run the risk of arriving at the wrong conclusions. This introduction to the chapter is not intended as an apology for, but rather as an explanation of, the broad lines upon which our discussion must be based.

Fortunately the starting point of our discussion is the one aspect of Early Minoan society for which we have direct evidence – namely the racial and physical make-up of the inhabitants of Crete in the Early Bronze Age.[1] Skulls found in eastern Crete and the Mesara provide us with information about racial groups in the island. Twenty skulls of EM I–II from Palaikastro, Zakro and Gournia proved to be predominantly dolichocephalic. Their indices were found to average 73·5 for males and 74·9 for women. But four of the group are either brachycephalic or nearly so. A group of nine

[1] For a summary of Minoan skeletal remains see Hutchinson *1962* 58–64; for particular skeletal groups see Duckworth *1903*, Xanthoudides *1924*.

skulls from Agia Triadha, Koumasa and other tholoi in the Mesara, and probably of EM III or MM Ia date, present a slightly different picture. Only one was brachycephalic, but four of the others were mesocephalic, having indices between 75·0 and 80·0. Finally there is a group of thirty-eight male and fourteen female skulls from MM I–II ossuaries at Palaikastro. The average indices of the male skulls was 73·1 and that of the female skulls 74·0. Of the fifty-two skulls only four were brachycephalic and about a dozen were mesocephalic. From these various groups a tentative picture of the racial make-up of the early Minoans may be drawn. The predominance of the narrow-headed or dolichocephalic people is clear. These were the so-called 'Mediterranean race', characterized by slender bones and medium build, dark hair and eyes, and a sallow complexion. Measurements of the long bones from the EM I–II group of skeletal material confirmed that the men in this group were not more than about 163 cms (5′ 5″) tall. A small brachycephalic element is already present, however, in the early group of skulls, and this represents people of the Tauric ('Armenoid') race. They are clearly in a minority throughout the period (and this is the case during the greater part of the palatial era) but nevertheless appear to have been an accepted element in Minoan society. The increasing number of mesocephalic skulls in the EM III–MM Ia, and MM I–II groups may perhaps represent increasing integration of the two races. It is a pity that we do not know when the Tauric element entered the island, for it might be possible to connect them with certain Anatolian or Syrian affinities in the EM I period, if we knew that it was at this point in time that they came to Crete.

Apart from the distinction between brachycephalic and dolichocephalic peoples, and the indications of stature, the skeletal remains tell us little else about the people of Early Minoan Crete. There is no reason to imagine that the balance of sexes in the population was not approximately even, except that of one hundred and four skeletons of the period which have been sexed, almost three-quarters were male. This may be the result of chance – which plays a large part in archaeological discoveries – or else of funerary customs. On the other hand it could represent a real situation; perhaps there were considerably more men than women in Crete at this time. As to their expectation of life there is really too little evidence to go on. Duckworth was able to estimate the age at death of three people from the Agios Nikolaos cemetery (Palaikastro).

One was a six-year-old child and the other two were both aged about fifty years. Apart from this we can say nothing, except perhaps to note that children's remains are rarely encountered in Crete at this time. This might suggest, surprisingly perhaps, that the mortality rate amongst infants was relatively low.

Having obtained some idea as to the most basic division in Early Minoan society – that of race – we might now consider the evidence as to the basis of social organization. The Gortyn Code reveals that in Crete the tribal system remained an important social factor down to the fifth century B.C. and beyond, and this would seem to be one of the many Minoan aspects of the famous code. Glotz thought that the Mesara tholoi were indicative of a tribal organization in the Early Bronze Age, but Hutchinson prefers to regard the tholoi as the tombs of individual clans.[1] This view has something to recommend it. The tholoi have often been found in groups of two or more. This is true of Koumasa, Platanos, Siva, Agia Triadha, Lebena, Apesokari, Drakones, Marathokephalo, Agia Eirene, Vorou, Kamilari, and Chrysostomos.[2] Although we cannot be sure, it looks as if on any one cemetery site all of the tholoi were in use at the same time. They may have been built at slightly different dates and they may go out of use at different times, but for the greater part of their life the tholoi on any one site are all in use together. This has been demonstrated at Lebena, Siva, Koumasa, Platanos and Agia Triadha and is probably true of the remaining tholoi. Once one has established that at least half of the cemeteries in the Mesara contained two or more tombs which were in use at one and the same time, then the existence of the clan system seems to be the most reasonable explanation of Early Minoan burial customs in this region. It seems most unlikely that if the tholoi were used by the whole village population without discrimination of any sort, that the villagers would have two large tombs in use at once. The evidence discovered in the tombs suggests that the labour of building the tholoi was such that the people on whom the responsibility for the erection of further tombs would fall, took every step to cram as many burials as possible into the existing one. The same basic objection may be

---

[1] Glotz *1921*; Hutchinson *1962* 232–3.
[2] Banti *1933* (Agia Triadha); Alexiou *1960* (Lebena); Matz *1942*; Megaw *1966* (Apesokari); Parabeni *1913* (Siva); Levi *1962* (Kamilari); Marinatos *1931* (Vorou); Chrysostomos unpublished but see fig. 38; for the remainder see Xanthoudides *1924*.

raised to any attempt to identify the tholoi as tribal burial places. That is to say, the population of any one village would have almost certainly belonged overwhelmingly to a single tribe. They would thus have no need of several contemporary tombs. Any members of the community who may have belonged to another tribe – if there were any at all – would presumably then be taken to the nearest village of their own tribe for burial. Finally, the alternative inter-pretation of the tholoi as the tombs of the leading families in a single village may be rejected on the grounds that the materials found in the tombs seem to represent all levels of wealth and compare well with the objects found in those few settlements which have been excavated. Thus, when all the alternatives are considered and all the evidence weighed, it seems most reasonable to regard the tholoi as the tombs of various clans, of which each village may well have had two or three.

The same situation may well have existed in the east of the island, where many of the ossuaries on Mochlos and some of those at Palaikastro are in use together. In the north of the island, where burials were often in caves, the evidence is not clear enough for us to come to a conclusion. It may be that other cave ossuaries remain to be found near the known examples in the north, like that at Kanli Kastelli. In the absence of evidence to suggest racial differences between the southern, northern and eastern parts of the island, one would expect the basis of the social organization to be the same throughout the island. In view of the persistence of the tribal tradition in Crete we might perhaps postulate that the clans were subject to the customs and demands of the tribe.

But the tribe would not be the only social unit to which the clans were responsible. In their own interests the clans would have duties to the community in which they lived, and indeed one clan might well be spread between two or three neighbouring villages thereby producing a conflict of loyalties perhaps. As the Early Bronze Age progressed, the conflict between clan and community must have grown, for the complexity of communal life grew considerably between EM I and MM I and the demands it made on its members must have grown accordingly. Equally as the communities expanded and various economic changes took place, the population must have become more mobile. People probably moved from one village or town to another much more freely and economic considerations would begin to attract people towards some of the more thriving centres. Inevitably some of the clan's social solidarity would be lost in the process – a process which has been repeated many times over with the same social effects throughout history.

Developments in the pattern of settlement and urbanization are thus of relevance to our discussion. The Minoans were by nature gregarious, a characteristic shared by their present day counterparts. On palatial frescoes we see them gathered together in great numbers, and already in the Early Neolithic period the settlers at Knossos lived in a village community. By the Late Neolithic period the houses at Knossos were being erected in blocks; that is to say the inhabitants of the village were fully committed to communal life.[1] By EM II the palace sites at Knossos and Phaistos were occupied by large villages, and in EM III the palace site at Mallia was completely covered by a settlement. Out of these villages developed the palatial towns of MM I. The difference between the villages of EM II and III and the palatial towns of MM I was not as great as we have often been led to think. We have seen in an earlier chapter that the villages at Vasiliki, Phaistos and Palaikastro consisted of well built houses and that in each case there is at least one building of large size and pretentious plan. The mansions at Vasiliki and Fournou Korifi clearly attest to the establishment of a class who could command the wealth and labour to erect dwellings superior to those of their fellow beings. In view of the architectural similarities between these mansions and the later palaces we can hardly doubt that these men represented, in embryo form, the occupants of the palaces and the central authority in the community.

Just how early such an authority emerged we do not know, but it may well have been during the EM I period; certainly we should not regard the mansions at Fournou Korifi and Vasiliki as necessarily the first of their kind. Before proceeding further, we should attempt to define what we mean by 'a central authority', for such a term need not imply a single man, or a despot, or a religious leader. Initially, the central authority in the Early Minoan communities was most probably an individual elected by the rest of the community or at least that part of it which was, by tradition, birth or wealth – or a combination of all three – the section which made communal decisions. There is no proof that this was so, but a system of this sort would not conflict with the evidence of the tombs or with the later developments of the earlier system, that is the system of

[1] Evans *1928* 1–21.

government during the palatial era. The Early Minoan tombs suggest that, within any one community, there were a large number of people who were considered to be of equal status, at least for the purpose of burial. If the central authority was imposed rather than elected, it is probable that those who held power would have had their own exclusive burial places. As it is, we find that the tombs yield evidence of having been used for the interment of large numbers of people whose material possessions vary little, and also for the burial of a smaller number of people who could go to their graves decked in gold ornaments. Gold had to be imported into the island and those who acquired it must have done so either because they had the wealth to exchange for it or else because it was part of the 'regalia' bestowed upon them when they were elected to a communal office.

In many cases the wealthy and the elected may well have been one and the same. It has long been thought that palatial Crete was governed by what Hutchinson calls a 'paternal theocracy' and the recent discovery at Mallia of a market-place close to the palace need not necessarily dispose of this theory.[1] On the other hand, the ritual role of those who ruled the palaces always seems to be more prominent than their political or economic roles, and we must recognize that the nature of the central authority in the second palatial era was probably very different from that of the communal leader in the Early Bronze Age. In EM II and EM III, as overseas trade grew and towns began to emerge from villages, the importance of the man who produced and controlled the main commodities of trade would increase greatly. Such men would naturally rise to prominence and be elected to office. It seems not unlikely that the period of tenure would be eight years. The legends which relate the octennial offering of Athenian youths to the Minotaur and the octennial departure of Minos to converse with Zeus are thought to indicate that this was the period of tenure during the palatial era and such an important tradition would very probably have its roots in the origins of the system, which seem to be in the Early Bronze Age.

The responsibilities of the communal leader in the Early Minoan period were probably very much different from those of 'Minos' in the palatial era. There was of course a great difference between the size of the Early Bronze Age community and that of the Middle

[1] Hutchinson *1962* 258; Willetts *1965* 57; Van Effenterre *1963*.

and Late Minoan 'city-state'. But the differences between 'Minos' and his Early Minoan counterpart were not just differences of scale. As we have said, the rulers of the palaces had a prominent role to play in the religious life of the community. The same cannot be said for the Early Minoan leader, for communal ritual other than funerary rites was still apparently of minor importance. It is not until EM III and MM I that the first peak sanctuaries appear and the 'Cycladic' religion of EM II is predominantly a personal religion, as it does not seem to be organized. Similarly the mansions at Vasiliki and Fournou Korifi do not appear to be the commercial centres that the palaces were. Store-rooms are found in these mansions but not whole series of magazines or quarters given over to use as workshops.[1] The impression one gains from the EM II mansions is that their occupants were wealthy rather than being the sole focus of commercial and economic life. Nevertheless with the coming of the palaces in MM I the functions of the central authority seem to have expanded to include the control of large scale commerce and, this being so, one imagines that a move in this direction began during the EM II and EM III phases. If, as we have suggested, it was the wealthy men indulging in trade who became the communal leaders, then this move to acquire for their office a measure of control over the economy and in particular over commerce is readily understandable.

The initial and continuing function of the central authority in the Early Minoan villages was presumably that of administering the 'law'. Whilst the political and economic unit was the village such 'law' probably remained relatively simple and was concerned principally with disagreements over property and land, adultery and rape, theft and murder. As the villages became towns and the towns were transformed into the 'city-states' of the palatial age the laws would of course become more complex, to cover the eventualities of an increasingly complex way of life. In particular, we should expect the central authorities to formulate laws which were intended primarily to protect and perpetuate their own position. It may well be that the first codification of law took place at the time of the erection of the palaces in MM I. With the emergence of the 'city-state' and the gathering together of innumerable small communities

---

[1] But Warren suggests that the mansion at Fournou Korifi may have been very much involved in the production of woollen materials, and certainly part of the site would seem to be industrial.

under a common political, legal, and economic leadership there must have been a multitude of legal anomalies to be investigated and removed. The codification of laws would be a natural corollary of such a process.

Equally inevitable as the result of the emergence of palatial civilization was the rapid expansion of two 'classes' of Minoan society – the officials and the domestic servants. On the one hand the economic, legal, and religious functions of the palaces could only be fulfilled if there was an efficient administration. On the other, the members of this administration and those under whose direction they worked would require a large domestic staff to take care of the day-to-day running of the palaces and villas in which they lived. I suggest that these two classes were expanded in MM I, rather than created at that time, for both probably existed in EM II and EM III. Houses like those at Vasiliki and Fournou Korifi in EM II, and Tylissos in EM III must surely have employed domestic servants and one imagines that the wealthy men who owned these mansions also employed a small staff of accountants and secretaries to oversee their commercial business. But the officials had probably not yet attained a superior social position to that of the majority of the village community. That is to say, in EM II and EM III there was no group of people in Crete who might be labelled as 'middle class' although the potential members of such a class already existed.

As to the political status of the domestic servants we are at a loss. I have refrained from referring to them as slaves, for there is no evidence of slavery in Minoan Crete and slavery would somehow seem to conflict with the spirit of Minoan civilization, at least in the Early Bronze Age. Nevertheless, it may well be that there existed a class of persons who had no political rights and curtailed legal ones. These would probably be those who had no land, those who for varying reasons had been deprived of their inheritance, or rejected by their clan. In any case, the erection of the palaces, the villas, the harbours and aqueducts in MM I would have required a large force of people who were expected to undertake heavy manual work and were used to doing so. Whilst the majority of the population could supply various building materials and were no doubt expected to do so, the actual transportation and construction work would be left to those who had nothing to offer but their labour. Those who owned land and grew crops or reared animals would need much of the year to deal with such things and their produce was vital to the economy and indeed to the success of the political and economic system which was evolving. The same was true of the metallurgists, the potters, the lapidaries, and the carpenters, but it was not true of those who had no land and practised no craft. Thus it was that these men with little to offer and few rights to protect them were probably the labour force which built the palaces and thereafter carried out many of the menial tasks involved in their everyday running. The erection of the palaces in MM I must therefore have led to a growth in social inequality and social distinctions.

The economic changes which had taken place in EM I–III had already begun to break down the uniformity of society. As we have seen in our discussion of the economy, the Early Minoan period saw the emergence of a number of specialized crafts and industries – metallurgy, carpentry, pottery and stone-working. Whilst all of these crafts could claim to be essential to economic progress, it has to be recognized that all indulged to some extent in the production of luxury goods. This implies two important social developments, namely, that people now sought after luxury items and that they were willing and able to support those who produced them. Thus there arose several new elements in society in addition to the officials and the domestic servants of the mansions. There were other developments in the social structure which could be traced to economic changes. With the growth of overseas trade and a fleet of ships to carry it, some men must have become sailors, others ship-builders, and still others must have become harbour officials. Equally, the economic developments which led to the emergence of towns and palaces inevitably led to further social distinctions – townsmen, villagers, and those who lived in the palaces. Thus it seems very likely that the various social distinctions introduced into Minoan society during the third millennium B.C. – whether the distinctions were made by political rank, by profession, or by habitation – were all basically the result of the economic changes which were taking place at the same time.

The importance of religion as a social factor in Early Minoan Crete has only been mentioned in passing. This is because, as we said earlier, communal ritual other than funerary ceremonies was apparently in its infancy in the Early Bronze Age, and the communal leader was therefore probably not involved in sacral affairs to anything like the same extent as his palatial successors. This is not to say, however, that religion was not a social factor in Early Minoan Crete. Though a common *organized* religion was lacking, until EM III or MM Ia, a common religion was not. The 'Cycladic' religion was widely followed, and the beliefs centring around the woman-vessels were also accepted throughout the island, it seems, for the examples we have come from Koumasa (in the Mesara), Mallia (on the north coast), Trapeza (in Lasithi) and Mochlos (in the gulf of Mirabello). The peak sanctuaries too attest to a uniformity of religious faith in EM III and MM Ia.[1] Such uniformity argues strongly for some measure of social uniformity between one region and another, and at the same time it was probably partially responsible for maintaining this consistency. Within any single community, however, religion had another important role to perform, and that was as the centre of social activity. In the chapter on religion I have already argued that the cemeteries were probably used for some communal ceremonies, such as those concerned with fertility and the seasonal cycle. The paved areas in the cemeteries at Koumasa, Apesokari, Mochlos, and Platanos, and the 'area' noted by Levi at Kamilari would have been suitable situations for ritual dances.[2] One of the models found in the large tholos at Kamilari apparently represented one of these dances. The Cycladic figurines playing pipes and lyres suggest the type of music provided as an accompaniment, and conch shells too may have played a part in such performances for they have appeared on several Early Minoan sites.

The social and political importance of religion is confirmed by its elevation to a palatial setting in MM I. The theatral areas of the palaces – assuming that those which survive had MM I–II predecessors – are clearly related to ritual performances and in particular, one suspects, to dances. In this sense they may replace the paved areas in the Early Minoan cemeteries. The religious aspect of the palaces and of their occupants' role in society became increasingly important, although this may have been a trend which the holders of office encouraged as a further means of safeguarding their position.

Whether or not the political, economic and religious functions of the central authority were associated with a fourth area of responsibility, leadership in war, we do not know. In some ways this

---

[1] For their distribution see Platon *1951* and Faure *1967*.

[2] Xanthoudides *1924* (Platanos and Koumasa); Seager *1912* (Mochlos); Matz *1942* (Apesokari); Levi *1962* (Kamilari).

is a strange situation because so many Bronze Age societies have left evidence which suggests that the military ability of their leaders was a matter of great importance to them. Minoan civilization reveals little interest in military affairs, although from MM III onwards offensive weapons and armour become more common. In the Early Bronze Age, however, weapons which one can confidently ascribe to military use are very few indeed.[1] Dagger blades are common, but there is reason to think that they were not used as weapons of war but rather as an all-purpose knife. Some of the longest daggers produced in EM III and MM Ia might perhaps be regarded as short rapiers. Apart from these there are perhaps half a dozen spearheads – which could have been used for fishing – and just two arrowheads, one of copper from Mochlos and one of stone from Sphoungaras. Clearly hostilities were rare and did not call for a civil leadership which was predominantly military in character.

So far we have discussed the emergence and role of the communal leader, and the various changes in society which were brought about by economic developments. That is to say we have been concerned with the importance of the male in Early Minoan society. As with many early peoples, however, it seems probable that the woman had an important part to play in Early Minoan communal life. Certainly women figure prominently amongst the figurines of the period, although some of these may perhaps represent deities rather than humans. Figurines like those from Petsopha, however, unquestionably show Minoan ladies in their elegant high-backed dresses. Nevertheless, the Early Bronze Age saw the economic role of the woman in decline. Traditional female tasks such as pottery making moved into the hands of specialists and one suspects that agriculture too became almost completely the preserve of the male. What then was the importance of the female in Minoan civilization? It was that Minoan society was, probably, matrilinear and the female therefore was the key to inheritance and descent. Her importance to both farmers and craftsmen and traders would therefore be considerable. However, it will be noticed that I have written that society was *probably* matrilinear. This is because direct evidence is lacking and the point has been one of controversy for many years.[2] A strong matrilineal tradition can be detected in the Gortyn Code,

[1] Branigan *1968* 27.
[2] For a recent discussion of this see Willetts *1965* 40, also Hutchinson *1962* 235-6.

however, as late as the fifth century B.C. and few doubt that this is another of the Minoan traditions which have become enshrined in the later code. This being so one may reasonably postulate that in the Early Bronze Age the matrilineal succession was practised, for most early societies seem to have been matrilineal originally and to have slowly become patrilineal. There are no known examples of the reverse process.

The remarkable fact about the social and political organization which emerged in MM I with the building of the palaces is that it was not brought about by a revolution but by evolution. In the course of the Early Bronze Age, Minoan society changed greatly but it did so in accordance with its own wishes and not under duress. Many of the changes which took place in society can be traced to the tremendous economic changes of the period, but it is equally true to say that without these social developments the economic ones could not have been consolidated and the palatial system could not have been evolved.

7 The art of Early Minoan Crete

In the Early Bronze Age of Crete we have no large-scale works of art like the frescoes of the palace period and 'art' is represented instead by decorated pottery, seal-stones and fine jewellery. In addition there are also some figurines, which, with some of the zoomorphic seal-stones, provide our only group of Early Minoan 'sculptures'. The range of Neolithic art in Crete was of course even more limited and there we are provided only with a few figurines, amongst which the fine stone example from Knossos is outstanding and a relatively limited repertoire of pottery decoration. Some of the Neolithic pottery is tastefully decorated and several pleasant shapes occur, but there is little that prompts one to speak of 'art' and it is perhaps true to say that Minoan art begins with the start of the Early Bronze Age.

In Early Minoan I art is represented by pottery alone, but this does not imply artistic poverty. Indeed, in the author's opinion, EM I pottery at its best is amongst the finest achievements of Cretan artists of any period. Decoration is relatively simple and limited in scope but it is often in excellent taste, whilst ceramic shapes are varied, finely proportioned and often interesting or even amusing in themselves. Nowhere do we see these qualities more clearly portrayed than in southern Crete. Amongst the standard shapes we find round-bottomed jugs with upswept spouts, two-handled tankards, two-handled bowls, and one-handled cups (pl. 4). In addition to these there are many unusual shapes – zoomorphic vessels, 'barrel' vessels, and cylindrical pyxides. All of the shapes just mentioned are associated with a type of decoration which we call 'Agios Onouphrios', after the site where typical vessels in this style were discovered by Sir Arthur Evans. This style consists of simple linear decoration in dark paints, usually red or brown, on a buff or cream ground. There are many varieties both in the colour of the paint and in the precise form which the decoration takes, and the ground too may vary, for some pots have a creamy white wash on them and others a buff slip. Despite these many variations the style is quite distinctive, however, and many of the best and apparently earliest examples are found in and around the Mesara. I have used the term 'standard shapes' in referring to the jugs, cups and two-handled vessels but this really conveys a false impression for one of the attractive qualities of Agios Onouphrios ware is that each and every vessel is an individual creation, and one can feel that they were indeed the products of artists. Some of the jugs, for example, have completely spherical bodies whilst others have very low waists and then narrow considerably to the neck. The necks themselves may be broad or narrow, upright or almost horizontal. Whatever the combination of neck and body, however, the shape is always balanced and well proportioned. The Agios Onouphrios shapes are enough in themselves to demand attention, but they are further enhanced by the painted decoration.

The outstanding feature of the Agios Onouphrios pottery from Phaistos, for example, is the quality of the paint and the painting.[1] The paint is usually an even brown or red, quite rich in colour and non-fugitive. Lines are painted evenly with a fine brush. The scheme is that widely adopted for the Agios Onouphrios style, a combination of vertical and horizontal lines around the vessels. On the jugs the lines sweep down from the neck, either in groups or else in an all-over effect, and gracefully emphasize the contours of the body. In contrast the neck is decorated with horizontal lines. Cups on the other hand are very often decorated with a chevron pattern from the handle upwards and with horizontal lines below it, so that they appear to flair from a stable base. Decoration of the tankards and two-handled jars provides a different combination of these elements, for the spherical bodies are again emphasized with vertical lines whilst the short, squat necks are painted with chevrons or triangular areas of paint. The attraction of Agios Onouphrios ware would seem to lie in this clever combination of well-balanced shapes and sympathetic decoration of simple type. The decoration is never overdone, even when the repertoire is expanded, as is the case at Phaistos (fig. 27). Indeed it is at Phaistos that we find the style applied very successfully to some large storage jars, vessels not particularly suitable for beautification.

[1] e.g. Levi *1965* pls LIVb and c, LVa.

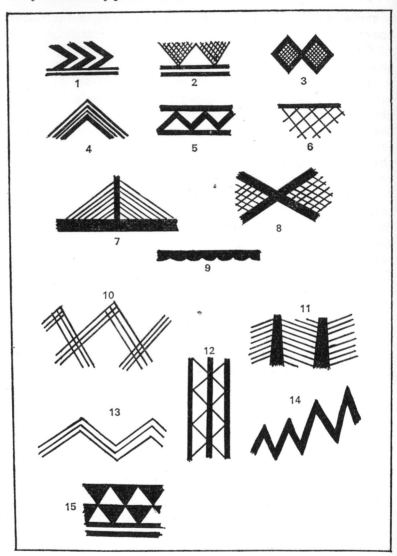

Figure 27 Agios Onouphrios I style. Unusual designs from Southern Crete

Contemporary with the Agios Onouphrios ware is a very similar style of pottery decoration which I have earlier suggested we call 'Lebena' ware. This is really little more than a reversal of Agios

Onouphrios, for it comprises linear decoration in white or cream paint on a red ground. The style is the same, but it appears on different shapes in general and often on some of the more unusual ones (pl. 4).

The Agios Onouphrios style also occurs in the north of the island, and some of the vessels in this style found at Kanli Kastelli and Pyrgos are the equal of the best produced in the south.[1] There are signs of a subtlety of decoration which perhaps surpasses the efforts of southern potters. Decoration is kept lively and interesting by the careful use of unpainted cordons or cordons which give a change of direction to the decoration, and the thickness of the painted lines is varied to produce a difference of 'texture' on the vessels' surfaces. Alongside these Agios Onouphrios fabrics in the north are a fine group of burnished chalices in what we call 'Pyrgos' ware. Although there is no painted decoration on these vessels we find that they reveal the same qualities as Agios Onouphrios ceramics – well balanced shapes with sympathetic decoration, albeit in reserve (pl. 3). There may indeed be some connection between these apparently widely differing wares, for on Pygros ware too we find the careful combination of vertical and horizontal lines.

Although the east of the island produced no pottery of equal merit to the Agios Onouphrios and Pyrgos wares during EM I, it developed very rapidly in EM II a distinctive form of pottery of its own. At its best this 'Vasiliki' ware is artistically as good as the best Pyrgos and certainly more inventive. It never appeals to the author as much as the finest Agios Onouphrios pottery, but that is probably a personal prejudice based on no sound reasons. The essence of the Vasiliki ware is that it is 'decorated' over its whole surface by a slip which is mottled during the firing. This technique was undoubtedly achieved initially by accident but its possibilities were quickly realized by the potters of the eastern region.[2] By exercising careful control over the differential firing, and by using slips of a different colour on a single vessel, these potters were soon able to produce pottery with a deliberately patterned mottling (pl. 4). Thus we find spouted 'teapots' with mottled designs on their body and the spout painted to represent a bird? with a ferocious row of teeth and small but watchful eyes. This sort of shape – the 'teapot' – suggests that it was initially a metal vessel form and was copied into ceramics, and

---

[1] e.g. Zervos *1956* pls 131, 133; Alexiou *1951*; Xanthoudides *1918a*.
[2] Seager *1905*, *1907*; Zervos *1956* pls 134–6; Frankfort *1927* II, 90–1.

this is true of several Vasiliki shapes – spouted jars and flagons, beakers with flaring rims, and some of the tall spouted-jugs (pls 4 and 5). Many of these shapes are decorated either with the small pellets which we have just referred to as 'eyes' on the 'teapot', or else with small rows of dots along or down the surface of the vessels. There seems little doubt that these represent rivets which, on the metal prototypes, held the vessel together. This being so it is logical to see the Vasiliki style as being itself an imitation of metal, and certainly the mottled brown and yellow tones of the style and the metallic texture of the slip are strongly reminiscent of bronze.

In contrast to the quality and ingenuity of the Vasiliki ware, the eastern varieties of Agios Onouphrios ware which appear in EM II are crude and entirely lacking in balance between decoration and vessel. Indeed the vessels themselves lack balance, possessing ugly spouts, flat, broad bases, and heavy bodies. The potters of eastern Crete appear to have had an enthusiasm for spouts in which they indulged to an excess, and excess is perhaps a characteristic of east Cretan pottery in EM II.[1] To some extent the same is true elsewhere in this period, for almost everywhere the Agios Onouphrios style is elaborated until its merits are very largely lost. Cross-hatching becomes a common feature of the style and the decorative motifs employed are seldom chosen to suit the pottery shapes on which they appear. The decoration, like the shapes, becomes 'heavy' for large areas are now covered with cross-hatching, and we may perhaps relate this development to part of a general trend in ceramic decoration at this time towards over-all decoration, as opposed to the selective, sympathetic decoration of EM I. In the north of the island EM II pottery includes both Vasiliki and Agios Onouphrios ware, but neither is of very good quality. The painted ware perhaps shows less tendency towards the over-all style than it does in the east and south, but only to go to the other extreme where a single motif is placed in isolation on a large jug or a few crudely painted bands are run around a vessel. On the whole the Agios Onouphrios style of decoration fares best during EM II in the south. At Phaistos indeed the style may perhaps have continued with little change well into the EM II period, but even elsewhere in the

---

[1] e.g. Bosanquet *1923* fig. 3 a–i, Seager *1905* pl. XXXIV, Boyd-Hawes *1905* fig. 1 (for excessive spouts); Hogarth *1901* fig. 52, Boyd-Hawes *1905* fig. 1 (for ill-conceived dark-on-light decoration); Xanthoudides *1924* pl. XXVIb (for Agios Onouphrios II style of EM II in Mesara).

Mesara where cross-hatching becomes popular, the shapes are still well balanced and the painted decoration is carefully executed and well distributed. The spouts are decorated in much the same way as they were in EM I, and here in the south the size and shape of the spouts is in keeping with the rest of the vessel. Vessels copying metal prototypes are rare in the Mesara, as is Vasiliki ware, and this may perhaps reflect the early development of metal-working in the Mesara – that is to say, the people of the Mesara had metal vessels and did not need to imitate them in clay.

The inventiveness of the eastern potters, as exemplified in the production of Vasiliki wares, is again demonstrated by the pottery of EM III. Pendlebury regarded the return to painted decoration in the east as an expression of the Minoans' inborn love of decorated, colourful materials, but this is not necessarily the case. Vasiliki ware could be more colourful than either EM I or EM III pottery, and equally decorative albeit in a less formal way. The decline of Vasiliki ware is probably due to several factors, including the emergence in EM III of eastern metal-working and the fact that the Vasiliki style had really been developed as far as it could go and now presented no new opportunities to the potter. At Vasiliki, Agia Photia, Pseira and (in northern Crete) Knossos, sherds of Vasiliki ware occur with white painted decoration over the mottled ground.[1] These sherds would seem to represent the first efforts to develop a new style at the close of EM II, and they may fairly be regarded as the prototypes of the white painted decoration on brown or black slip which characterizes EM III pottery.

The new style evolved very rapidly and shows few points of contact with the previous Minoan styles. A few of the motifs employed on the later Agios Onouphrios wares survive or are re-adopted, but the style is notable for producing a large range of new motifs, and motifs which are not restricted to a rectilinear form. To describe these new motifs would take up much room and not really do them justice; it is far easier and more effective to refer the reader to plate 5, where two vessels in the new style are shown. The most striking feature of the new range is the predominance of curvilinear designs, particularly the spiral. There has been much discussion concerning the origins and diffusion of the spiral in the

[1] Seager *1905* 215 (Vasiliki); Boyd-Hawes *1905* 183ff. (Agia Photia); Seager *1912a* 17 (Pseira); Knossos sherds unpublished, seen in the Stratigraphical Museum.

ancient Near East and I have no intention of adding to this volum-
inous material. In the case of Crete and the appearance of the spiral
on the pottery of EM III, there can be little doubt that the motif
had been introduced to the island from the Cycladic islands.
Borrowed as it may have been, the eastern potters adapted the spiral
to their own particular designs and did not attempt to copy the
over-all spiral decoration popular in Early Cycladic II art. In the
pottery of eastern Crete the spiral, and several adaptations of it,
appears as the element in a continuous frieze which more often
than not is one of several friezes. Spiral friezes are sandwiched
between other friezes of dots and horizontal bands, and are rarely
a focus of the decoration but rather form part of its frame. The
motifs which form the focus of attention are often the circles with
interior hatching in various attractive varieties, rows of concentric
semi-circles, or semi-circles with partial decoration of the interior.
These features are noted mainly on the larger vessels–the teapots and spouted jars–whilst the new shapes, particularly the
small cups, rarely have a major element but are decorated with
simple bands of paint and cordons of curvilinear designs. These
cups are perhaps the pleasantest of the eastern vessels at this time,
for the teapots have lost any charm they ever possessed and the
spouted jars have not yet attained the fine proportions which they
acquire during MM Ib and MM II. The lack of balance in the
shapes is matched very often by a similar lack of balance between
the various motifs and almost always by a lack of sympathy between
the painted decoration and the vessel on which it appears. Inventiveness is not matched by artistic sensibility and the decoration is
rarely in sympathy with the ceramic shapes and is carelessly executed with a broad brush. Thus the freshness and enthusiasm
which characterizes eastern pottery in EM III is marred by a lack
of discipline in execution and an absence of appreciation of spatial
relationships such as we see in the early Agios Onouphrios ware.

Recent excavations at Knossos have proved once and for all the
existence in northern Crete of an EM III phase, and there are
various other sites in the region where there is pottery which we
may safely attribute to EM III. Some of the best light-on-dark
pottery of EM III is in fact found at Mallia where the paintwork
matches the best found in the east–at Gournia. The schemes of
decoration at Mallia are very similar to those employed in eastern
Crete and are better executed in the main. Pottery shapes too are

more carefully produced and retain some of the balance found in the shapes of EM II. Pottery of similar quality was found at Tylissos and it will be interesting to see the quality of the material from Hood's excavations at Knossos.[1] In the inland areas of the north there are signs of conservatism and lower standards. At Gournes for example we find heavy, unpleasant shapes decorated in both light-on-dark and dark-on-light schemes. Amongst unbalanced goblets and squat, splash-decorated jugs with broad bottoms from this site there is one jug of particular interest. This is painted in the dark-on-light scheme associated with Agios Onouphrios ware, but the style of decoration is clearly derived from the EM III pottery of eastern Crete – sprays set diagonally in space. This vessel and one or two others to a lesser extent seem to represent a mixture of EM II and EM III traditions in pottery decoration.[2]

In the south of the island EM III light-on-dark pottery is not common, but although none was reported from the tholoi at Lebena it should not be thought that no EM III pottery is to be found in the south, or that there was no EM III period. The small amount of EM III light-on-dark pottery found in the south is little more than a reversal of the Agios Onouphrios style. There is little sign of the curvilinear designs of the east but rather a continuity of the rectilinear tradition of the south, although this shows little of its former quality.[3]

We have commented in an earlier chapter on the difficulty which has always surrounded the differentiation of EM III and MM Ia pottery, and although certain points of distinction were suggested as being generally valid it was also admitted that a great deal of light-on-dark pottery manufactured in the late third and early second millennia B.C. probably belonged to a transitional style between the true EM III and MM Ia styles. Apart from technical differences – such as the quality and colour of the paint, the fabric and the wash – there are developments in the handling of colour, the spatial relationships of motifs, the texture of the surfaces with which the painted decoration was associated, and the relation of the decoration to the vessels on which it appears.

In the east of the island we find less repetition of motifs and less regularity in their disposition. Designs are applied more freely, the

---

[1] Demargne *1945* pls Vd, XIIg; Hazzidakis *1921* pls XX–XXI.
[2] Hazzidakis *1914* fig. 3, centre top.
[3] Levi *1958* fig. 353; Pernier *1935* p. XIII; Zoes *1967a* pl. KH.

limitations of the parallel cordons being partially withdrawn. Most of the motifs were originally presented in EM III and are simply developments within the general trends of the period. Thus there is less emphasis on the curvilinear motifs, particularly the spiral, whilst hatched triangles and diamonds again become popular. These were of course two of the motifs commonly used in the later stages of the Agios Onouphrios style and their re-adoption is paralleled by the return of dark-on-light decoration. That is not to say that there is a return to the Agios Onouphrios style itself; there is a return to the form of Agios Onouphrios style but not to the spirit which made the style what it was. Many of the designs are those seen on EM III cups – inverted triangles with single hatching for example – and the style is certainly closer to EM III light-on-dark than EM I or II dark-on-light.[1]

In the north of the island too we see the re-emergence of dark-on-light decoration. Festoons of dark paint neatly draped around handles or shoulders are common, but more ambitious designs involving lozenges, 'butterfly' motifs, and concentric circles or ovals are also found and point to a blending of the rectilinear and curvilinear traditions. Some of the shapes and decoration of vases from the houses beneath the west court at Knossos are amongst the finest products found in the north since the Agios Onouphrios pottery of the EM I deposits at Pyrgos and Kanli Kastelli. An attractively shaped bridge-spouted bowl for example is decorated with simple vertical lines so spaced that they enhance the shape of the vessel.[2] In the south too, the quality of MM I pottery is mixed. Some vessels are well proportioned and tastefully decorated, whilst others lack balance and often become grotesque when painted. The most pleasing vessels are perhaps the low dishes with linear decoration and low spouted bowls, examples of which turn up in some of the tholoi tombs. The successful matching of vessel shape and painted decoration on these vessels is in contrast to the more 'floral' decoration of other vessels which does not show the same restraint or good taste.

It is in the south of the island that we find the appearance of new fabrics with different surface textures, the encrusted, rusticated, or barbotine wares (pl. 6). The best of these wares are not unpleasant

---

[1] e.g. Seager *1907* figs 9, 10; Seager *1912* figs 28, XI, 11; 32, XIII, h; 37, XVI, 9.

[2] Evans *1921* figs 118, 117; *1935* fig. 53, 7.

and are reminiscent of metal jugs – the shape with which the new fabrics are particularly associated – but as with the EM III light-on-dark style, the adoption of a new technique was followed by an excess in its application and many of the barbotine and rusticated vessels are heavy and ugly. Where the vessels themselves are well proportioned then they are able to carry the decoration tolerably well, but jugs with small spouts and large bodies are unsuited to such elaborate decoration.[1] It is perhaps unfortunate that the introduction of these fabrics was contemporary with a great increase in the use of polychrome decoration. Polychrome had made a limited appearance as early as EM III, when one finds experiments in the east of the island which produce a polychrome effect by applying the dark wash to only the sections of pot which are painted with simple designs in white. Thus decoration is produced in black, white and buff. It may well be that Vasiliki ware had first aroused an interest in polychrome decoration, for that could, on occasion, be very highly coloured indeed.

With the start of the MM I period polychrome suddenly achieves popularity. The range of colours used is still small, usually red and white on a brown surface or wash, but grey is sometimes used as well. Polychrome and rusticated fabrics are combined on some jugs and rarely produce a pleasing effect, for there is inevitably a richness of decoration which is hard to appreciate. Nowhere is this better illustrated than on the jugs found at Koumasa where one feels that the potters have attempted to use every available space to demonstrate their skill with these new techniques. This was a temptation which seems to have overcome potters in the north and east as well, but the introduction of polychrome decoration should not be regarded as a regression. As with the new motifs and styles of EM III it was misused initially but nevertheless came to play an important part in the development of Minoan art of the palatial era. Before MM Ia has run its course fine polychrome decoration of restrained type is appearing throughout the island – delightfully painted bowls and beakers, and, perhaps most significant, sprays and floral decoration which are clearly related to the Kamares style of MM II[2] (pl. 6).

The development of floral motifs from the curvilinear designs of

[1] e.g. Xanthoudides *1924* pl. XLI 4953, 4955-7.

[2] Xanthoudides *1924* pl. V, 4972, 4973, 4105 (Koumasa); Evans *1935* fig. 57, 9 (Knossos); Chapouthier & Demargne *1962* pls IIId, IVı (Mallia).

EM III is an important stage in the evolution of Minoan art, for previous to this development the art of the Early Minoan potters had shown little inclination to any sort of representational style, at least in two dimensional decoration. A small group of EM III sherds has been found, mainly in the east but also at Mallia, which show stylized goats. The degree of stylization varies considerably, and the most realistic animal is to be found on a sherd from Mallia, but all of them show an individual handling of a new theme and preserve something of the animal's liveliness. Apart from these goats the only creatures appearing in pottery decoration are some fish, which swim around vessels from Vasiliki and Palaikastro, and a solitary human being (fig. 28). This scarcity of representational

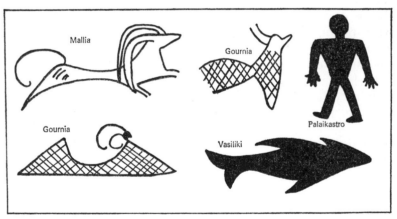

Figure 28 Representational motifs on Early Minoan III/Middle Minoan Ia pottery

art in pottery decoration is in contrast to its abundance not only on contemporary seal-stones but even in pottery shapes and plastic ceramic decoration. Furthermore, when this type of art evolves in the decorative motifs of MM Ia it is dealing with floral motifs rather than animal ones. It looks very much as if the Minoan potters, after a brief experiment with animal motifs in EM III, found that they could not be adapted to the style of decoration which they were evolving; floral motifs on the other hand suited the emerging style very well.

Despite the abstract motifs employed on pottery, Early Minoan potters nevertheless managed very often to endow their products with a certain vitality or even dynamism. This is not seen so much in the Agios Onouphrios and Vasiliki styles as in EM III and MM I, and certainly the adoption of curvilinear motifs and particularly the spiral encouraged this spirit. But it goes deeper than the motifs employed, to the way in which they are used. The principle of torsion in Early Minoan art was recognized long ago by Matz, and it underlies much of the painted decoration of pottery in this period. In its initial stages of development it might perhaps be recognized in the diagonal lines decorating some of the early Agios Onouphrios ware, but it seems more likely that torsion was introduced into pottery decoration in EM III when we find cordons of both rectilinear and curvilinear motifs set diagonally across the surface of a vessel in such a way as to suggest that the vessel is, or should be, turning. Even individual motifs – such as sprays – are set diagonally in space. A fine example of torsion is an EM III jug in basic polychrome recently discovered at Palaikastro (pl. 3). Here the effect is achieved by simple but skilful use of colour and line.[1] Jugs are certainly well suited to the application of the principle and in MM I many of the encrusted ware jugs are decorated in accordance with the principle (pl. 6).

It is perhaps surprising that the principle of torsion appears in ceramic decoration only from EM III onwards for it is already apparent in EM II in some of the designs carved upon seal-stones, and certainly we find here an interest in representational art which is in marked contrast to the abstract designs found on the pottery. Although seal-stones from pure EM II deposits are rare there are many stones from mixed deposits which we may confidently attribute to EM II, by comparison with the few certain EM II seals which we have and with seal-stones and sealings from the mainland of Greece. Nevertheless it is difficult to trace the development of glyptic in Early Minoan Crete for there is such a variety of design and style in both the motifs and the seal-stones themselves.

If we look at the small group of seals which we may probably date to EM II we find that two distinct styles emerge. The one is disciplined and is based upon the principle of symmetry. Geometric and abstract designs are the only motifs, and these are almost invariably some simple variation on the cross (fig. 29, 1–3). On a seal from Mochlos we find a simple cross, on others from Sphoungaras and Trapeza superimposed crosses, and on an example from

[1] Popham *1965* pl. 72b (Palaikastro); Xanthoudides *1924* pl. XXXV, XLI.

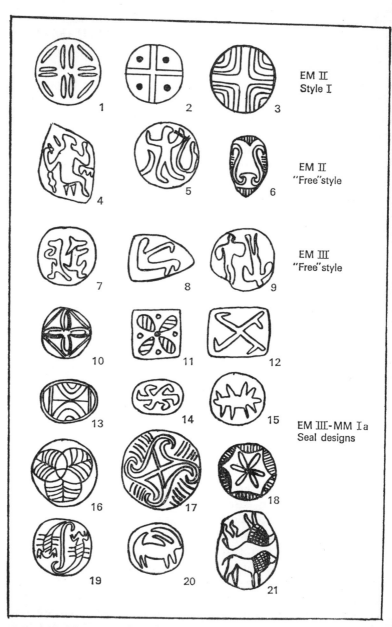

EM II
Style I

EM II
"Free" style

EM III
"Free" style

EM III-MM Ia
Seal designs

Figure 29 Early Minoan seal-stone designs

Phaistos a cross with diagonals between the angles. Similar designs were found on seals or sealings during the excavations in the EM II house at Fournou Korifi.[1] The appearance of this style in EM II is thus beyond doubt. It is of course a simple style, requiring no greater ability of the cutter than that to make a series of short, straight incisions and in these early examples there is certainly nothing which requires further comment or appreciation.

The other style is of considerably greater interest, though represented in EM II by only three or four examples. This style differs from the first in both spirit and content, and very probably in origin. It is characterized by representational and/or curvilinear motifs which are cut in a fluid and vigorous style (fig. 29, 4–6). Compared to style I we might well call this the 'free style' for it shows none of the preoccupation with symmetry, the designs being allowed to wander over the field at will. Undoubtedly the two best examples of this style are HM 774 from Mochlos (fig. 29, 4) and HM 939 from Sphoungaras (fig. 26d). On both of these seals we see a human figure, drawn in outline in a single flowing line. On the Sphoungaras seal we see in addition a snake and what appears to be a quadruped, identified by Kenna as a dog.[2] These seals argue very strongly indeed for a Near Eastern origin for this style and these motifs. Seal-stones of the late fourth millennium B.C. from Tell Asmar and Tepe Gawra provide very close parallels indeed to the seals from Mochlos and Sphoungaras.[3] Whilst the seals of style I find parallels elsewhere in the Aegean at this time (Troy and Chalandriani for example) style II is restricted to the island of Crete. This is true of other features of Early Minoan civilization which appear to have some connections with Syria-Palestine and with which we shall be concerned again elsewhere. The similarity of style and motif between the Near Eastern seals and those of Mochlos and Sphoungaras (as well as others of EM III date) is such that despite some chronological disparity, the author would himself regard glyptic of style II as very probably of Syrian inspiration if not of Syrian origin.

Apart from seal-stones of styles I and II there are others of EM II date which do not really fall into either category. Amongst those we find the first expressions of torsion, such as the loose spirals on the

[1] Kenna *1960* fig. 18 (Mochlos); Hall *1912* fig. 25b (Sphoungaras); Pernier *1935* fig. 57 (Phaistos); Warren *1968* (Fournou Korifi).

[2] Hall *1912* fig. 25a (Sphoungaras); Kenna *1960* fig. 20 (Mochlos), 15.

[3] Amiet *1961* pl. 2, 38, 45; pl. 7, 137, 151.

seal from tomb II at Mochlos (fig. 29, 6) and the three small spirals on the seal, possibly imported from Crete, found at Agios Kosmas in Attica[1] (fig. 43, 9). This amorphous group of seals grows larger in EM III and MM Ia as the art of cutting seal-stones improves. The free style on the other hand is never common, although it persists throughout the Early Bronze Age. In EM III, examples from Mochlos and Platanos display figures drawn in the same fluid style as we see on the earlier seal-stones, but signs of a development in the style are evident (fig. 29, 7 and 9). No longer are the figures allowed to wander freely across the whole field; now they are carefully and deliberately placed where they may be seen to the best advantage. Thus whilst the style of drawing shows continuity from EM II 'free-style', there is a trend towards a more disciplined approach particularly to composition. This trend is hardly surprising when one considers the sort of style emerging in the remaining (and far larger) field of glyptic. The simple geometric style of EM II had achieved symmetry by virtue of its basic design, the cross motif. In EM III and MM Ia this motif rarely appears, being replaced by a variety of abstract designs and representational motifs. Yet symmetry remains the guiding principle of the compositions whatever the type of motif (fig. 29, 11 and 21). Simple star patterns and flowers, successors of the cross-motif, are still used to quarter the field but frequently the field is divided into only two or three equal areas within which there is a careful balance of filling decoration. Alternatively the field may not be subdivided at all. In this case we find a single central motif enclosed by a border, or a running frieze which itself encloses a subsidiary design. Even where the field carries only a single animal motif there is a conscious effort on the part of the engraver to produce a balanced design. Agrimi for example are drawn in such a way that they tend to divide the field in two, and yet the lines flow from one end of the animal to the other in a way which brings the animal and the field as a whole into a single entity (fig. 29, 20). These seals depicting the agrimi are of particular interest, for they are three-sided seals of MM Ia date and represent the last appearances of the 'free-style'.

The 'free-style', as we have seen, was associated throughout with representational motifs, but the more disciplined symmetrical style was initially used only for abstract patterns. Whilst these were still used during EM III and MM Ia, in more sophisticated forms

[1] Seager *1912* fig. 12; Mylonas *1959* pl. 166.

and compositions, there was, as we have noted, a marked increase in representational motifs. By far the most common of these new motifs are agrimi, lions and scorpions (fig. 29, 19–21). Why these particular creatures should have been chosen is not clear, although we have seen in a previous chapter that the agrimi probably played an important part in Minoan religion at this time. The scorpion may well have been a favourite simply because it could be so easily adapted for use as a pattern rather than a representation pure and simple, and the same may be said of the fish which make their appearance on EM III and MM Ia seals. The same cannot be said however of the lion, for this animal does not have the same potential for use as a pattern and indeed the seal engravers make no attempt to use it in this way. The lion is always represented in a realistic manner, more so in fact than any other motif found on Early Bronze Age seal-stones. It is here that the skill as well as the artistry of the Minoan seal engraver can best be seen. Whilst the agrimi appears in pairs or alone, and the scorpion in two's and three's, the lions more often than not are shown in groups of four or more. Thus on a field less than two centimetres in diameter there may be as many as six or eight lions, each engraved in a highly realistic manner. Even on these diminutive drawings the strength and nobility of the animal are successfully evoked (fig. 29, 21). The popularity of the lion as a motif may well have been due to the notable increase in contact with the eastern Mediterranean during EM III and MM Ia, and there may be other manifestations of this contact to which we may return shortly.

To relate the development of Early Minoan glyptic to that of the Middle and Late Minoan phases, and to the development of Minoan art as a whole, is not an easy task. In the seals which we have so far considered there is little or no attempt to portray either scenes or events. Although there are many seals bearing representational motifs these motifs are almost invariably used to form a pattern. They are presented without a scenic background and are themselves the central motif rather than part of a larger scene. This is of course in contrast to the seals of the neo-palatial era, and even in MM II we find that some indication of background is often given. The earliest signs of this development are perhaps to be seen on some of the MM Ia seals which depict Minoan ships and fish swimming about their hulls. On the Middle Minoan seals and sealings which carry only a single animal or figure, and those which are decorated only with abstract designs or flower-like patterns it is possible to see a clearer line of continuity from the Early Bronze Age sealings. The cutting is infinitely finer and often results in miniature low-relief 'sculptures' of exquisite realism, but the essence of the style is found in the seal-stones of MM Ia where flower-like designs are developed and where we have already noted the development of realistic animal representations as opposed to the 'impressionism' of the 'free-style'. Nevertheless the superb artistry of the seals of MM II onwards is so far superior to that of MM Ia that it can only be explained in terms of much improved working techniques which freed the artist from the limitations of size and material.

Amongst the earliest seal-stones we find several of green steatite – from Mochlos, Siva, and Trapeza – and others of limestone and ivory. Ivory and steatite, mainly black, are the commonest materials in both EM III and MM Ia although other forms of stone are also used occasionally. The marked increase in the use of ivory in EM III may again be taken as an indication of increasing contact and trade with the eastern Mediterranean.[1] So too may the adoption of the stamp seal – a Syrian type – and, in MM Ia, the imitation of the Egyptian scarab.[2] The signet seal on the other hand, appearing in MM II, need not be regarded as a sign of Anatolian influence for its ancestry may perhaps be found in Crete. The earliest Minoan seal-stones are either of the 'bottle' variety or are else pyramidal or conical in shape. Either of these forms could have developed towards the signet type and there are indeed a group of seal-shapes which we may regard as developments of the 'bottle' type[3] (fig. 30). Whether or not we may also regard them as predecessors of the signet seal is less certain.

Apart from the various seal-stone forms just mentioned there is also a large group of zoomorphic and anthropomorphic seal-stones which are fully worthy of study as miniature sculptures in their own right. Minoan Crete never produced monumental sculptures, even

---

[1] I cannot agree with Kenna who perceives a dropping off in the use of ivory at the start of the Middle Minoan I period. Kenna *1960* 32, fn. 8. Approximately 70 per cent of the seals of MM Ia are made of ivory, compared to about 30 per cent of the seals of EM II. This is what we should expect, for the evidence of metallurgical and ceramic imports and exports clearly points to a marked increase in trade with the east from EM III onwards.

[2] Hutchinson *1962* 149; Xanthoudides *1924* pl. XIII, 1034; pl. XIV, 1075; pl. XV, 1058, 1124.

[3] Xanthoudides *1924* pl. XIV, 1130.

at the height of palatial civilization, but on the contrary has a long tradition of miniature sculptures of the finest quality. The length of the tradition was eloquently illustrated by the superb marble figurine found in the Early Neolithic deposit at Knossos only recently, and the continuity of the same tradition through the Early Bronze Age is nowhere better illustrated than in the seal-stones.

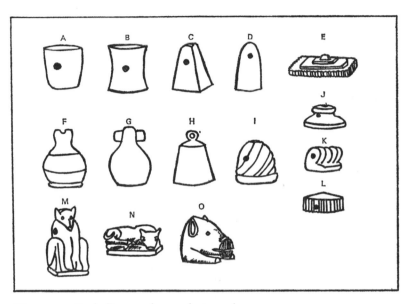

Figure 30   Early Bronze Age seal-stone shapes

The variety of animal life portrayed is staggering. Apart from domestic animals such as ox and pig, we find a variety of wild life which includes not only creatures native to Crete but also lions, monkeys and apes of east Mediterranean origin. Sea-creatures are represented by shell-fish. In addition there are seal-stones modelled after human beings, both male and female (fig. 23). The quality of the modelling varies but at its best it is excellent. Here, surprisingly, we find the same skilful rendering of limbs and muscles which we see in the actual seal engraving of the neo-palatial era. The realism is tempered however by a humour which we shall note emerging in other fields of artistic expression and by a remarkable ability to portray the character of the animal as well as its physical features. For example a trio of zoomorphic seal-stones from Platanos includes a pig, a monkey and a cow. The pig, with tiny eyes, raised ears, and blunt snout looks slightly stupid; the monkey, on the other hand, has an air of alertness and mischief about him, whilst the cow looks placid and docile (fig. 30, m–o).

A similar grasp of the 'personality' of different species is evident in the ceramic sculptures of the period. This is true not only of clay figurines themselves but also of clay vessels modelled in the form of animals and humans. These vessels form a distinctive group ranging over the whole period, but the earliest of them are perhaps the most charming of all. In the EM I stratum at Lebena Alexiou found a series of oddly shaped vases which represented both animals and plants.[1] Outstanding amongst this group of unique vessels was a small one in the shape of a pig. The rotund body, four stout but tiny legs, and the thrusting, blunt snout all contribute to produce a charming caricature of the animal. A jug of EM II date from Koumasa, in the form of a bird, is equally interesting but in a different way.[2] In this piece the effect is achieved not by the combination of several individual features but by the emphasis of one of them (pl. 12). Looking at the piece one is oblivious of its four legs, its handle, its tiny wings and tail; only the long neck, the large gaping beak and the big staring eye hold the attention. The artist has clearly seen young birds in the nest, stretching up for food and has brilliantly re-created in clay not merely the visual image but the very essence of their selfish, overwhelming demand for food.

In comparison to these items, those of EM III and MM Ia seem rather uninspired. One wonders if this is to be connected with the religious function which many of these later vessels, in the form of bulls or birds, appear to have. Did the artist feel that ritual vessels should be more restrained, or was he simply preoccupied with depicting the animals accurately? We do not know, but certainly these bulls and birds, charming and skilfully made as they may be, lack the artistic perception evident in the Lebena pig and the Koumasa bird[3] (pl. 11). They do, however, attest to the continuity of this tradition from the beginning of the Bronze Age to the start of the palatial era. During the period of the palaces the zoomorphic rhyton reaches perfection in the well known bulls' heads of stone. Stoneworking has a very long tradition itself in the Aegean and we have already looked at the production of stone-vases in Early Minoan

---

[1] Alexiou *1960*.   [2] Xanthoudides *1924* pl. II, 4121.
[3] Xanthoudides *1924* pl. II, 4141, 4126, pl. XIX.

Plate 13

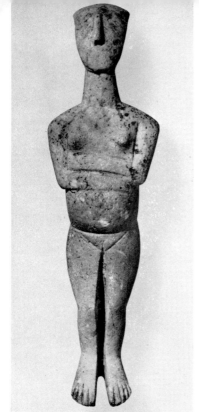

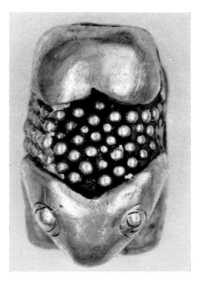

a Cycladic figurine from Koumasa. EC II

b A small gold toad with granulated decoration from Platanos. MM Ia

c Gold brooch featuring two bees (or wasps?), from Chrysollakos ossuary at

Plate 14

a ?Minoan stone pyxide with running spiral decoration, Maronia. EM II

b A frying-pan similar to Cycladic vessels of this type, from the Giamalakis Collection. EC II?

Crete in a previous chapter. Similarly we have discussed the engraving and sculpture of stone and ivory seal-stones in the present chapter. Before we leave either the medium of stone or the subject of zoomorphic vessels, however, we must comment briefly on the remarkable pyxide lids from Mochlos and Zakro[1] (pl. 12). The two lids are almost, but not quite, identical, each being of green soapstone with incised decoration of hatched triangles. On both lids the handle is carved in the form of a dog, stretched out but alert. The dog is long and lean, a close relation – as Seager noted when he published the Mochlos lid – of the dogs found in present day Cretan villages. There are several notable features on these lids, the most prominent perhaps being the posture in which the dog is portrayed. One might expect the animal to be aligned across the circular lid, but it is not; instead we find it with its forelegs thrust forward and its rear legs spread sideways, at rather more than ninety degrees to the body and forelegs. The animal thus forms a figure seven on the top of the lid, but the balance of the piece is preserved by the tail which curves round and away from the rear legs. The modelling is equally interesting. Whilst the legs and tail are treated summarily, the body is carefully worked and preserves a fine contour along the back from the rump to the crown of the head. Again, however, there is no attempt to achieve symmetry, for the head is kept low and thrust forward whilst the rump rises abruptly and forms the highest part of the handle. The posture and modelling together evoke very clearly the image of some Cretan dog resting beneath an olive tree. Thus the lids from Mochlos and Zakro, the work, one imagines, of a single Minoan master, typify three of the distinctive features of Early Minoan art – imagination, a command of spatial relationships and the ability to grasp the essential characteristics of the native fauna and re-create them in stone, clay or ivory.

Having found such an abundance of artistry in the representation of animals, it is surprising to find a lack of it in the modelling of clay figurines of humans. In the chapter on religion we divided the human figurines into three groups – the Cycladic group, the schematic group with pointed bases, and the realistic group. In a discussion of Early Minoan art only the last group need closer study. Most of the figurines in this group are of clay but there are a small number from the Mesara tombs which are made of ivory. Apart from the attempt to portray the human body more or less

[1] Zervos *1956* pl. 146; Platon *1964*.

realistically there is nothing which holds this collection of figurines together as a group. They are, for the most part, poorly proportioned and modelled. There is, one feels, a complete lack of interest on the part of maker, so much so that one is loathe to use the term 'artist'. This is particularly true of EM II, and the best of a poor bunch (fig. 24) illustrate the point quite clearly. The small figures from Koumasa and Porti are both stiff in posture, unsophisticated in modelling and badly proportioned although their diminutive size may partially excuse these shortcomings. Better proportioned, the fragmentary figure from Siva is so primitively modelled that it can claim no significance whatever as a work of art.[1] Only in EM III and MM Ia do we find figurines which, if lacking in inspiration, are at least competently modelled and properly proportioned. Amongst these figurines there is perhaps some sign of uniformity though this is probably due to the similarity of dress rather than the emergence of a common style. Koumasa, Tylissos, and Petsopha all produce female figurines with long dresses and spreading hats.[2] There is little advance in the representation of features over the EM II figurines, but in addition to the improvements in proportion and modelling, the light-on-dark painted decoration of these figures gives them a freshness and clarity which partially compensate for their artistic limitations (pl. 10). The male figures share the faults of the female figurines, but not the improving effects of the light-on-dark decoration. Nevertheless, the best of them are not unpleasant and seem to convey an air of nobility and pride on the part of Minoan manhood at this time. This is perhaps the only link that these figurines have with the superb ivory figures and the proud 'princes' depicted on the frescoes of the later palatial era.

In the field of gold jewellery the situation is different, for during the Early Bronze Age Crete produces fine jewellery as exquisite as the best that the palatial era can boast. It occurs particularly in EM II, and is undoubtedly part of the same trend we see in the Cyclades, Troy, and on the mainland of Greece in the second phase of the Early Bronze Age. Although the gold jewellery is found throughout the island, it is best known from the tombs of Mochlos and certainly it is in the material from these tombs that we see it at its best. The jewellery from the Mesara tholoi is perhaps a little

---

[1] Parabeni *1913* fig. 17.

[2] Xanthoudides *1924* pl. XXX, 5050, 5655; Hazzidakis *1912* fig. 37; Myres *1903* pls IX–XII.

later in date, but it is very similar in type and good pieces certainly occurred in the EM II strata at Platanos (tholos A) and Lebena.

Amongst the hundreds of pieces of jewellery found in these deposits there are very few rings – perhaps a dozen – and only two pins, both of silver. The majority of the pieces are either beads, pendants or diadems and attachments. Most of the beads are cylindrical or barrel shaped and are beaten from gold sheet, but in addition to these there are others of highly coloured or attractive stones – rock crystal, limestone, carnelian, and serpentine – which are far more varied in form. Variety is brought to the gold beads by decoration in the incised, repoussé or appliqué techniques (fig. 31). At Platanos all three techniques are represented and torsion is the principle on which the decoration is based. Repoussé and incised designs twist around the cylinders and barrels, or double running spirals form a continuous frieze. For craftsmanship a small cylindrical bead with such a frieze found at Kalathiana is difficult to equal.[1] It meets its match perhaps in some of the pendants such as those found at Platanos, Mochlos and Sphoungaras (fig. 31, 8–14). All of these pendants dangle from delicate chains, each formed of tiny individual links. The pendants themselves are cut from sheet gold in the shape of hearts, triangles or leaves. Some of these pendants were probably attachments for the diadems rather than pieces of jewellery in their own right, for many of the diadems have holes in them where additional decorations were fixed. Dozens of the decorations have been found in the same deposits as the diadems and amongst them we find some of the finest achievements of the Early Minoan gold worker. Most of the diadem attachments are in the form of flowers or petals beaten from sheet gold. There is a wide variety of shapes represented amongst the leaves or petals which are often simply decorated in repoussé (fig. 31, 15–20). The diadems themselves are normally broad bands which taper from the centre outwards (fig. 32). Their length is such that they were clearly not intended to encircle the whole head but were probably held on the forehead by fine gold wire which was tied at the back of the head. Strands of gold which may have been used for this purpose are commonly found in the same deposits as the diadems. The simplest diadems are undecorated or perhaps have a border of a single row of repoussé dots, but many are decorated with diamonds, crosses, arrows or triangles. Of particular interest are two of the

[1] Zervos *1956* pl. 201.

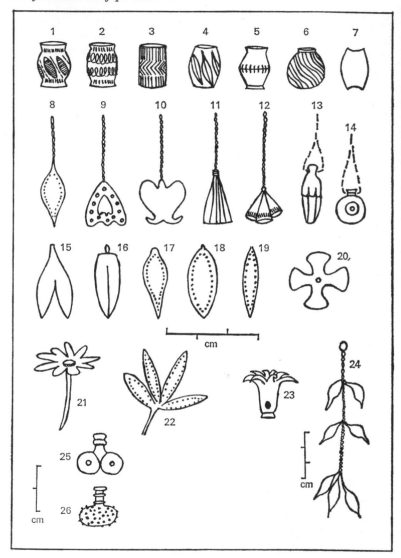

Figure 31   Early Minoan gold beads and pendants

Mochlos diadems, one of which sports a pair of eyes and the other three quadrupeds (fig. 32, 1 and 3). The animals seem to be dogs and the diadem is very similar to a silver one found in the Cyclades.[1]

[1] Tsountas *1899* pl. 10, 1.

Finally, attention should be drawn to a fragment of an openwork diadem found at Kalathiana, the only example of this style of work found in Early Minoan Crete (fig. 32, 9).

The supreme achievement of Early Minoan goldworking is the

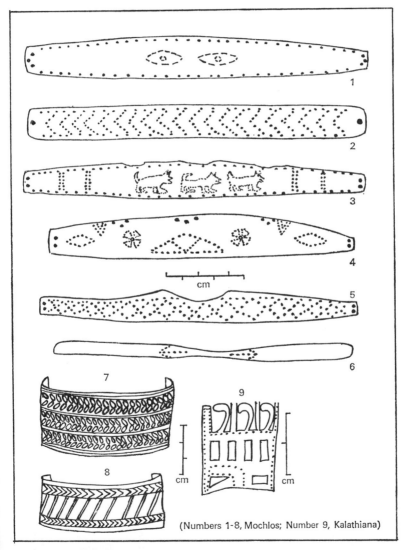

(Numbers 1-8, Mochlos; Number 9, Kalathiana)

Figure 32   Early Minoan gold jewellery

splendid brooch found in the Chrysolakkos cemetery at Mallia. It is made in the form of two wasps? sampling a berry (pl. 13). From their wings and tails hang three small circular pendants and between their legs they hold a fourth circle. The eyes, and abdomens of the wasps, and the four discs are all decorated with granulations, or small beads of gold. This is a technique not found before MM Ia and seen again on a small gold toad found in tholos B, Koumasa[1] (pl. 13). The workmanship of the Mallia brooch is superb, but it is equalled by the artistry of the man who made it. Here again we see all that is best in the art of Early Bronze Age Crete–imagination, control, and good taste. It is particularly true of the gold jewellery that its merits lie not in the workmanship but in the taste which it displays. The workmanship is always competent but it is never pretentious and only rarely does it show the brilliance revealed in the Mallia brooch. But the taste is always irreproachable. Where gold is used together with stone the colours are always complementary;[2] where gold is used alone it is always simple in style and decoration, never flamboyant in either size or design.

The development of Early Minoan art should not be seen as a smooth progression from the primitive to the sophisticated. At the very outset of the age we see good taste and discipline displayed in pottery of the Agios Onouphrios style, and a lively interest in problems of texture and form. Imagination and invention are revealed in contemporary zoomorphic vessels. The same features are all present in the art of EM II. In the Vasiliki pottery we see the invention of a new technique and a new, metallic texture. On the other hand there is a noticeable decline in the quality of Agios Onouphrios style ceramics, and although the discipline seen in EM I pottery is maintained in Vasiliki ware, amongst the earliest seal-stones we find a small group which represents a trend in the opposite direction. The outstanding artistic innovations of the EM II phase are the principle of torsion and experiments with polychrome, the first expressed on seal-stones and the second in Vasiliki pottery. Torsion is developed rapidly in EM III and invention and imagination play a full part in painted decoration at this time. But enthusiasm introduces a lack of control which results in a conflict between pottery shapes and decoration and a general

---

[1] Zervos *1956* pl. 201; Marinatos *1960* pl. 13 bottom.
[2] e.g. Zervos *1956* pl. 201 (gold and rock crystal–a combination repeated in the Agios Onouphrios deposit).

decline in good taste. There is a gradual transition to MM Ia, during which control and discipline are reinstated. A short-lived experiment with zoomorphic and anthropomorphic motifs in pottery decoration is rejected and a gradual evolution towards geometric and flower-like motifs begins. Further simple experiments in polychrome during EM III are developed into the beginning of the full Middle Minoan polychrome style, whilst yet another experiment in texture is represented by the encrusted and rusticated wares. Amongst the sealstones and figurines we can trace perhaps the initial formation of the styles and principles which characterize Minoan glyptic and minor sculpture of the palatial era. But although these links with the art of the palatial period are evident, the art of Early Minoan Crete is more than an introduction to Kamares pottery, Minoan fresco painting, and Middle Minoan glyptic. Early Minoan art is a vital and colourful experience in itself.

8   Funerary architecture and ritual

Our knowledge of Minoan civilization in the Middle and Late Bronze Ages is mainly derived from the discoveries made in the great palaces and villas in which the Minoans of these times lived. The palaces and their contents have proved so magnificent that the testimony offered by the contemporary tombs has been to some extent overshadowed. In the case of the Early Bronze Age, however, the tombs and their contents provide by far the most complete testimony as to the nature of life and death in Crete at that time. This has been apparent throughout the previous chapters, where almost all of the objects discussed have been those found in Early Minoan tombs. Whilst the chapter on domestic architecture and settlements was, of necessity, largely concerned with a few fragmentary remains, a discussion of funerary architecture is in no way limited by a lack of material. And yet we shall find that, despite a large number of excavated tombs of varying types, we know very little about the rituals which would seem to have accompanied burials.

The method of burial which seems to have been practised throughout the island during the Late and sub-Neolithic phases was that of inhumation in a cave or rock shelter.[1] Thus in the west we find the caves of Ellenouspelio and Kumarospelio, in central Crete the cave at Skaphidia and the rock shelter of Kastelli Tzermiadhon, and in the east the rock shelters of Agios Nikolaos, all used for the interment of the dead. Only in the region of the Mesara do we lack evidence for Late Neolithic burials of this type, and this is the case during the Early Bronze Age as well. Several rock shelter inhumations have been found at both Agia Photia and Zakro, dating to EM I and EM II. A single burial of the EM II phase was also

---

[1] Marinatos *1928* 5ff. (Ellenospelio); Matz *1942* 1ff. (Kumarospelio); Duckworth *1903* (Agios Nikolaos); Pendlebury *1938* 5 (Skaphidia) 8, 13 (Kastelli Tz.).

discovered in the rock shelter at Vrokastro. In the plateau of Lasithi the continuity of the tradition is evidenced by the much disturbed burials which Pendlebury found in the cave at Trapeza. Elsewhere in the centre of the island we have the numerous EM I burials in the cave at Kanli Kastelli and equally numerous inhumations dating to EM I and probably also to EM III at Pyrgos. It seems probable that the burials in the cave at Kumarospelio are contemporary with those at say Kanli Kastelli, but the single burial found in a cave at Ellenes Amariou attests quite definitely to the continuity of this type of burial into the EM I period of at least south-western Crete.[1] No doubt further work in this much neglected part of the island will yield many more instances of cave burials.

Apart from the re-use of the rock shelter at Pyrgos during EM III, the only other EM III–MM Ia inhumations found in caves and rock shelters occur in the east of the island, at Gournia, Ayios Ionnes and Mochlos.[2]

Almost all of the burials referred to had suffered badly from later disturbance and often from natural erosion as well. The only example which gave a clear indication of the actual method of inhumation was Ellenes Amariou where the single interment was found to be lying on its back in an extended position. But at Kanli Kastelli there is no sign of later intrusion and the only natural disturbance is the collapsed section of the roof which fortunately sealed the deposit for us. The confused state of the skeletal remains in this deposit therefore calls for an explanation other than later or natural disturbance. The excavator of the site, Dr. Alexiou, is in no doubt that the disturbance is really due to the burial rites which accompanied the successive burials, rather than to the cave being used as an ossuary. That is to say, he believes the burials to be primary. The large number of pots recovered from the deposit might perhaps support this hypothesis, although in eastern Crete some Middle Minoan ossuaries, Roussolakkos for example, also produced large numbers of pots. It could be argued that the fine preservation of the pottery at Kanli Kastelli is indicative of a minimum of rituals taking place in the cave, which might suggest use as an ossuary rather than for primary inhumation.

[1] Hogarth *1901* (Zakro); Boyd-Hawes *1905* (Agia Photia); Hall *1914* (Vrokastro–Agios Andoni); Pendlebury *1936* (Trapeza); Alexiou *1951* (Kanli Kastelli); Xanthoudides *1918a* (Pyrgos); Marinatos *1932* 177 (Ellenais Amariou).

[2] Boyd-Hawes *1905* 56 (Gournia) (Agios Ionnes); Seager *1912* (Mochlos).

However, there can be no doubt at all that considerable disturbance must have been caused by ritual practices, for which considerable evidence was found. Clear traces of burning were noticed,
particularly on the bones of both animals and humans. Alexiou
recalls that similar burning had been noticed at the other cave
burials at Pyrgos, Zakro and Trapeza. At the latter site Pendlebury
emphasized this fact and said that some bones looked as if they had
been almost completely incinerated. There is no question of
cremation being involved, as the unburnt bones clearly attest. We
are therefore left really with two possibilities. Either the tombs were
fumigated at times when it was considered necessary, or else ritual
practices included a funerary feast or the offering of burnt sacrifices within the tomb. The fact that burnt bones do not occur in all
of the cave and rock shelter burials would suggest that a common
funerary ritual involving the use of fire was not practised during the
Early Bronze Age. There may have been local customs which were
observed and which account for the burnt bones in the deposits
mentioned, but it seems at least as likely that the burning is the
result of fumigation. Some further light may be thrown on this problem when we come to discuss the tholos tombs of the Mesara and
rather similar evidence for burning which has been found in them.

There is nothing in any of the cave burials which gives us good
reason to think that the communities using these caves propagated
a cult of the dead. The cave at Trapeza produced some objects which
would seem to be offerings, but it is impossible to say whether they
were intended for the dead or for a local deity believed to occupy the
cave. Many caves, of course, achieved a sacred status during the
Middle Minoan period, and there is nothing in them, nor elsewhere
in the island, to suggest that the deities to whom they were dedicated
were in any way connected with the ancestors who might be buried
somewhere within their depths.

Contemporary with the cave and rock shelter burials in eastern
and central Crete from the start of EM II onwards, were rectangular
chamber tombs which we might regard as the equivalents to the
tholos tombs of the Mesara. These have been regarded by successive
authorities as imitations of houses used by the living. In particular
both Pendlebury and Hutchinson thought that they were modelled
after the houses of the ancestors, that is to say after the Late Neolithic houses.[1] Some of the tombs at Palaikastro (figs 33, 35) could

[1] Pendlebury *1939* 63; Hutchinson *1962* 145.

perhaps be compared with the Neolithic house at Magasa which we have already discussed in chapter three, but the so-called 'but-and-ben' design is so simple that its use for a burial chamber is to be expected and certainly need not imply a conscious attempt to copy dwellings. The design of the rectangular ossuaries varies considerably in detail but falls into two broad groups, one characterized by square or oblong rooms and the other by a series of long, narrow chambers running parallel to one another. In the former group we may include one of the ossuaries at Gournes (fig. 33b), several of those at Palaikastro (figs 33, 35) and some of those at Mochlos (fig. 35). The second group comprises the ossuaries at Roussolakkos (Palaikastro), Arkhanes and Gournes (fig. 34). There is no obvious chronological difference between the two types and at Palaikastro and Gournes both types are found on the same site.

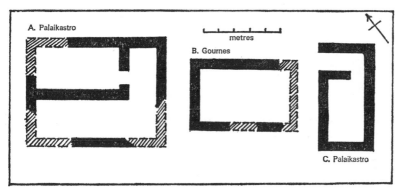

Figure 33   Early Minoan ossuaries

It is presumed that the ossuaries with long, narrow chambers were never roofed over but left open. Beams to support a simple roof of branches and mud plaster could easily have been laid across the closely aligned walls but no traces of these have ever been recorded and at Roussolakkos and Arkhanes some of the chambers at least had no entrances. These ossuaries with narrow chambers can hardly be interpreted as imitations of contemporary houses, for not only have no comparable houses been found but the design would of course make no sense at all if applied to domestic architecture. The other group of ossuaries could be imitations of dwelling houses, and the appearance of both types of ossuary together at Palaikastro and Gournes might perhaps suggest that burial was a two stage process, involving burial in the mortuary 'house' and subsequent removal of the bone remains to one of the narrow-chamber ossuaries.

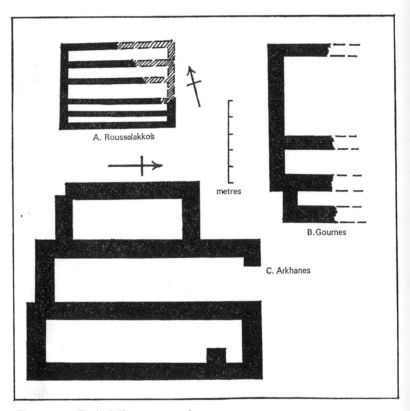

Figure 34   Early Minoan ossuaries

In this case the mortuary 'houses' should not, of course, be regarded as ossuaries at all. The mass of bones found in them, however, and the condition in which they were found, do not support this attractive hypothesis, and despite the distinction between the two types of ossuaries, it seems that they were manifestations of a single concept.

The only convincing arguments which suggest that the concept was that of a domestic dwelling are centred on some of the 'house' tombs from Mochlos and Palaikastro, and upon the observations of

Dawkins in one of the simple tombs at the latter side.[1] This was a tomb occupied in EM II–MM Ia which had an outer, L-shaped room and a rectangular room fitted into the right-angle (fig. 33a). Only one burial was found in the tomb, and that was within the small rectangular room; but no pottery was found here, all the pottery was in the outer room. It could be reasonably argued that the burial was made in this way in order to perpetuate the idea of an inner bedroom and an outer living-room, where the man would eat his food and drink his wine from the vessels which were left for him. This arrangement might also imply, of course, a cult of the dead.

The same interpretation could be placed on the design of the 'but-and-ben' chambers and the chamber tombs at Mochlos, but here the mixed distribution of bone and ceramic finds does not suggest such a conclusion. In the case of the Mochlos tombs it is the architectural refinements which suggest a derivation from domestic architecture. Unlike the walls of the ossuaries at Palaikastro and Khorion Gournes, which are built of small stones for the most part, those of the chambers on Mochlos are strongly built of either horizontally laid courses or else of upright slabs. The doorways have projecting jambs such as we might expect to find in palace and villa architecture, and the doors themselves are represented by large upright slabs. Such refinements, it may be argued, are surely indicative that the tombs were regarded as more than mere repositories for the bones of the dead.

There are, however, good reasons why we might regard these chambers as nothing more than repositories. Chambers I, II, IV, V, and VI at Mochlos are all long, very narrow rooms (fig. 35) which have no parallel in domestic architecture except in the magazines. Furthermore it is in the magazines of the palaces and villas that we find the projecting door jamb most commonly used. The Mochlos chambers are in fact only refined examples of the ossuaries at Khorion Gournes, Roussolakkos and Arkhanes, where we find the same long, very narrow rooms in use. There is no evidence from Mochlos to suggest that the chambers were regarded as houses for the dead. Indeed, the only tomb to present any clear evidence of the attitude towards burial was tomb V where 30 skulls were found piled up in a heap at one end. This situation was repeated at Arkhanes where almost 200 skulls were found in heaps. This would seem to strengthen our hypothesis that these chamber tombs were regarded as repositories

[1] Dawkins *1905* fig. 2.

for the remains of the dead and not as houses in which the dead were expected to dwell.

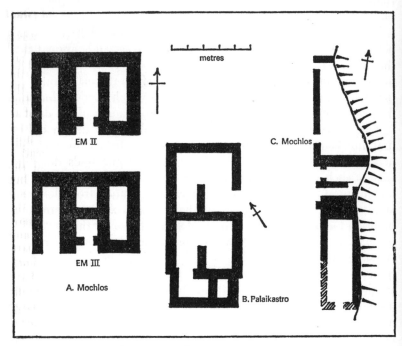

Figure 35   Early Minoan ossuaries

This is implied also in the history of the tomb complex comprised of chambers IV, V and VI (fig. 35a). In EM II chambers IV and VI were a unit which could perhaps be interpreted as an imitation of the 'but-and-ben' house type. In the succeeding period, however, the doorway between IV and VI was blocked and IV was divided into two sections, the rear of which was also completely blocked off from the front of the tomb. It is thus quite clear that, in EM III at least, this particular tomb was not regarded as a house for the dead, but rather as a repository for them with enough room left at the front to take new burials. Chamber V, of course, could never be interpreted in terms of house architecture.

Finally we might recognize that these long, narrow chambers in the Mochlos, Khorion, Gournes, Arkhanes and Roussolakkos tombs may well be related to the long narrow cells which are placed outside some of the Mesara tholoi (see fig. 40, Platanos 'A' for example). We shall have to discuss these cells in detail when we examine the tholoi with which they are related, but it will suffice here to say that there is every indication that they are intended to be store-rooms for both objects and human remains.

The ultimate form of the rectangular chamber tomb or ossuary is represented by two large ossuaries found near Mallia on the north coast.[1] The smaller of the two tombs, Agia Varvara 'B', was about thirteen metres square. Into this area were packed at least seventeen 'cells', of irregular shape and size. Originally the ossuary may have comprised five or six large cells but these had apparently been subdivided in order to accommodate more burials. Large as the Agia Varvara ossuary may be when compared to the EM II and III ossuaries at Roussolakkos, Arkhanes, Gournes and Mochlos, it is dwarfed by the other MM I ossuary at Mallia. This is known as 'Chrysolakkos' – 'the gold hole' – and it seems likely that the name is derived from the great wealth of the tomb deposits. The superb bee or wasp pendant was found here during the excavations, but most of the deposit had been looted and it is thought that the famous 'Aegina treasure' may perhaps have been stolen from here in antiquity.[2] Chrysolakkos is more than forty metres long and thirty metres wide. Surrounded by a paved walk and, along the east side at least, a pillared portico, it must have been a most impressive monument when it was erected (fig. 36). The inside has been much disturbed by the action of looters and we cannot be sure how many cells eventually filled the interior but about forty remain and one imagines that there were once at least twice that number. These ossuaries clearly represent a departure from the earlier ossuary practice of building chambers to take many bones. The multiplication of cells suggests that originally at least, each cell may have been intended to hold a single burial. We might therefore relate the concept behind the Mallia ossuaries to that represented in the larnake and pithos burials which begin to appear during EM III. At Mallia we may be seeing a compromise between the communal ossuary and the individual burial.

A similar phenomenon may perhaps be recognized in the Mesara tholoi, where in EM III and later, larnake burials are sometimes placed inside these great circular tombs.[3] To date over seventy of these tombs have been recorded at some forty-five different

[1] Demargne *1945*.　　[2] Higgins *1957*.　　[3] e.g. Kamilari, Porti.

locations[1] (fig. 39). Of this total, fifty have been examined archaeologically. There are certainly many unrecorded tholoi still to be examined. Travelling in the Mesara, one often hears of tholos tombs whose existence has gone unrecorded. I understand that there may be as many as eighty tombs which have not yet been put on the distribution map. This figure should not surprise us, for a total of one hundred and fifty tombs to cover a period of almost a millennium (and in some cases more) is hardly excessive!

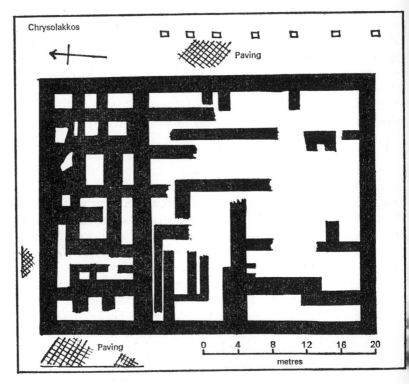

Figure 36 Chrysolakkos

The tholoi certainly have no Neolithic precedents in the island and appear suddenly in EM I. How many of the known tholoi date

[1] The best excavated of the ones discovered early in this century are published in Xanthoudides *1924*. Later excavations are published in Matz *1942*, Levi *1962*, Alexiou *1958*, *1960*.

Plate 15

a The tholos tomb at Kamilari after excavation. MM I-LM

b Fallen vaulting stones of the Kamilari tholos. MM I-LM

Plate 16

a The antechamber and door-stone of the Kamilari tholos. MM I-LM

b Funerary remains in the Kamilari tholos swept up against the wall of the tomb. MM I-LM

to this phase is not certain.[1] Salame, the two tholoi at Siva, Agia Eirene, Chrysostomos (fig. 38) and Lebena II all contained EM I material, and evidence shows that many of the other known tholoi were also first constructed in this period. But some are clearly later constructions. Drakones and Vorou seem to be built during EM III and Apesokari (fig. 41) and Kamilari not until MM I.

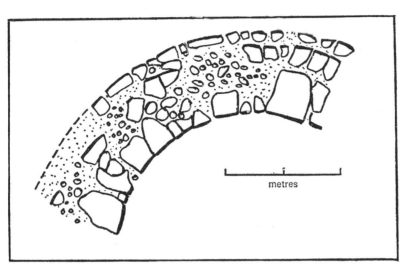

Figure 37   Details of Tholos wall construction, Lebena

However, the appearance of up to three tholoi on any one site does not necessarily indicate that they succeeded one another. Platanos, Koumasa, and Lebena have several tholoi but in each case we find that all the tholoi at some time overlapped with each other in usage. Indeed, there is now good reason to think that the tholoi on any single site were all built at approximately the same time. For example, the two tholoi at Siva were both built in EM I, whilst Lebena I and Ib were both erected in EM II. All three tombs at Platanos were probably built in EM II as well. Only at Yerokambos (Lebena II/IIa) can two adjacent tholoi be shown to have been constructed at different times (EM I, EM II respectively).

[1] Xanthoudides *1924* (Salame, Agia Eirene); Alexiou *1960* (Lebena); Parabeni *1913* (Siva); Xanthoudides *1924* (Koumasa E); Marinatos *1931* (Vorou); Matz *1942* (Apesokari); Levi *1962* (Kamilari).

These points are of some importance as they may help us to determine for whom the tholoi were built. Glotz suggested that they were tribal tombs but Hutchinson preferred to regard them as each belonging to a 'genos' or clan.[1] A third, obvious, alternative is that they were quite simply the communal tombs of the villages with which they were, most probably, associated. This is perhaps the simplest, and hence most attractive theory, but it is hard to reconcile with our conclusion that on those sites where more than one tomb exists, they were all in use together for at least a certain period of time. This would favour Hutchinson's suggestion that the tombs each belonged to a 'genos'. If this were so, then it would induce some speculation about the social structure in the Mesara villages. However, at this point in our discussion there is little evidence to support any of the theories and we should perhaps turn to questions of construction and the method in which the completed tomb was used. From our discussion of these subjects there may emerge some new light on the problem we have just examined.

Basically, the tholos tombs of the Mesara consist of a circular stone wall which has a single entrance on the east side. Many of the tholoi form the main element of a complex of enclosures but despite considerable variety in these elaborations, the tholos tombs form a remarkably homogeneous group, both geographically and architecturally. The main wall of the tholos is built, in most cases, of a rubble core of small stones and earth faced both inside and out with large unworked blocks (fig. 37). Some of the latest tombs, such as Kamilari, have roughly worked and shaped blocks as facing, but this refinement does not seem to occur in the earlier tholoi. The tholos tomb at Kalathiana has the appearance of using worked blocks but this is apparently due to the nature of the local stone which was used to build it. Some of the smallest of the early tombs do not even employ a faced rubble wall but simply a wall built of large blocks of stone. Such is the case with the small tholos tombs found by the author at Chrysostomos on the south coast (fig. 38). The thickness of the walls, whatever their manner of construction, is naturally greatest in the tombs with the biggest diameter. Thus we find that tholos A at Platanos, which is thirteen metres in diameter, has a wall which is almost two and a half metres thick. This contrasts with the wall of the tomb at Salame which is less than one metre wide and has a diameter of about five metres.

[1] Glotz *1921*; Hutchinson *1962* 232.

These details of wall construction are not of inconsiderable significance for they must be borne in mind in any discussion of the method by which these tombs were roofed over. This has

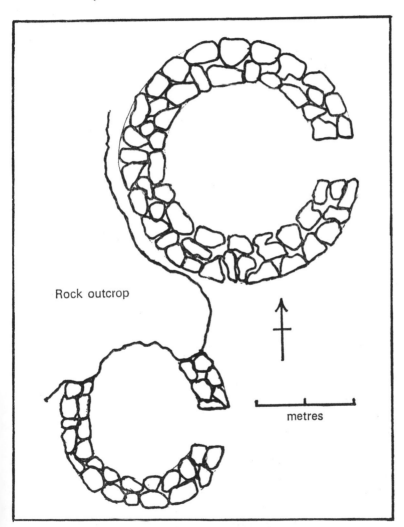

Rock outcrop

metres

Figure 38 Early Minoan I–III tholoi at Chrysostomos

remained an unsolved problem ever since Xanthoudides first excavated these tholoi. He himself was apparently in little doubt that the tombs were vaulted, for he titled his report on their excavation 'The Vaulted Tombs of the Mesara'. As evidence for this assertion he pointed to the inward curving walls of several of the tholoi which were reasonably well preserved, and also to the mass of fallen stone he found in tholos B at Platanos. This apparently amounted to some twenty-five cubic feet of material. Pendlebury pointed out that this amount of stone, however, would only account for another eighty centimetres in height, and even if we make an allowance for the earth in the rubble core it is clear that the material found in tholos B could never have constituted a complete stone vault. We must remember, however, that just as many of the grave goods were looted over a period of almost four thousand years, so too, in all probability, was the building stone. The evidence is therefore inconclusive!

Those who argue that these tombs could never have been vaulted do so for good reasons. The rather careless manner in which most of these tholos walls were built, and the small stones used in them, do not suggest the use of a vaulted roof. But of greater importance is the fact that the tholoi are free-standing structures above ground level. There is no trace of covering earth over any of the tholoi nor of external buttresses. (The so-called buttresses at Platanos on one side of tholos A will be discussed shortly.) This being so, it is quite clear that many of the tholoi, if not all, could never have withstood the outward pressure of a full stone vault. For this reason various alternative solutions have been suggested.[1]

Sinclair Hood believes that many of the larger tombs may have had their vault finished off with mud-brick. But no traces of mud-brick have ever been observed in the debris from the tombs. From this point of view a more plausible explanation is Pendlebury's. He suggests that the tholoi may have had a roof of branches or wood, and draws a comparison with a Macedonian hut. Hutchinson follows Pendlebury and adds a Hebridean hut to the comparative material. The author has himself seen small rock-built huts in the hills outside Hebron in Jordan which are roofed in precisely the same manner. Clearly this method of vaulting a low-sided building is satisfactory and well proven. It is a satisfactory solution to our problem as well, for the use of organic materials for the roof would explain why we have found no trace of the roof. Indeed, Pendlebury suggests that the traces of severe fire in some of the tholoi

[1] Hood *1962b* 224; Pendlebury *1939*; Hutchinson *1962* 152ff.

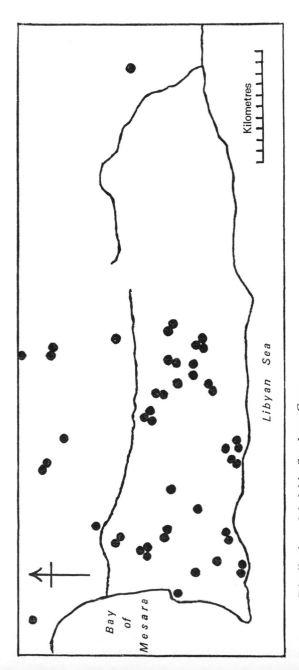

Figure 39 Distribution of tholoi in Southern Crete

are evidence for a roof of the type he suggests which during funerary rites had been set alight by mistake. At Kamilari Professor Levi found burnt pieces of wood amongst the debris (pl. 16b), but we do not know whether the wood here came from torches, objects buried with the dead, or from the roof structure.

Kamilari, however, is one of the three tholos tombs where good evidence has been found for a full stone vault. When the earth over the tomb was removed, Levi discovered that the centre of the tholos was full of collapsed masonry (pl. 15); and it had collapsed in such a way that it had clearly come from a corbelled vault. The larger stones, and those that still faced the inside of the wall, were wedge shaped to make the task of corbelling easier. Evidence of a very similar nature was found in tholoi I and II at Lebena by Dr. Alexiou. Again the slabs were discovered still in the position into which they had fallen, and Alexiou was convinced that the tombs had been fully vaulted with stone. These three tombs and the evidence they provide for corbelled stone vaults might suggest that those who argue for a less substantial roof have no case. But the amount of stone found at Lebena and Kamilari inside the tombs was still not enough to complete a stone vaulted roof and more important, there is still no evidence to show how the outward thrust of the vault could have been sustained. Thus in the author's opinion it is still advisable to think in terms of the vault being completed by a wooden construction.

It has been suggested that projecting slabs found, in varying numbers, on the outside of some tombs were intended to help anchor a covering mound of earth. Were this so, then the main argument against a fully vaulted roof of stone would be invalidated. But not only do no traces of such covering mounds exist but these small slabs placed about one metre above ground level and about the same distance apart could hardly be of any value in keying down a complete covering mound. Such slabs would need to be built into the wall at regular intervals right up to the top if they were to be effective. Few tholoi have produced more than the single row of slabs, just above ground level. It seems therefore that other reasons for the slabs' existence must be sought.

There seem to be very few constant factors in the manner in which the slabs were employed. The number of slabs recorded on any one tholos vary from only four at Apesokari to twenty-four at Platanos on tholos B. There is no pattern at all in the positioning of the slabs. At Koumasa, tholos B has five on the north side, whilst tholos E has twelve on the east. Tholos E at Agia Eirene and tholos B at Platanos have slabs on the southern side. At Porti there are six slabs on the north-east side and three on the south-west. Neither can the use of slabs be attributed to a particular period. Porti was probably built in EM I, Koumasa B was built in EM IIa, Platanos B in EM IIb, Koumasa E most probably in EM III, and Apesokari in MM I, all of these tombs have projecting slabs. The absence of a single common factor in the way these slabs were used is enough to discount any suggestions which have yet been made as to what that use was. Xanthoudides, who believed that they helped to bind a covering mound, also thought that the slabs were in some way connected with the actual construction of the tomb, perhaps a sort of elementary scaffolding. Alternatively, it has been suggested that the wooden roof was anchored by cord to these slabs. The other possibility which springs to mind is that the slabs had some ritual significance. Perhaps it was intended that offerings should be placed on them. But objections can be raised to each of these suggestions, particularly the objection we have stressed throughout – the lack of uniformity of practice.

In contrast to the slabs, the doorways of the tholoi are remarkably uniform in size, orientation and construction. We have already mentioned that all the doorways face eastwards, which is surely indicative of some particular funerary belief. Most of the doorways are constructed of a trilithon and are about one metre high. A few are larger, such as Kamilari and Drakones Z, and some use large slabs only for the lintel, the sides of the door being built of laid courses. A particularly good example of this sort of structure is the doorway of the Kamilari tholos (pl. 15). The doors themselves appear to have been large, flat slabs of stone (pl. 16a) although those tombs where such slabs have not been found may possibly have had wooden doors. The most unusual doorway is that to tholos B at Koumasa which has a central dividing stone set into the ground so that there is in fact a double doorway. There is no apparent explanation for this deviation from the norm. This doorway is also of some interest as holes were found in the side of the doorway where wooden bars were once placed, one assumes, to hold the door in position. None of the doorways were small enough to suggest that burials were made through the roof as some people have suggested. This practice may have suggested itself to these authorities because of the possible relationship which exists between the Mesara tholoi and the contemporary Cycladic cist graves.[1] In many of these it is clear that the doorway was purely representational and that the bodies were placed in the tomb through the roof. In the Cyclades the cist graves were most commonly made of stone slabs, but examples which were made by building a small circular wall which was given a corbelled roof are by no means scarce. These cist graves were of course dug into the ground and cannot be compared to even the smallest of the Mesara tholoi, but there are also examples of similarly built tombs which stand above ground and one of these in fact has been discovered in Crete at Krasi in Pediadha.[2] Ordinary cist graves have also been found at Mochlos and Zakro and these facts, together with other manifestations of Cycladic influence in Early Minoan Crete such as grey incised pottery, various small jar shapes, and of course 'Cycladic' idols, have suggested to some people that the Mesara tholoi might be adapted and improved Cycladic tombs. But the gap between the two types is so large that a close relationship seems unlikely. We should also expect to find most of the tholos tombs in the northern coastal area if they were introduced to Crete from the Cyclades. In this respect Sir Arthur Evans's theory of a Libyan origin would seem to fit the geographical distribution of the Minoan tholos tomb far better. And indeed the Libyan parallels to the Early Minoan tholoi are interesting. In particular we notice that the Libyan structures share with the Minoan, the feature of a rectangular vestibule in front of the doorway.[3]

The vestibules in front of the tholoi are small and can never have been used for any elaborate rituals (pl. 16). That in front of Koumasa A for example is only one and a half metres long and less than a metre broad. Furthermore, many of the tholoi show no trace of having had a vestibule. The vestibules however do seem to be primary structures whereas some of the auxiliary cells and rooms which we find attached to several tholoi are certainly secondary. Such would seem to be the case with the rectangular rooms outside tholos A at Platanos (fig. 40), rooms AN and D at Lebena and rooms b and c at Porti. All of these rooms not only give the appearance of

---

[1] See Mylonas *1959* 64ff. for a discussion of burial method in the cist graves at Agios Kosmas.

[2] Marinatos *1929*.

[3] Cf. Koumasa tholos A (Xanthoudides *1924*), Evans *1928* 37, fig. 17a–c.

being added on to an existing structure but all of them produced late pottery. In the case of Platanos A, the fragmentary walls on the south side were considered by Xanthoudides to be buttresses, but this interpretation ignores the curving wall which is clearly intended to join these cells to the rectangular block of magazines on the east side. It seems certain that these fragmentary walls are the remains of further magazine-like rooms.

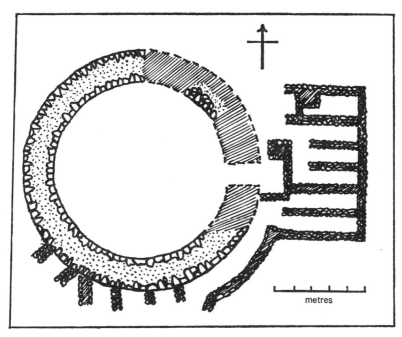

Figure 40   Tholos 'A' at Platanos

Within these rooms at Platanos, Xanthoudides found both objects and bones and it was apparent that the cells were regarded simply as store-rooms for the dead and their belongings. There can be little doubt that these cells were added to the tholos at a late date, probably in EM III, when the burial chamber had itself become too full to use. This was quite clearly the case at Porti where room b contained fragments of pithoi and larnakes. Room c seems to have been used principally as an ossuary and it may be that the bones here were from earlier burials which had been cleaned out of the main burial chamber. There is ample evidence for such clearing out operations having taken place.[1] Tholoi B and E at Koumasa both contained groups of bones which had been swept into one area and there heaped up against the wall. Levi found similar evidence at Kamilari (pl. 16). Many of the bones removed from the Koumasa tholoi were probably buried in one of the ten trenches which were found there, all of them full of bones and objects. Two trenches jammed with bones and personal objects were also discovered at Platanos. Such treatment of ancestral remains raises serious doubts as to whether the Early Minoans practised elaborate funerary rituals and even more as to whether they propagated a cult of the dead. The complete confusion of human remains in every tholos yet excavated suggests a complete disregard for the dead. Yet in spite of the evidence seen above there are still several indications that this was not in fact the case.

One such indication is the nature of the objects found in the tholoi along with the bones. These can be divided into four main groups, vessels, tools and weapons, jewellery, and seals. All of these groups of material are large enough to suggest that it was the common practice to bury the dead with personal belongings and with food and drink. The sealstones, necklaces, diadems, dagger blades, razors, and small toilet blades and tweezers, all show clear signs of having had a working life before they were deposited in the tombs. That is to say, they were objects which actually belonged to the deceased and had actually been used by them; they were not objects which had been specially made for funerary use. This is true also of the majority of pottery vessels, which in shape and decoration are identical with vessels found on occupation sites. Most of the vessels are jugs, pyxides, dishes, and storage jars which could have contained drink, oil, and various foods. The only certain evidence that they did contain these things was found by Alexiou at Lebena. Here he found olive seeds, the teeth and bones of animals, and various seashells, which bore witness to the sort of food which was left with the dead. This evidence for food and drink being left with the dead, along with their personal belongings, must surely imply that although we have never found articulated skeletons in the tholoi but only confused masses of bone, the dead must have been buried as bodies. It clearly argues against any suggestion that the tholoi were simply ossuaries.

[1] See Xanthoudides *1924* on Platanos, Koumasa, Porti.

Some of the clay vessels found in the tombs, however, were obviously of ritual significance and so too were most of the small stone vases. The latter are almost all too small to have served any practical use, and like the clay vessels in question are noticeably absent from settlement sites. This does not mean that all the vessels involved were made exclusively for funerary rituals, however, for some are clearly connected with the veneration of the bull, with fertility, and with other beliefs that are concerned as much with the living as with the dead. These vessels were discussed in the chapter on religion. There are other vessels though which can only be interpreted in terms of funerary practices, particularly the kernoi (which often bear a remarkable resemblance to modern condiment sets) and the small stone bowls and straight-sided cups. As we have said, these are far too small to have had a practical use, and their appearance in hundreds both in the tholoi and in the outside chambers and trenches can only imply that they were used for funerary feasts and possibly for subsequent rituals as well. Their funerary function is quite clearly established by Alexiou's discovery at Lebena of dozens of clay cups which had obviously been used in a burial rite and which seem to have been used in place of their stone relatives on this particular site.

Whether or not the extensive signs of burning which have been noticed in many of the tholoi are to be interpreted as further evidence for funerary feasts is a matter for discussion.[1] Xanthoudides reports that he found a large hearth in the centre of tholos B at Koumasa and another fire-place by the south-east section of the wall. Hearths and fire-places are surely to be connected with feasts or sacrifices of the sort we have mentioned. Unfortunately, no photographs or plans of these 'hearths' exist so that we cannot judge their precise nature for ourselves. But in tholos A at Platanos, where extensive signs of fire were noticed on both the bones and the floor, the signs were found to be most marked in the centre. There is no mention of a hearth in this case. It seems likely to the author that these signs of intensive burning at the centre signify not a burial feast but fumigation. Two points of evidence suggest this solution. All the tholos tombs which have produced evidence of burning have produced it not only on the floor of the tomb but also on the human bones. Secondly all the four tombs where a clearing-out operation

[1] Traces of fire have been noticed at Koumasa B, Porti II, Drakones D, Platanos A, C (all Xanthoudides *1924*) and Kamilari (Levi *1962*).

is clearly indicated are found to be tombs with signs of burning in the tomb. We have already mentioned the traces of fire in tholos B at Koumasa, where the bones had been swept to one side and the skulls heaped up. At Kamilari Levi found the same thing had happened and published a photograph which shows some of the burnt bones and pottery swept up against the wall of the tomb. In tholos A at Platanos the signs of excessive burning were found to accompany a complete cleaning out of the earlier burials and the sealing over of what odd scraps remained by a layer of white earth. We find the same happened at Lebena in chamber IIa where the EM II burials were burned and overlaid by a spread of white sand. Above this sand the new (MM I) burials were made.

Whether or not the white earth has some significance we do not know, but apart from Lebena and Platanos A, it was also found covering swept-aside burials in tholos E at Koumasa; and in the small graves on Mochlos in the east we find a filling of white clay which is said to have been taken to the small island from the mainland.

Perhaps the clearest indications that the Minoans were in fact much concerned with the dead are to be found in three particular tholoi, two comparatively late in construction. These tholoi are Platanos B (EM II), Apesokari (MM I) and Kamilari (MM I). The evidence is best preserved at Apesokari (fig. 41). Here we find that, joined on to the tholos itself, the builders constructed a rectangular complex of rooms. One entered the complex through a narrow vestibule which led into a square room which would seem to have been the focus of the ritual practices. From this room entrance to the tholos was gained through a second narrow cross-room. Two altars are associated with the complex, one in the square room and another standing just to the right of the outer entrance on a small area of paving which there is good reason to think would have originally covered the whole area in front of the tholos. It would be senseless to attempt any detailed interpretation of the ritual complex, but the two altars most probably indicate one of two things. It is possible that they imply the existence at any ritual performance of two distinct groups of people, one of whom would be allowed to enter the square building and make sacrifices or offerings on the altar there. The distinction may have been between those with religious authority and the rest of the population, or between the village dignitaries and the other villagers. It is quite possible that the village dignitaries were also those in religious authority. But the simplest distinction, of course, would be between the close relatives of the deceased and the neighbours and friends, or perhaps if we think in terms of 'genos' tholoi, between the close relatives and the rest of the clan. The alternative explanation of two altars is just as attractive however. They may well indicate that the complex served two different functions. The inside altar and the complex in which it stands would be used during the more complicated ritual of burial, whilst the outside altar would be used daily by those who came to make offerings to the dead or perhaps to intercede on their behalf with some great spirit.

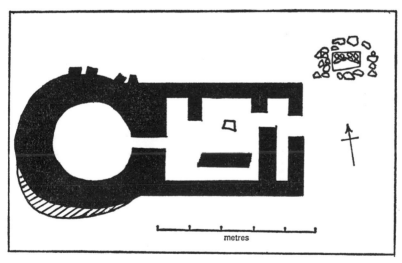

Figure 41   MM I tholos at Apesokari

This interpretation admits the existence in Early Bronze Age Crete of a belief in the after-life and perhaps of a cult of the dead. Fortunately the evidence from Apesokari is to some extent substantiated by discoveries elsewhere. At Platanos traces of a very similar rectangular complex were found built on to the front of tholos B. The walls only survived in fragments but those fragments which were found certainly suggest that here too the complex had an inner room. Outside the rectangular structure an area of green slate paving was found, much better preserved than that found at Apesokari. At Koumasa an even larger stretch of paving was found, and for about ten metres the wall which separated the paving from the tholoi area was found still in place. The paving, however, ran right up to the vestibule of tholos E, perhaps suggesting that the small vestibules found on the front of several tholos tombs are to be equated, in function, with the complexes found on the front of the tholoi at Apesokari and Platanos. These areas of paving found in front of the tholos tombs surely imply that the cemetery area was divided into two quite distinct sections, the burial area and the ritual area. At Kamilari Levi found no paving but a semi-circular area, marked out by stones, in which offerings had been made. This area surrounded the square chambers which we might equate with the ritual complexes at Apesokari and Platanos B.

Within the tomb at Kamilari, however, Levi found a clay model which is perhaps the most eloquent testimony to a cult of the dead.[1] A rectangular structure is seen, open on three sides but with a high wall at the rear. No roof is preserved but there is evidence that originally the roof was supported on the rear wall and on the two columns which stand at the front of the structure. Seated against the rear wall are four human figures. In front of each is a small column which we might interpret either as an altar or as a table. In front of the 'tables', and facing the four seated figures stand two more human figures. Professor Levi suggests that this scene represents the living standing before the dead, perhaps having made offerings to them. This is an attractive interpretation of the scene and one which we cannot disprove.

There are, however, one or two features of the model which suggest that other interpretations might be made. Particularly interesting is the construction of the 'shrine'. It has every appearance of being a temporary structure rather than being a building of the type we have found at Apesokari and Platanos. Of course it might be argued that the reason we have not found similar buildings at other cemeteries is because they were temporary structures of the type seen in the Kamilari model. The appearance of four deceased figures is also somewhat puzzling. A single man or woman, or else a man and wife combination, would seem to make far more sense, than having four deceased figures. In fact there is no reason why we should not interpret the standing figures as the deceased and the seated as deities or spirits. Equally, the whole scene could be representative of a ceremony which took place in life rather than

[1] Levi *1962* pl. 170 a–f.

death. Interesting as the Kamilari model is, it does not provide us with incontrovertible evidence that a cult of the dead existed.

Thus we find that the tholos tombs of the Mesara and the material found within them fail to provide us with any coherent picture of funerary ritual and belief. Throughout our discussion of the tholoi we have found that variations in the rites and customs are suggested by the evidence. This is particularly true of the evidence relating to the attitude of the living towards the dead. We have seen that the dead were buried with their personal belongings, probably amid ritual which included sacrifices or offerings. There is some evidence to suggest that offerings may have been made long after burial as well and that rituals performed outside the tholos tombs in the rectangular buildings or on the paved court were not always of a funerary nature. Yet it is quite clear that earlier burials were usually swept on one side, or even out of the tomb chamber altogether, to make room for later burials. The subsidiary cells and trenches at Platanos and Porti, packed with masses of bones, remind us of the situation in the narrow chambers of the Mochlos tombs. There seems to have been no regard for the remains of the deceased, and it is possible that many tholoi were subjected to at least one fumigation during their history.

These apparent contradictions could be explained in terms of the limitations of our knowledge and in particular of the fragmentary nature of our evidence; in some cases no doubt they are. But it seems to me that even if we allow for such cases, we are still faced with two alternative conclusions about funerary rites and beliefs in the Mesara. Either we must see them as being entirely localized, differing from one village to the other and without any semblance of uniformity within the region, or else we must admit that they are far more complex and sophisticated than we have previously imagined. I am inclined to favour the latter solution, for the concentrated geographical distribution of the tholoi and their association with a rather indistinct but nevertheless recognizable 'Mesara culture' would seem to imply that there was probably some considerable degree of uniformity in burial customs. So too does the strict adherence to the eastern orientation of the tholos tomb doorway. The fragmentary and much disturbed evidence is insufficient to allow us to delve into the complexities of these rituals and beliefs or even to draw a complete profile of them. But one point may, I think, be made. The burial of the dead with their personal belongings, food, and drink, the subsequent disregard for their skeletons, and the continuing practice of offerings to or on behalf of the deceased, taken together can only imply that the Early Minoans possessed beliefs which were mature enough to envisage a spiritual after-life which was not necessarily dependent on the survival of the physical body.

During Early Minoan III two new methods of burial were introduced. One of these was the use of larnakes or clay coffins.[1] These seem to be introduced throughout the island, although it may be that they did not find acceptance in the Mesara until MM I. Fragments of larnakes in tholos D at Drakones were unfortunately accompanied only by a few other objects which were perhaps found in the burial stratum below the larnake fragments. These finds included two seals which are certainly not earlier than MM I.

In northern Crete larnakes from Pyrgos and Gournes are also indecisively dated, being EM III or MM I. The Pyrgos deposit is most probably to be dated not later than EM III and this would bring the occurrence of the larnake at this site into line with its single occurrence at Pachyammos in the east. This was a child burial and the larnake in question was a small oval one. Recently, larnake burials were found in the top level of an EM II–MM Ia ossuary at Arkhanes. At present too little is known about the introduction of the larnake to Crete during the Early Bronze Age to allow a worthwhile discussion of the subject. Rutkowski however has suggested that larnakes such as the one from Pachyammos are adapted domestic utensils, though it is difficult to point to any Early Minoan clay vessels which might be regarded as the antecedents of the Pachyammos larnake.[2] His suggestion that the Pyrgos larnake type was derived from wooden troughs does however seem a reasonable one which might well be correct.

For some reason Rutkowski regards the practice of pithos burial as a continuation of Early Minoan tradition and contrasts it to the appearance of the larnake. This is strange for apart from a child burial in the cave at Stavromyti, probably of Late Neolithic date, there are no pithos burials in Crete until EM III. Furthermore, the appearance of the pithos and the larnake as burial containers is

---

[1] Xanthoudides *1924* 76 (Drakones); Xanthoudides *1918a* (Pyrgos); Seager *1916* (Pachyammos).

[2] In a paper to the Second Cretological Congress 1966 (published in the *Proceedings*).

linked not only chronologically but also geographically.[1] At the four sites discussed above, where larnake burials appear in EM III or MM I, we find also that pithos burials make their appearance. The adoption of this method of burial throughout the island is testified to by the discovery of MM I burials of this type at Khania in the far west. The largest cemetery to come to notice so far is at Galania Kharakia where Platon found over three hundred rope-ornamented pithoi, standing on their heads. He believes that the cemetery dates to the EM III–MM I period, but several of the finds suggest that the latest burials may be as late as MM III.

Rutkowski makes two important points about larnake burials which also apply to some extent to pithos burials as well. The appearance of the first larnakes in Crete is contemporary with several other notable events in the fields of metallurgy, stone-working, and architecture. In particular it would seem to coincide with the appearance of large urban settlements. This point may be connected with the second, which is that larnake burials (and those in pithoi) would seem to represent a growth in individualism, which might in turn represent a reaction to the loss of it which urban life demanded. Whether this is so or not, the use of the larnake and the pithos for burial certainly becomes increasingly popular during the hey-day of the first palaces.

Prior to the introduction of the larnake and the pithos burial there was, as we have seen, a distinct difference in the funerary architecture of the south and that of the rest of the island. Certain small scraps of evidence from Mochlos, such as the white clay fill in some graves, the heaping up of the skulls in one corner, and the building of a paved forecourt to at least some of the tombs, suggests that the differences in ritual may not have been so marked. So too does the evidence of the burnt bones at Kanli Kastelli and elsewhere. However, the evidence for ritual is too tentative to allow us to be at all certain on this point. What we may be reasonably certain about is that in the Mesara at least the funerary architecture and ritual show no social distinctions other than those, perhaps, of clan. It seems clear from the Mesara tombs that the village chieftains were buried in these tombs and that so were large numbers of other people of lesser rank. No tholos site has yet produced evidence which might indicate that the poorest members of the community were denied burial in the communal tholos. The evidence from the

---

[1] Daux *1960* (Galania Kharakia); Matz *1942* 79 (Khania).

north and east of the island is not so clear, but the contrast at Mochlos between the well built chamber tombs and the simple cist graves might perhaps suggest that here social distinctions were observed. These regional differences in tomb types and perhaps in the attitudes of the people towards death persist well into the Middle Minoan period, indeed we have seen that some of the tholoi are not built until MM I. But the introduction of the pithos and larnake as funerary containers in EM III is the first step to a uniformity which only becomes fully manifest much later.

9 Trade and communications

Although we have little evidence to prove it, there can be little doubt that extensive trade was carried on between villages and between different regions of the island. The villages on the small coastal plains would have been able to produce more than enough grain for their own purposes, and villages situated on the coast itself would no doubt have been able to produce a surplus of sea food. Fish and wheat would have found a ready market further inland, and in return the villages on the hill slopes could provide the lowland communities with pigs and, if required, with goats and cheese. The villages situated on the hill slopes further inland would also have access to the vast supplies of timber which the coastal people in particular would wish to acquire. It is true, of course, that we cannot be sure that natural resources such as timber were subject to any sort of 'ownership' at all. The boat- and ship-builders may have been able to go to the forests and take whatever they needed, and in the case of raw timber this is perhaps the most likely situation. On the other hand the communities living on the edge of the forests would have engaged in wood-working and carpentry to a greater extent than those living in the plains and on the coasts, and a trade in woodenware may have arisen for this reason. One raw material which was almost certainly traded and kept for the use of those who controlled its sources was copper. Whilst copper is common along the south coast of Crete, in the extreme west of the island and, to some extent, in the region of Rogthia, it is very rare – if not completely absent – in the east and north of the island. Thus the copper objects found in these areas, if they are made of Cretan copper, must be made of metal brought from other parts of the island. There is some indication in fact that a particular sort of long dagger was made at Platanos in the Mesara and traded to other villages in the Mesara, north and east.[1] Any trade which was pursued must

[1] Branigan *1968* 14 (type V).

initially have been carried on foot, but no later than MM I four-wheeled wagons were in use. A model from Palaikastro illustrates one of these carts. The wheels were apparently solid and the floor would appear to have been made of thick planks. A heavy vehicle such as this was presumably drawn by oxen. The use of the ass may have already been introduced, but the earliest representation of the animal is on a prism bead of EM III–MM Ia.[1] Whatever the pattern of trade and means of transport during the period of time occupied by Early Minoan I to Early Minoan III, the building of the palaces and the emergence of the social and political system which went with them must have brought many changes. The construction of the palaces required the transportation of large quantities of stone and timber, and the centralization of authority must have led to a similar centralization of control over raw materials and trade. At the same time it must have given further impetus to overseas trade.

The question of 'imports' and 'exports' is a difficult one to discuss. Organic imports and exports perished long ago, and the quantity of inorganic objects of trade surviving to us is so small as to be of little significance. Furthermore, it is hard to distinguish between objects of trade and those which were gifts made between friends. For these reasons, whilst we may speak with confidence about the various overseas contacts of Early Minoan Crete, it is very difficult to interpret these contacts in terms of trade and commerce.

There is no better illustration of this than the relations between Crete and north Africa, particularly Egypt, during the Early Bronze Age. When the Early Minoan settlements and tombs were first excavated it was to Egypt that Xanthoudides and Evans looked for comparative material.[2] They did not look in vain, for various similarities between Early Dynastic Egypt and Early Bronze Age Crete can be recognized.[3] Many Early Minoan stone bowls are similar in shape to contemporary Egyptian ones, foot-amulets occur in both countries, carinated and pierced maceheads are shared by both cultures, 'kernoi' from each country are closely comparable and so too are figurines with pointed bases. There are many other points of similarity, and taken together these were thought to represent perhaps an actual influx of people from

[1] Kenna *1960* K. 50.
[2] Xanthoudides *1924* 128ff; Evans *1921*.
[3] For detailed references of comparable material see Xanthoudides *1924* and Evans *1921* 56ff.

Egypt and north Africa. Much of the enthusiasm with which these ideas were presented and accepted in the first three decades of this century has been replaced by an awareness that Minoan civilization owed far less to Egypt than we use to imagine. But contacts between Crete and Egypt most certainly existed in the third millennium B.C., and they were almost certainly direct ones.[1] Fragments of Egyptian stone vases were found in the Late Neolithic levels at Knossos, and during the Early Bronze Age Egyptian objects appear on many sites throughout the island. The finds from Knossos came mainly in disturbed deposits including material of the Middle and even Late Minoan periods; but they are predominantly Old Kingdom in date, and it seems highly probable that they were 'exported' to Crete during the Early Bronze Age. Excavations at Knossos have produced about twenty complete or fragmentary Egyptian stone vessels of Old Kingdom and First Intermediate date, including a very fine series of bowls made of gabbro, diorite, syenite and porphyry (fig. 42, 2 and 3). Egyptian 'imports' were found elsewhere in the north of the island at Gournes and Katsambas. Whilst the latter site yielded three more stone vases assignable to Dynasties III–IV, the former produced two scarabs and some XIIth Dynasty faience beads. In the east of the island similar beads and a fragment of a bowl were found on Mochlos, whilst at Palaikastro a late predynastic jar and two ivory figurines, possibly of XIIth Dynasty date, were discovered. Excavations at the nearby site of Zakro have so far produced two Old Kingdom bowls. Several of the Mesara tholoi have yielded Egyptian 'imports', the latest discoveries being at Lebena where several scarabs and an imitation of an Old Kingdom claw foot goblet were found (fig. 42, 4). Vases of IVth and VIth Dynasty type were found in burial deposits at Porti and Agia Triadha, the latter also producing three scarabs. Scarabs seem to be amongst the most plentiful of Egyptian 'imports' in Crete and other Mesara sites yielding examples include Marathokephalo (1), Agios Onouphrios (4), and Platanos (3) (fig. 42, 1). Excluding the zoomorphic sealstones from the tholoi—sometimes labelled as Egyptian imports—there are thus more than four dozen known objects of Egyptian derivation imported during the Early Bronze Age. The 'imports' fall into two distinct groups—vases and jewellery—both of which are luxury items, and both of which were manufactured in

---

[1] Collected references in Pendlebury *1932*; see also Alexiou *1958, 1960*; Hutchinson *1948, 1954*; Warren *1965a*, 28–34.

quantity in Crete itself. These items might thus have been brought to the island as trinkets and souvenirs and we cannot be certain that they represent the Egyptian half of Minoan-Egyptian trading relations, indeed they may well be little more than a by-product of them. There were other commodities which the Minoans may have sought in Egypt – gold, dates, and possibly even grain – which are difficult for us to recognize archaeologically, apart from the gold jewellery perhaps. The quantity of Egyptian material is such, however, that we must postulate regular trading contacts between Crete and Egypt, even if we cannot speak with confidence of the main imports obtained from the Nile valley.

The influence of trading contacts with the Levant is less pronounced perhaps than that of Egyptian contacts, but it makes itself evident in seal types and motifs – particularly the lion, and in metallurgy.[1] From EM III onwards Syrian dagger types and Syrian hafting techniques were copied in Crete, and indeed Syrian daggers form the largest group of Syrian objects 'imported' into the island. Two tanged Syrian daggers were found at Platanos (fig. 42, 6) and a fragment of another at Agia Triadha. Further examples of the same type were found in Lasithi – at Psychro and Trapeza – and a sixth dagger may be represented by a broken tang found at Knossos. A tangless dagger found at Koumasa is of a type which appears to be Syrian (fig. 42, 9). Apart from these metallurgical 'imports' there are several cylinder seals which date to the early second millennium B.C., including examples found at Platanos, Knossos, Arkhanes, Agia Triadha and Iraklion. As in the case of Egyptian 'imports', however, one suspects that the main commodities for which the Minoans traded are no longer surviving in a recognizable form. The ivory used for Minoan seal-stones from EM II onwards very probably came from Syria, and the 'imports' of metal objects may well reflect increasing Minoan interest in the copper resources of Cyprus. As we shall see shortly, there is some evidence to suggest that both Crete and Syria may have had commercial interests in Cyprus.

If the nature of Early Minoan contacts with the eastern Mediterranean is difficult to understand, it is still much clearer than that of similar contacts with the western end of the basin. In the copper age of Italy, Sicily, Malta and Sardinia there are abundant traces of contact with the Aegean and eastern Mediterranean, but it is

[1] Branigan *1966*, *1967*, *1968a*; Evans *1928* fig. 158; Hutchinson *1962* 157.

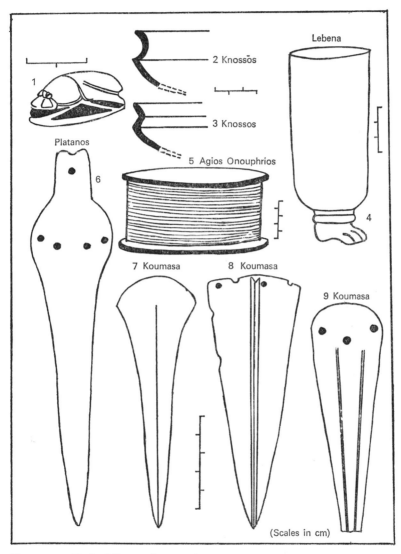

Figure 42 Early Minoan 'imports'

seemingly impossible to define the nature and origin of these contacts more closely.[1] The manifestations of contact are widely spread.[2] Rock-cut tombs in Sardinia, Sicily and peninsular Italy probably testify to Aegean or eastern connections. Stone figurines in Sardinia and Malta cannot be dissociated from 'Cycladic' idols, and similarly a connection must be recognized between embossed bone plaques from Altemura, Casteluccio, and Malta and others from Troy and Lerna. So too there are visible relationships in ceramics. Incised lids of Gaudho Chalcolithic compare closely with ones of Early Minoan type, and Cellino Chalcolithic flasks have close affinity with Cypriote examples. Finally the contemporary Remedello and Rinaldone cultures reveal very clear metallurgical connections with the Aegean and particularly with Crete. Despite these widespread traces of contact, there is little to indicate what commodities were exchanged between the two regions. The only identifiable Italian 'exports' to Crete are three silver daggers (two of triangular form) found at Koumasa (fig. 42, 7 and 8), a similar dagger in copper found at Agios Onouphrios, and a flat dagger found on Mochlos.[3] There was one commodity, however, which Italy and Sardinia could supply which was probably not obtainable elsewhere in the Mediterranean, and that was tin. Both Tuscany and Sardinia have tin deposits, although we do not know when they were first exploited, and it has recently been suggested that the Sardinians at first imported their tin from Spain.[4] Apart from tin, Sardinia also had natural resources of silver, and the peoples of the Aegean may well have obtained their supplies from here or again from Spain.[5] The traces of Aegean influence are so widespread in Chalcolithic Italy and its environs that one imagines that even if the tin and silver were obtained from Spain, it was through the inhabitants of Italy, Sicily and perhaps Sardinia.

As one should expect, the greatest amount of Minoan overseas trade seems to have been centred on the Aegean. In the third millennium B.C. the Aegean was the home of four thriving centres

---

[1] Mosso *1910* was particularly impressed by the similarities between Minoan and Italian religion of the prehistoric era.

[2] See Guido *1963* (Sardinia); Trump *1966* (Italy); Bernabo-Brea *1957* (Sicily); Evans J. D. *1959* (Malta). But I am much in sympathy with the views expressed by Renfrew, *1967*.

[3] Branigan *1966b*.

[4] Guido *1963* 153.

[5] But see Renfrew's comments *1967a* 4–6, and Branigan *1968b*.

of culture – Crete, the Cyclades, the Troad and environs, and the Argolid and central Greece. These cultures – each with its own characteristics yet all sharing certain fashions in pottery, religion, jewellery and art – together constituted a wealthy and willing market for each other's products. As Renfrew has said, there was an international spirit abroad in the Aegean during the second phase of the Early Bronze Age and in Crete we find many indications of this. Cycladic 'imports' are numerous.[1] Melian obsidian had been brought into Crete ever since the Early Neolithic period, some three and a half thousand years earlier. Throughout the Neolithic period it had been a vital material used in the production of razors, knives, and sickles, and even with the advent of copper and bronze its usage continued. Blades of Melian obsidian occur widely on Early Minoan sites and it is clear that it had two valuable advantages over copper. It was more easily obtained and it was harder than unalloyed copper. Cores and flakes like those found on Pseira show that the obsidian was brought to the island in its unworked state and then manufactured into the various implements required. Renfew has recently raised doubts as to whether the Cycladic peoples ever traded obsidian, and suggested that they may have allowed people to simply sail to Melos and the other sources in the Aegean and take whatever they wanted. Other Cycladic 'imports' are common enough, however, to suggest that regular trade was carried on between Crete and the Cyclades, and it is unrealistic to think that the Melians did not exploit the remarkable source of wealth at their command. The volume of obsidian transported may have been small, but it presumably went along with other commodities. Apart from obsidian, Cycladic marble was also exported to Crete in the form of 'idols' and stone vases. Both of these Cycladic industries go back to the Neolithic, as the excavations on Saliagos and Keos have illustrated. Although there were many imitations of Cycladic idols made locally – examples from Tekes, Agios Onouphrios, and Lebena for instance – there were also some figurines of this type made of Cycladic marble and imported from the Cyclades as finished products. An excellent example is the fine figurine from Koumasa (pl. 13). Probably contemporary with the

[1] Renfrew et al. *1965*; Seager *1916* 10 (Pseira); Renfrew et al. *1965* 52; Xanthoudides *1924* pl. VII, 122; Renfrew *1964* pl. ET, 3 (Agios Onouphrios); Zervos *1956* pl. 144–5 (Maronia); Zervos *1956* pl. 128 (Marathokephalo); pl. 82; Xanthoudides *1918a* (Pyrgos); Marinatos *1960* pl. 5 (Giamilakis Coll).

importation of these idols in EM II was a trade in Cycladic stone
vessels. The date of a marble pyxide lid from Knossos is uncertain,
but the complete pyxide from Agios Onouphrios is almost certainly
of Early Cycladic II date. This is a cylindrical pyxide decorated
only with horizontal ribbing (fig. 42, 5). In addition to stone vessels,
several Cycladic clay vases also appear in Crete. Notable amongst
them are the five 'bottles' found at Pyrgos. Apart from these, however, there is a small juglet from Marathokephalo, a high-necked cup
from Lebena and the curious 'frying-pan' in the Giamilakis collection (pl. 14). The design on the base of this vessel is unique and
cannot be closely paralleled at all in the Cyclades; for this reason its
authenticity should not be assumed. Other vases with Troadic
connections, like the barrel vessels from Koumasa and Lebena,
appear to be Minoan imitations rather than actual 'imports',
although a simple chalice of uncertain provenance is unlike any of
the typical 'Pyrgos' chalices and may almost certainly be referred
to a Troadic origin (cf. Poliochni). Despite the Cycladic lead in
metallurgy, metallic 'imports' from the Aegean are very few in
number. A long dagger from Platanos has a rather angular base
which would be commoner amongst the EC II long daggers than
the Minoan ones, but the attribution to the Cyclades is uncertain.
The other two objects are of dubious provenance and authenticity.
Two lead plaques were published by Evans in *Cretan Pictographs*,
said to have been found near Iraklion and almost identical with
a female figure and two superimposed cross designs on a mould
found at Selendj in Western Asia Minor. The female figure com-
pares closely with a lead figurine found by Schliemann at Troy and
we may here be dealing with two genuine 'imports'.

In discussing the various objects of foreign origin which have
been found in Crete, and the various commodities which may have
formed the principal Minoan 'imports' during the Early Bronze
Age, I have deliberately avoided any reference to Minoan 'exports'.
Objects of Minoan manufacture do turn up however in foreign
contexts and provide us with further confirmation that Early
Minoan Crete was in contact with the countries of both the east and
west Mediterranean, indirect though the contact may have been in
some cases. The evidence from the Syrian coast is sparse, and mainly
dates to the very end of the Early Bronze Age (in Crete) or the
start of the succeeding period.[1] The earliest items are probably a

[1] Branigan *1967*; Money-Coutts *1936* 139; Hutchinson *1962* 105.

small scraper (fig. 43, 7) and a votive agrimi horn, both of bronze, and a green-stone pyxide lid, similar to those from Mochlos and Zakro. All of these were found at Byblos. Minoan pottery begins to occur in deposits at Byblos shortly afterwards and before long appears also at Ras Shamra. It is not surprising, therefore, to find that Minoan objects were also finding their way into Cyprus at this time.[1] Some of the finest Minoan dagger blades of the period have been found not in Crete but in the tombs of Lapithos and Vounous, where two Minoan daggers were found in each cemetery (fig. 43, 1, 2). In addition a Minoan razor was found at Lapithos in the same tomb as one of the daggers (fig. 43, 5). Another tomb in this cemetery contained an MM Ia bridge-spouted jar. It is perhaps of interest that the Lapithos tombs also produced three daggers of Syrian type, and it may well be that Minoan contact with the ports of Syria was channelled, at least partially, through the island of Cyprus.

Discoveries of Minoan objects in Cyprus and Syria are about as numerous as those of Syrian and Cypriote objects in Crete. We might therefore expect to find many examples of Minoan 'exports' to Egypt, but this is not the case.[2] The earliest Minoan pottery appearing in Egypt is of MM II style, fragments of which were found at Lahun and Harageh and a complete bridge-spouted jar at Abydos. Previous to this the only possible Minoan 'imports' at present recognized are the famous metal vessels in the Tod treasure, which may date as early as MM Ia – if they are indeed of Minoan manufacture. Surprisingly the situation is little different in the Aegean, where we should expect the exchange of small objects to be quite common and widespread.[3] Sherds of Minoan pottery occur in small quantities (or singly!) at Poliochni (EM II), Phylakopi (EM III and MM I), and Lerna (MM Ia). Foot amulets from Zygouries and Agios Kosmas are very probably Minoan (fig. 43, 3 and 6), for the type is extremely common during the Early Bronze Age in Crete where more than a dozen have been found. Similarly the bottle-seal from Agios Kosmas may be identified as Cretan

[1] Catling and Karageorghis *1960* (but see Branigan *1966*) Branigan *1968* 61.
[2] Hutchinson *1948*, *1954*; Chapouthier *1953* – but see Branigan *1968b*.
[3] Bernabo-Brea *1964* 585 (Poliochni); Dawkins and Droop *1912* 9; Atkinson et al *1904* 127 (Phylakopi); Caskey *1964* 38 (Lerna); Blegen *1928* pl. XX, 3 (Zygouries); Mylonas *1959* pl. 166 (Agios Kosmas); Schachermeyr *1964* 326, Heath *1958* (Lerna sealings); Frodin and Persson *1938* 236 (Asine); Blegen *1950* pl. 408, Schliemann *1880* 601, No. 1407 (Troy).

(fig. 43, 9) and compared to examples from Platanos, Krasi, Mallia, Mochlos, Agia Triadha and several other Early Minoan sites. On the other hand the sealings from Lerna are not closely comparable

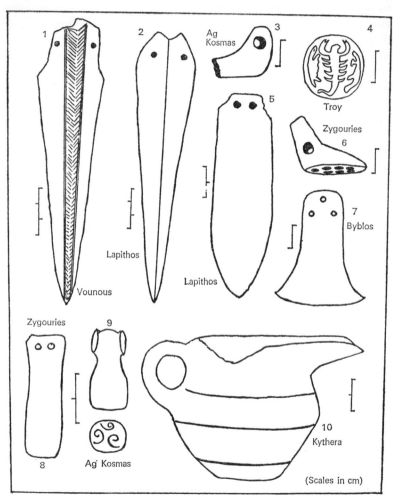

Figure 43 Early Minoan 'exports'

to Early Minoan seal designs. Schachermeyr would regard them as either Minoan or else of Minoan inspiration, but Heath's exhaustive analysis of them concluded that they were non-Minoan, and with this view I find myself in agreement. This being so, one must question whether or not the sealings from Asine might not also have been made with seals produced on the mainland. These seals were thought by Frodin and Persson to be indicative of Early Helladic trade with Crete, possibly for woollen goods, and they are thus of considerable importance. The seal which is central to the argument for a wool trade, number four, does not have close parallels in Crete, and in particular the spider does not appear as a motif on Early Minoan seals. Seals two and three on the other hand could be Minoan in origin. Apart from the Agios Kosmas seal, the most acceptable evidence for Minoan seals and sealings travelling abroad is found in the city of Troy. The spiral design of an impression on an imported jar finds a very close parallel on a seal from Platanos and the general style is certainly Minoan. An ivory seal depicting a scorpion, found on the surface during Schliemann's excavations, is a Minoan seal of EM III–MM Ia (fig. 43).

These Minoan objects from the Aegean region are not particularly numerous and indeed they cannot all be accepted as Minoan without some degree of uncertainty. It is therefore with relief that we can point to one part of the Aegean where direct contacts with Crete can be spoken of as a matter of fact rather than probability. It has long been known that the Minoans colonized the island of Kythera, off the coast of Laconia, but until recently it was not realized how early the colonization began.[1] A marble jug from the island which was clearly an import from Crete could be paralleled in Crete by a jug from Mochlos probably dating no later than EM III (fig. 43, 10). Professor Huxley's recent excavation on Kythera has now revealed that strong connections with Crete were established as early as EM II. The establishment of a colony on Kythera would seem to be connected with Minoan interest in overseas trade and is indeed one of the best pieces of evidence for it.

If we look back over the list of Minoan 'exports' we find that there is little there to argue for extensive Minoan trade in the Aegean and east Mediterranean, during the Early Bronze Age. Daggers to Cyprus, seal-stones and amulets to the Aegean and a few pots here and there! A worthwhile foreign trade could hardly have been based on the market for sealstones and amulets, and 'exporting' metal objects to Cyprus is rather like the proverbial coals to Newcastle or sand to Egypt. These items, and most of the imported objects found in Crete, must surely be regarded as the

[1] Zervos *1956* pl. 167; Megaw *1966* 21; Huxley and Coldstream *1966*.

by-products of a trade in more valuable but less durable commodities. We have already discussed some of the commodities which Crete might well have sought abroad – gold from Egypt, ivory from the Levant, obsidian in the Cyclades and tin and silver in the west. Now we might briefly consider what the Minoans would have offered in exchange for these goods. The only foods which they may have been able to offer abroad were olives – and the oil from them – and dried grapes or alternatively wine. Grapes and wine may have found a ready market in the western Mediterranean and olives and oil in the east. In addition we know that by the Middle Dynastic period, the Egyptians were importing lichens from the Aegean to use in bread-making. We have already mentioned the suggestions that the Minoans exported woollen goods to Asine, and although the evidence from there is not convincing it seems very probable that woven goods were indeed traded by the Early Minoans. Their rapid development of colourful and interesting patterns has been illustrated and certainly if they tried to trade their woven goods there is little reason to doubt that they would have been successful. Finally the Minoans of the Early Bronze Age commanded vast resources of wood, and particularly of Cypress wood. This was highly valued and much used and would have found a ready market, if the Minoans were capable of transporting it.

The question of transport is obviously of paramount importance in any discussion of overseas trade. Even if we accept that the Minoans traded the commodities mentioned above – and the evidence is lacking – we cannot be sure that the actual trading and transportation was not carried on by the peoples of the Cyclades or Syria, unless we can show that the Minoans at this time had the capability to do these things themselves. Fortunately the evidence exists.[1] The famous Cycladic ships with many oarsmen but no sails probably had their Minoan counterparts, and the small model ship from Palaikastro may represent an Early Minoan vessel of this sort (fig. 44b). It has the distinctive high prow and low stern which characterize the Cycladic ships. This sort of vessel, however, without sails, was not really suited to long sea journeys such as trade with Egypt and Syria would require, even though the routes to these regions would probably be coastal ones. Furthermore, ships depending on manpower for propulsion over long distances were unlikely to take on large loads of heavy materials such as timber.

[1] Zervos *1956* pls 204, 218–19; Renfrew *1967a* pl. 3; Zervos *1956* pl. 142.

It is thus significant that the great expansion of foreign contacts which seems to begin in EM III is contemporary with the appearance in Minoan art of sailing vessels (fig. 44, c and d). Not surprisingly these vessels are very similar to the ships of the preceding period, retaining the high prow and low stern. It is clear too that the oarsmen were still carried to be used for manoeuvring and when the ship was becalmed, for some of the ships seen on EM III and MM I seal-stones have eight or ten pairs of oars indicated along their sides. At the rear the rudder projects. The ships have a single,

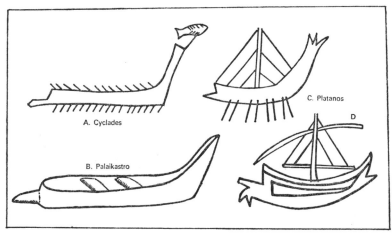

Figure 44   Early Minoan shipping

central mast from which 'ropes', probably made of leather thongs, lead to the spreader yard. From the details on some of the seals the yards appear to be formed of two spars. The 'lifts' (or ropes) suggest that a large square sail was used in conjunction with a heavy spreader yard extending its foot. Ships of this sort were capable of carrying heavier loads over longer distances than the earlier ships, and at a faster speed too. That is not to say that they had no shortcomings, and in particular the lack of fore-and-aft sails must have severely limited the choice of sailing routes if the advantages of this type of ship were to be realized. Thus Hutchinson is very probably right in suggesting that Minoan ships intent on trading in the east Mediterranean sailed in a circular route to Egypt first and then to Syria, Cyprus and the Dodecanese.[1] In this way they could take

[1] Hutchinson *1962* 95.

advantage of the prevailing summer winds blowing from the north. Trade within the Aegean on the other hand could have been carried still in vessels propelled by oarsmen alone, for here the distances travelled between ports were much smaller and the cargoes would probably not have included timber.

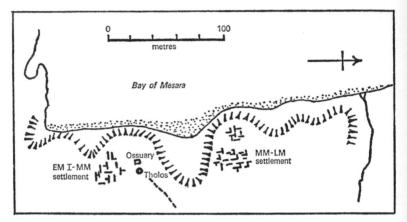

Figure 45   The Early Minoan port at Komo

The Minoan ports from which these trading vessels began their journeys were probably very numerous, and evidence for Early Minoan occupation on good harbour sites is accumulating. On the south coast the suitable sites of Lebena and Limenes have both produced evidence of Early Bronze Age occupation within the last decade.[1] So too have Arvi and Myrtos, and in the extreme south-west of the island the sites at Khrisoskalitissa (pl. 2) and Thrimbokambos. The most interesting harbour site on the south coast however is that at Komo in the bay of Mesara (fig. 45). Evans surveyed this site and found two separate settlements, one occupied in the Early Bronze Age and the other from MM I onwards. In addition the Early Minoan site contained an ossuary, the remains of a tholos, and possible traces of a road going towards Phaistos. The importance of Komo as a port is clear not only from these remains

---

[1] Alexiou *1960* (Lebena); fig. 38, p. 163 for unpubd. EM tholoi near Limenes; Hood et al *1964* 92, 95, Warren *1968* (Arvi and Myrtos); Hood *1965* 101–2 (Khrisoskalitissa, Thrimbokambos); Evans *1928* 88 (Komo); Marinatos *1929* 95, *1930* 91 (Amnisos); Seager *1912* (Mochlos), *1916* (Pseira); Hall *1914* pl. XVII (Priniatiko Pyrgos); Dawkins *1904*, *1905*. Popham *1965* (Palaikastro).

but also because it stood at the entrance to the Mesara. Behind Komo stretched the rich hinterland of the 'Mesara culture', and many of the foreign objects 'imported' into Crete during the Early Bronze Age have been found in the tombs of the Mesara. It was probably from Komo therefore that many Minoan ships began their

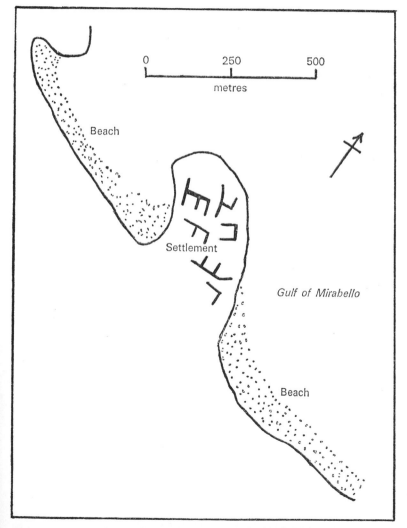

Figure 46 The Early Minoan harbours at Priniatiko Pyrgos

voyages to Egypt and Syria. On the north coast there were other ports of almost equal importance and perhaps handling a greater quantity of trade. Amnisos is perhaps the best known of these northern harbours and was one of the earliest founded. Further east in the Gulf of Mirabello were other thriving ports–Mochlos, Priniatiko Pyrgos and Pseira. Mochlos and Priniatiko Pyrgos are characteristic of a group of Minoan ports which could offer harbourage on whichever side of a peninsula was the most favoured at the time of the ship's arrival (fig. 46). This is true also of the port of Palaikastro on the east coast of the island–another settlement founded early in the Early Bronze Age.

The importance of these ports, and the ships which sailed from them, to the development of palatial Crete and Minoan civilation

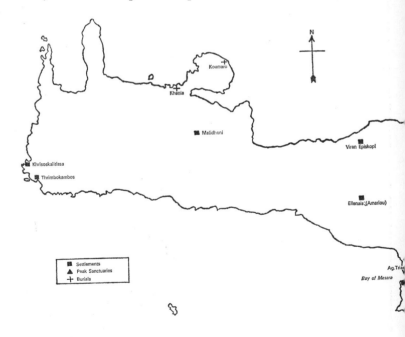

Figure 47 Map of sites mentioned in the text

should not be underestimated. Through these ports flowed not merely gold, ivory, copper, tin and silver, but new ideas – from all over the Mediterranean. Every aspect of life in Crete during the Early Bronze Age must have been in some way affected by the foreign contacts which became increasingly common as the third millennium drew to a close. From irregular and probably indirect exchanges of goods at the start of the Early Bronze Age, the peoples of the Aegean evolved a regular trade between themselves and indeed with other parts of the Mediterranean. That Crete shared in this development is witnessed not only by Minoan 'imports' and 'exports' discovered in archaeological excavations, but by the nature and characteristics of the civilization which emerged in Crete at the start of the second millennium B.C.

This book has been designed to illustrate the development of the individual elements which together make up the culture and civilization of Crete in the Early Bronze Age. Inevitably this sort of approach denies the reader a clear concept of the broad historical development of the period. The individual strands of which that history is composed are perhaps understood, but the historical pattern into which they were woven remains obscure. Our first concern in this concluding chapter is, therefore, to sketch briefly the historical pattern which would seem to emerge when our 'strands' are brought together.

In the introductory chapter we saw that there is a major controversy as to the date, and thus in the circumstances to the origin, of the start of the Early Neolithic period in Crete. That is to say that we cannot be sure of the origins of the Cretan population as it existed at the start of the third millennium B.C. Fortunately this is not a major disaster because the inhabitants of Crete in the Neolithic period had already developed a very individual culture of their own. They had thus become to all intents and purposes 'Cretans' rather than 'Anatolians' or 'Syrians' or any other label one cares to give to the first Early Neolithic settlers. The problem for us is to decide whether it was this 'Cretan' population which evolved into the society of the Early Bronze Age, or whether there was an influx of people from outside at the crucial moment who speeded up and changed the process of evolution. That there were outside *influences* we cannot doubt. Cycladic connections are clear, and in particular one suspects that it was from the Cyclades that the people of Crete learnt about metallurgy. Other connections, with the Troad, the Greek mainland, Cilicia, Syria, Palestine, and Egypt, may be postulated. However, even if all of these connections were proven – and it is very unlikely that they were all in being c. 3,000

B.C. – the problem would remain. There may well have been influence, probably indirect in most instances, without an actual influx of people.

This is in fact the sort of impression which emerges from a study of the sub-Neolithic material and in particular from a study of the pottery found by Levi at Phaistos.[1] Pottery shapes, an interest in plastic ornamentation (Trapeza ware for example), the experiments in pattern burnishing, production of buff wares, the first signs of an interest in painted decoration – each of these developments would seem to be a prelude to some aspect or the other of Early Minoan I ceramics. In addition, we find in EM I deposits not only those fabrics whose existence the Phaistos sub-Neolithic pottery would seem to foreshadow, but also several fabrics which are clearly of the Neolithic tradition, in particular the 'wiped' wares. Apart from the evidence of the pottery one may point to the continued use of stone axes and maceheads, the smooth development of domestic architecture, and the continued unbroken occupation of several sub-Neolithic sites into the EM I period, as evidence of the continuity of population.[2]

However, this is a rather thin array of evidence, and it fails to account for several distinctive features of Early Minoan I culture. The Mesara tholoi, and collective tombs in general, the introduction of metallurgy and the production of the 'triangular' blades in particular, many of the pottery shapes decorated in the Agios Onouphrios style, and above all the spirit of that style – these are innovations which cannot easily be traced to sub-Neolithic source and for which inspiration may be sought abroad. Cycladic connections are clear, as we have said earlier, and Hutchinson believes there may have been Cycladic immigrants who came to Crete at the start of the Early Bronze Age.[3] Certainly Minoan metallurgy seems to owe something to the metalworking of the Cyclades, but Cycladic metallurgy provides no prototypes for the Minoan 'triangular' dagger. Equally although the small built tomb at Krasi (dating from EM I) can be compared to the Cycladic-built graves, it is hard to follow the suggestion that such tombs were developed in Crete into the tholoi such as we find in the Mesara. In particular their distribution, concentrated in the south of the island, is just the opposite of what one would expect if they were of Cycladic

[1] Levi *1965*.   [2] e.g. Knossos, Phaistos, Trapeza, Melidhoni, Amnisos.
[3] Hutchinson *1962* 139–40.

inspiration and were to be connected with the tomb at Krasi in the north of the island. Finally, the hypothesis of a Cycladic immigration provides no prototypes for Agios Onouphrios and Lebena ware. Neither does the theory of an immigration from western Anatolia! In recent years Caskey, Hutchinson, and Schachermeyr have all suggested that there may have been Anatolian immigrants entering Crete in EM I – or just before.[1] Such claims can be supported only on the evidence of a few pottery shapes. Admittedly the most typical pottery form associated with the Agios Onouphrios style is the beaked jug, which certainly has close relations in western Anatolia. Other EM I shapes which have relations in western Anatolia, or those islands adjacent to it, are the single-handled cup, the 'barrel' vessel, 'eared' lids, and the chalice. These shapes are, for the most part, distinctive ones, and their appearance in Crete clearly implies that influence from the north-west corner of the Aegean was reaching Crete in the sub-Neolithic and EM I period. Pottery forms alone, however, are not sufficient to warrant the recognition of an actual immigration taking place. Two of the distinctive features of Early Minoan I culture – collective tombs and dark-on-light pottery decoration – are completely at variance with the traditions of the north-western Aegean at this time. One would expect Cycladic and Anatolian influence to be found in Crete at the start of the Early Bronze Age. It is quite clearly there, but there is nothing to suggest that it results from an actual immigration.

The case for an immigration from North Africa is based almost entirely on the similarity between the Mesara tholoi and the Libyan mapalia. The distribution of these tholoi in the south of Crete is perhaps significant in this respect. It is mainly from the tholoi in the Mesara that the 'triangular' daggers and figurines with pointed bases come, and both of these have parallels in predynastic Egypt, the one in flint knives or lanceheads and the other in clay figurines. Finally foot amulets occur very early in the Minoan Early Bronze Age and these too have their parallels in the Early Dynastic period. A migration from north-western Egypt to Crete at the time of the Early Dynastic period would fit in very well both with our tentative chronology for the start of EM I and with what we know of political events in Egypt at this time. There are two occasions when such a migration might have begun. At the start of the Dynastic period

[1] Caskey *1964* 32, Hutchinson *1962* 140, Schachermeyr *1964* Chapter I.

when Scorpion and Narmer achieved supremacy for the South over the North, there may well have been refugees fleeing westwards looking for a new place to settle. This would have been c. 3,000 B.C. Over the course of the next three and a half centuries there were, it seems, several attempts by the North to re-assert itself.[1] For a short time, c. 2,750 B.C. it may have been successful and Egypt may have reverted to two kingdoms. Before the end of the Second Dynasty, however, the South had finally regained control of the whole country, and at the time of its victory there may again have been a number of refugees fleeing westwards. Egyptian immigrants would have brought the arts of metallurgy with them, of course. Despite the attractions of this hypothetical immigration it does not provide by any means a complete explanation of the culture which emerged in EM I. In particular we are again faced with an immigration by peoples who favoured neither collective tombs nor a dark-on-light tradition of pottery decoration, such as we find in EM I. It is true that the last of the predynastic cultures in Egypt, the Gerzean, produced pottery with decoration in dark paint on a light ground, but it is predominantly representational decoration and totally different in style and approach to that of Agios Onouphrios ware.

The only area producing pottery which we might compare with Agios Onouphrios ware in the period preceding its appearance in Crete, is Palestine. Jirku and Weinberg have both argued for connections between the Ghassulian Chalcolithic culture of Palestine and the sub-Neolithic, Early Minoan I culture of Crete.[2] Ghassul can indeed provide some interesting parallels with Early Minoan I. Pottery shapes which are common to both cultures include the chalice, 'bird-vase', and straight-sided, flat-bottomed bowl. This pottery is decorated with dark-on-light linear patterns including cross-hatching and hatched triangles. The Ghassulian culture, however, seems to fade out some time after the middle of the fourth millennium B.C., and its sites are no longer occupied. It is therefore possible to argue that these people in fact began a migration initially perhaps north-west towards Syria and that some of these

---

[1] In the First Dynasty during the reigns of Udimu, Enezib and Semerkhet, and in the Second Dynasty in the reigns of Aka and Sekhemib-Perabsen (see Branigan 'The Social and Political History of Archaic Egypt', unpublished B.A. Dissertation, University of Birmingham 1963).

[2] See Weinberg in Ehrich *1954* 96ff.

migrants eventually found their way to Crete. However, the succeeding 'Proto-Urban' culture in Palestine is chronologically more compatible with the start of the Early Minoan period, for it lasts until the start of the third millennium B.C. This culture produces pottery which is in many ways a better parallel to Early Minoan I fabrics than is Ghassulian pottery.[1] In particular we meet for the first time a style of decoration which is in the same spirit as that of Agios Onouphrios ware. Painted in red on a buff ground, the decoration is predominantly composed of vertical and diagonal groups of lines running down the side of the vessel. On the neck or shoulder there is often a change of direction as the lines run horizontally. Bowls are often decorated with a cordon of chevrons. Amongst the shapes we may compare with EM I shapes are spouted bowls, two-handled jars, and handled and lipped cups. Of particular significance, I feel, is the Palestinian preference for two-handled vessels. This is something that one meets with in EM I pottery and which cannot be paralleled at this time in the Aegean area. There is one further interesting point of contact between EM I Crete and the Proto-Urban culture of Palestine, and that is the practice of collective burial. In Palestine this is in caves or rock-cut tombs whilst in Crete it may be in caves or in tholoi. The Proto-Urban 'A' tombs at Jericho also provide a detail which is strikingly similar to what was noted in some of the tholoi and at Arkhanes, namely the stacking up of skulls when the tomb was cleared to make room for more burials. There is the possibility too that the Proto-Urban people of Palestine might also provide the link between the Minoan tholoi and the Halafian 'tholoi' from sites such as Arpachiyah.[2] These Halafian structures are very similar indeed to the Mesara tholoi, although they were not used as tombs but as shrines, and archaeologists seeking the origins of the Minoan tholoi have often looked wonderingly at them. The problem has always been that they dated no later than early fourth millennium B.C. and that they occurred in northern Mesopotamia. The Proto-Urban 'A' people, however, appear in Palestine about the middle of the fourth millennium B.C. and it is thought that they arrived there from the east. They might therefore provide us with a link with the early fourth millennium structures at Arpachiyah and elsewhere on the one hand and, as we have seen, with Crete on the other.

[1] Kenyon *1960* fig. 12; Albright *1960* fig. 12.
[2] Mellaart *1965* fig. 106.

All of this is very tentative and potentially dangerous thinking! Are we really to postulate that a group of people left Palestine at the start of the third millennium B.C. and that their descendants arrived in Crete about two centuries later, bringing with them their old pottery styles and shapes – in modified form – their burial customs and the memory of structures which their ancestors had seen a millennium earlier? It seems very unlikely that this is what happened, but *if* we are to find an outside source for the inspiration which brought the Early Minoan culture into being it seems to me that Palestine would best fill the role, allowing also for the influence of the Cyclades and western Anatolia.

There remains however the possibility that what happened in Crete was a spontaneous reaction to the stimulus which came with the spread of metallurgy. Sinclair Hood has suggested that the Agios Onouphrios jugs are perhaps copies of gourds, initially, and this would certainly provide us with a plausible origin for the style.[1] Several of the shapes we have already seen to be in use in the north-west of Anatolia at the start of the third millennium B.C. and these may well have found their way to Crete. Some of the sub-Neolithic shapes seem to have Anatolian affinities too. I have already suggested that Pyrgos ware may have had its (?Minoan) ancestors made of wood, but even if one rejects this hypothesis, Levi's pattern-burnish sherds of sub-Neolithic date argue that this EM I fabric at least is indigenous. As for the Mesara tholoi it is not unreasonable to argue that these are the result of the people of the Mesara attempting to compensate for the relative scarcity of caves in their region in which people could be buried. Certainly the two small tholoi I discovered at Chrysostomos (fig. 38), both dating apparently from EM I – to judge by surface finds – were very primitive structures which more closely resemble rock shelters than the tholoi at Platanos or Kamilari! The Chrysostomos tombs were, in fact, both built up against a rock face and were not unlike small caves in appearance. The idea of collective burial may well have evolved during the sub-Neolithic phase in response to social developments. Bearing in mind the problems which are raised by each and every one of the 'immigration hypotheses' it is perhaps wisest in our present state of knowledge to regard the culture which emerges in EM I as indigenous, though owing something to the Cyclades and north-west Anatolia. It will be many years before we can really begin

[1] Hood *1965* 229.

to understand the process which produced the Early Minoan culture.

The one feature of this process which we can observe very clearly is the speed with which it took place. In Early Minoan I we already see many of the features which characterize the Cretan Early Bronze Age as a whole. Socially the Cretans began to emphasize the clan as the important unit within society, and the earliest tholos tombs appear during EM I. At the same time the proliferation of specialized industries – metal-working, pottery manufacture, carpentry – led to the breakdown of the social equality which seems to have persisted throughout the Neolithic. An interest in overseas contacts was expressed in the founding of the harbour towns of Komo, Mochlos and Amnisos and can also be traced, as we have mentioned above, in Aegean pottery forms and the early metal types. Artistically the Minoans were already showing an interest in geometric and linear decoration of pottery, ceramic textures, and zoomorphic pottery forms. We may also see perhaps the first interest in torsion expressed in the Agios Onouphrios style of decoration. Although the Early Minoan I period still remains in the shadows, its details hard to define and its outline rather indistinct, we can recognize enough of its character to see that it is truly a part of the Early Bronze Age.

This is a conclusion of some importance for it helps us to see the developments of Early Minoan II in some sort of perspective. It has been customary to regard the second phase of the Early Bronze Age throughout the Aegean as the period when a sudden flowering of civilization takes place. Renfrew has written of the 'international spirit' of this period in the Aegean, and Caskey has called it a 'prosperous era'.[1] Both are correct and these are matters we shall ourselves discuss in a moment, but it is important that we should realize that EM I laid the foundations for the rapid advances which were made in EM II. Those advances were certainly notable ones, and can be traced principally, one suspects, to the widespread contacts and trade which Crete enjoyed at this time. In Early Minoan II deposits we find the marble figurines which appear both in the Cyclades and on the Greek mainland, the gold jewellery comparable to that from Troy, and Zygouries, the Minoan variety of the 'urfinis' pottery being used on the mainland and in the Cyclades, and black-burnished 'fruit-stands' which I suspect may be a Minoan equivalent of the Cycladic 'frying-pans'. On the Greek

[1] Renfrew *1967a* 15ff.; Caskey *1964* 37.

mainland 'bottle' seals and foot amulets confirm that Crete and southern Greece were in contact with one another and were sharing common cultural fashions. Above all there is an over-all unity in Aegean metallurgy, despite the existence of clearly defined regional 'schools'. Renfrew is surely correct in regarding the rapid development of Aegean civilization at this time as being fostered principally by the impact of metallurgy.

Inevitably the economic results of the new contacts led to social developments and within the EM II period, probably in its initial phases, the first mansions appear. That these belonged to men of enterprise who had exploited the social and economic situations which the onset of the metal age had brought about we cannot doubt. Both the social and architectural seeds of the Palatial era are sown in EM II. Whether or not such men were directly responsible for the setting up of a Minoan 'colony' on Kythera we do not know but one suspects they were.

Certainly we may recognize their initiative in the rapid expansion of Minoan overseas contacts in EM III. Renfrew is a little dubious as to the continuity of the 'international spirit' into the third phase of the Aegean Early Bronze Age, but recognizes that its character may have changed.[1] In the case of Crete this seems to be true. Crete was quite clearly developing a distinctive culture of her own, and having absorbed the best of what the Aegean had to offer she had adapted it and modified it to fit into the pattern of her own culture. Now, in EM III, she was looking elsewhere for new ideas, new trading opportunities, and above all, I think, for new metal sources. She found the trade in the eastern Mediterranean, the metal in the western, and the ideas in both. Visible signs of trade with Syria, Cyprus, Egypt and Italy can be observed. The Minoan 'merchant navy' was apparently growing and trading expeditions were probably becoming regular and regulated. This, and the organization of the various industries within the island to produce commodities which found a ready market abroad, must have required supervisory officials acting on behalf of the authority who controlled such matters. Thus, in EM III, the evolution of palatial society is taken a stage further. A reaction to this increasing control of all aspects of life is perhaps represented by the first of the pithos and larnake burials. Certainly they may be taken to represent one other result of the economic developments, namely the further breakdown of

[1] Renfrew *1967a* 17.

social unity and the importance of the clan. Some of the peak sanctuaries were probably begun at this time and these represent a further sphere of activity where the individual was being brought into an organized framework.

The EM III phase of development was superseded, with little apparent disturbance, by the MM Ia phase. Whilst in pottery, metalwork, and seal-stones we can distinguish, though often with difficulty, the products of EM III from those of MM Ia, socially there is little to mark the beginning of MM Ia. The climax of the social development which began in EM I and was given a new impetus in EM III does not come with the start of MM Ia but a little later, with the building of the palaces. That is to say that although there were changes in art and in fashion that enable us to distinguish the beginning of a new cultural phase, there was no change socially or politically but rather a continuation of the process of evolution. It is for this reason that MM Ia must be studied as part of the Early Bronze Age, and that palatial civilization must be seen to have its roots in Early Minoan Crete. The MM Ia phase should be seen as the climax of the Early Bronze Age rather than as the beginning of the Middle Bronze Age. The process of social development had seen the original social interests of the central authority first integrated with economic interests in EM II, then subjugated to commercial interests in EM III, and finally, in MM Ia, integrated with both political and religious interests to produce palatial society. Thus, as we have said earlier, the society of palatial Crete, like its art, architecture, religion, economy, and crafts, was brought about not by revolution but by evolution. This was perhaps the finest achievement of Early Minoan Crete and its most valuable contribution to palatial civilization.

The historical development which I have outlined was not of course identical all over the island. In contrast to Hutchinson and Caskey I believe that the Mesara was more developed than either the east or north in EM I and for the duration of EM II as well.[1] EM I in the east is very shadowy indeed, and in the north it is clearly still closely akin to the sub-Neolithic phase. The east of Crete is much more prosperous in EM II, at least around the Gulf of Mirabello where many ports were springing up to deal with the Aegean trade. In the Mesara, however, there is already a distinctive culture which shows an advanced stage of metallurgy and con-

[1] Hutchinson *1962* 148; Caskey *1964* 32.

siderable prosperity. The Mesara possessed many advantages for the Early Bronze Age inhabitants. The plain itself was fertile, and the foothills immediately surrounding it were suitable for grapes and olives as well as grazing. In the plain runs one of Crete's few permanent rivers, the Yeropotamos, whilst at the west end of the plain lies the sea, within easy access of the whole plain. Apart from the sea, however, access to the Mesara is quite difficult and in the Early Bronze Age the inhabitants must have led a relatively sheltered existence. Thus the geographical setting was such that a distinctive regional variation of Minoan culture was inevitable.

The same is true of both northern and eastern Crete. The east was isolated from the north and south by high mountain ranges, Dicte completely cutting off access to the Mesara and only the gorge of Selinari allowing it to the plain of Mallia. For contact with the rest of the island the east must therefore have depended very largely on coastal communications. With the expansion of sea communications in EM II and the extension of overseas commerce in EM III the east thus received the impetus needed to develop a standard of culture comparable to that in the Mesara. The agricultural and mineral poverty of the east, however, may well have had its effects upon social development in this region. It seems likely that here the accumulation of wealth could not have been achieved from agriculture or control of metallurgy and metal sources, but rather from control of commerce. This may explain why the two earliest mansions known in Crete are both in the east of the island, at Vasiliki and Fournou Korifi. Both of them date to EM II, the period when trade with the Aegean is rapidly expanded and the east is coming into its own.

In the north the situation is a little different. The narrow coastal strip and the two small plains around Mallia and Iraklion are relatively fertile, and from the plain of Iraklion a series of small valleys stretch southwards into the central range of mountains. Economically the situation was rather similar to that in the Mesara, although there is very little copper in the north. The north, however, lacked the geographical unity of the Mesara, and perhaps this is why no distinctive culture seems to have developed here until EM III and MM Ia. Nevertheless it is still difficult to understand why the north suffered a retarded development in EM I and EM II, particularly when one recalls that this is the region where one can trace the settlement of the island back to 6,000 B.C. As for the west, an area representing about forty per cent of the total area of the island, we can really say very little. There is no reason to think that it must have been sparsely settled during the Early Bronze Age. Indeed Sinclair Hood's surveys indicate that there were many Early Minoan settlements in this area.[1] It may be, however, that social and political development, and thus ultimately economic and commercial development, was held back by the mountainous nature of the terrain.

Clearly there is a great deal we still need to know about Early Minoan settlement in the west of Crete, and indeed about the Early Minoan period throughout the island. Much of what I have written in this book is, of necessity, a tentative attempt to reconstruct the events and processes of the Early Bronze Age. There is still an insufficiency of reliable evidence which prevents us from speaking with conviction on many points. It might therefore be profitable to conclude our survey with a brief discussion of the major problems which remain and the methods whereby they might be solved.

Undoubtedly the greatest need facing students of Early Minoan Crete is for a series of stratified deposits from several sites in all four regions of the island. From such a series it would at last be possible to construct a sound relative chronology within the island, to recognize local variations in pottery styles, and, with good fortune, to obtain a reasonably large corpus of closely dated seal-stones, stone vessels, amulets, jewellery and metalwork. Such a corpus would, in turn, enable the large body of unstratified material we have at present to be confidently identified chronologically. However, it will take many years for such a stratified series to be assembled, and meanwhile we should perhaps be satisfied with the publication of the Early Minoan deposits from Knossos, Lebena and Fournou Korifi. From a close study of these, the pottery styles of all three Early Minoan phases and of MM Ia should be better understood and related to one another. In particular we might expect to distinguish two or more sub-phases of EM II and to see more clearly the distinction between EM III and MM Ia.

There are two types of site about which we need to know much more. No Early Bronze Age settlements have been excavated in anything like their entirety, and in particular it would be valuable to have the plan and history of a village in the Mesara. Whilst Vasiliki and Fournou Korifi tell us something about social and

[1] Hood *1965*; Hood et al. *1964*; Hood and Warren *1966*.

political developments in the east we know nothing of such developments in the Mesara, which was probably the most technologically and economically advanced region in EM I and II. The expansion of overseas trade and the relationship between commercial and political progress would be better understood if there were the excavation of an Early Minoan port.

Seager published few details of the houses he excavated on Mochlos, and Hawes devoted just two lines to the excavations she conducted on the EM II harbour at Priniatiko Pyrgos. Undoubtedly the most suitable site to excavate would be that at Komo. Here Evans noted two settlements, one dating EM I–MM I and the other MM I–LM.[1] Thus Komo would provide the complete history of a Minoan port and at the same time throw some light on the vicissitudes of life in the Mesara as a whole during Minoan times. The port at Komo was that through which the vast majority of overseas imports must have passed into the Mesara, and as such it should yield rich finds. Of particular importance and interest would be objects of foreign origin which would help to establish a more satisfactory absolute and relative chronology for Early Minoan Crete.

There are some problems which can be tackled, however, without resort to further excavation. The compilation of catalogues of Early Minoan seal-stones, jewellery, figurines, and other small finds would in itself be a major advance and if accompanied by a full study of these artifacts would be invaluable. Until five years ago one could have included in this list above, all the other major groups of artifacts – pottery, stone vases, obsidian, and metalwork. Renfrew has done much to enlighten us as to the obsidian sources utilized by the Minoans, however, and Warren has completed a comprehensive study of the stone-vases. Both Zoes and Cadogan have made close studies of Early Minoan pottery, and I have myself completed a study of metalworking.[2] All of these studies have yielded valuable new information and there is no reason to think that similar studies of the other artifacts would not produce similar results.

There is, too, the problem of terminology. Unsatisfactory as it may be, I have used Evans's terminology throughout this book, in

[1] Evans *1928* 88.
[2] Renfrew et al. *1965*; Warren *forthcoming*, *1968a*; Zoes *1967*; Cadogan unpublished (see forthcoming reports on the excavations at Knossos); Branigan *1968*.

order to avoid confusion. Up to the present time material of the Minoan Early Bronze Age has always been classified and described according to Evans's scheme,[1] and to suddenly introduce a new scheme without a full explanation of the way in which it is put together and the way in which it relates to Evans's system would indeed result in confusion. On the other hand, to present a full explanation of a new scheme would involve the reader and myself in the sort of technical and very detailed discussion which is better suited to the pages of a learned journal than to those of a broad survey of the type presented here. The time has come however when I, and all those like me who have consistently pushed the problem on one side and continued to use Evans's scheme because it is convenient, must come to grips with the problem. Much of the trouble springs from the fact that we use Evans's terms – Early Minoan I, II and III and Middle Minoan Ia – to distinguish both pottery styles and periods of time. Thus, when two styles overlap in time we may have a confusing situation. This is the case with EM III and MM Ia. Whilst the north was using pottery of the MM Ia style, the east was using pottery of the EM III style. As Evans's scheme is used at the moment, this is a contradiction in terms – two styles may be contemporary but not two periods which succeed one another! There are several solutions to the problem. We could, for example, retain Evans's terms for pottery styles and introduce the simple terms Early Bronze I, II, III etc. with any sub-divisions which seem justified. But this too will lead to some confusion, simply because the dual standards of Evans's scheme have become engrained in our jargon and in our minds. It seems that the best hope is to abandon Evans's terms altogether and to use type sites for all the pottery styles and the Early Bronze I, II etc. for the periods. Working on this basis it should be possible to reconstruct Evans's framework with the necessary adjustments. In particular I feel that just as it has become increasingly clear that MM Ia is farther removed from MM Ib than is MM II, so it will slowly become apparent that EM III is closer to MM Ia than to EM II.

But these are complex problems into which we need not enter further at the moment, and which we must not allow to obscure the picture of Crete in the Early Bronze Age which has, I hope, emerged

---

[1] But recently the scheme of 'Prepalatial', 'Protopalatial' and 'Neo-palatial' has been widely adopted. For the Early Bronze Age however it is too imprecise to be of value.

as our survey progressed. We began our discussion of Early Minoan Crete with the views of Levi and Aaberg who said, in effect, that it did not exist. I think we may end it with the certain knowledge that Early Minoan Crete was a vivid reality and that it laid the foundations for the yet more brilliant era which succeeded it.

Appendix
Early Bronze Age sites open to visitors

Most excavations in Crete are left open after excavation, and theoretically all Early Bronze Age sites are open to the public. However the inaccessibility of many sites is a serious obstacle to all but the most determined students, whilst several of the remaining sites preserve little or no trace of the Early Bronze Age structures found there. The list given below is intended to cover only those sites which are both accessible and well preserved.

HOUSES

Fragments of houses can be seen at Phaistos and Knossos. At Phaistos the foundations of a room and possibly a corridor of EM I or EM II are preserved on the peak of the palace site. The MM Ia houses found in the West Court at Knossos are partially preserved at the bottom of the koulouras in the court. However the only two houses which are really worth visiting are those at Vasiliki and Fournou Korifi.

Vasiliki. The modern village of Vasiliki lies on the west of the road from Gournia to Hierapetra, some five kilometres south east of Gournia. On leaving the Hierapetra road one passes a small hill on one's left (south) and it is here that the Early Minoan II–Middle Minoan I settlement was situated. It is a walk of only two or three minutes from either the main or the subsidiary road to the top of the hill. Here the authorities have recently restored the EM IIb mansion (Seager's 'House-on-the-Hill'). Most of the east wing can no longer be seen but a portion of it survives along with the whole of the excavated part of the south wing.

The first thing to notice is that only a portion of this house seems to have been excavated and one is therefore looking at only a fragment of an EM II mansion. Note that the house was built into the hillside and the slope of the ground utilized to provide stories. In general the south wing was built on higher ground than the east wing and at its eastern end the upper floor rooms of the south wing extend over the lower or ground floor rooms of the east wing. In the south-western corner of the building some of the lower floor rooms survive to their full height and red plaster may be seen adhering to the walls in places. Also at the eastern end of the building the well can still be seen (although for safety's sake it has been filled in) standing in what was probably a small open court. Two semi-circular footholds are preserved just below the rim.

Most of the rooms are truly rectangular but it is difficult to assess the quality of the construction since so many walls have been rebuilt by the authorities. To the west of the south wing is a paved court the limits of which have never been determined. It at once recalls the west court of the palaces, and here the visitor might take note of the excellent and commanding position occupied by this building. A final point of interest is that many sherds of the typical EM II ware called after this site can be seen scattered over the surface. (It is an offence under Greek law to remove them however.)

Fournou Korifi. This site is a little difficult to reach but well worth a visit. It lies about ten kilometres west of Hierapetra on the south coast. The most convenient route is to follow the road to Myrtos, a little further west, and then take the coast road back to Fournou Korifi. A bus to Myrtos can be caught in Hierapetra. Fournou Korifi is itself a small but prominent hill overlooking the sea and can be approached from the small plains on either side of it. The excavations conducted by Dr. Warren revealed an extensive mansion of EM II date.

Along the slope, running north-south, a complex of rectangular rooms back on to a sheer cliff. Defensively the site is excellent. Running east-west, and facing out on to the Libyan sea is a long suite of well built rooms which perhaps represent the best architecture on the site. There is little similarity to the plan of Vasiliki – as Vasiliki is known – but this may be because the shape of the hill at Fournou Korifi is very different from that at Vasiliki. However the *scale* of the building is similar to Vasiliki and one imagines it must have been occupied by a man of similar wealth and status to the one who lived in the House-on-the-Hill. The small white hill just north of the site contains copper-bearing pebbles which seem to have been utilized during the EM II period.

TOMBS

Several tholoi still survive and the rectangular chamber tombs of Mochlos can still be seen, but the latter are difficult to reach. Good representative examples of the tholos and the rectangular ossuary are Kamilari and Arkhanes respectively. These are chosen because both are relatively easy to reach and both have been excavated recently and are therefore still in good condition.

Kamilari. Levi excavated the large tholos at Kamilari for the Italian School of Archaeology. There are in fact at least three and possibly more tholoi in the immediate vicinity. The 'cemetery' of Kamilari lies less than two kilometres from Phaistos and is best reached from the palace site. If one takes the small road from Phaistos to Agia Triadha and branches off across the countryside shortly before reaching the latter site a track leads past the hill on the side of which stands the large tholos.

Built in MM I, the tholos was used for several centuries and in fact represents the latest extant tholos of Mesara type. Despite its late date it is typical of the Mesara tholoi in every respect. It is a little larger than most (but not all) and certainly the best preserved. Points of importance and interest are the signs of vaulting to be noted on the walls, which survive to about two metres in height, and the traces of burning which mark the wall in places. Whether or not these were caused by fumigation, funerary rituals, or a wooden roof which was accidentally destroyed by fire we do not know (see Chapter 8). The method of construction can be seen clearly enough–a rubble fill with facing of roughly worked stones which are tapered so that they can be used to construct a circle. Outside the tholos itself is a complex of small rectangular chambers which may be compared with those at Porti, Apesokari, and Koumasa. To the north east of the tholos is the open space which was found to be marked out as a 'sacred area'.

Whilst visiting Kamilari the student can easily visit the remains of the two tholoi at Agia Triadha. Neither are well preserved but the smaller example still retains some of the mysterious slabs, set into the wall on its southern side. The other complex well worth visiting is at Lebena, overlooking the Libyan Sea, but this site is difficult to reach and will add little to what one can see at Kamilari.

Arkhanes. Arkhanes lies approximately fifteen kilometres south of Iraklion from which it may easily be reached by a frequent bus service. The visitor can see in the village the fragmentary remains of a villa or 'palace' recently excavated, before moving off north-westwards out of the village towards the tombs. These are situated on a hill nearby from which one obtains a good view both of the town and of Iuktas. The interest of Arkhanes is perhaps the continuity of burial customs which can be traced at the cemetery site. Here the visitor can see two superimposed 'tholoi' of the palatial era, with a complex of chambers outside, and a little to the north of these the great domed tomb in which the rich 'royal burial' was found. For the student of the Early Bronze Age however, the particular point of interest is situated just behind the two superimposed tholoi where stands a small but well preserved example of an Early Minoan ossuary. The long, narrow cells with projecting door jambs illustrate well the magazine-like nature of these ossuaries. Dr. Sakellarakis, the excavator, found a typical assortment of Early Minoan material here dating from EM II onwards.

PALACES

There is of course no Middle Minoan I palace surviving to us, all of the palaces having undergone alterations, sometimes very considerable ones, in their later stages. However a clear idea as to what the Middle Minoan I palaces may have been like and the sort of atmosphere which may have pervaded them can be grasped from a visit to Mallia.

Mallia. Mallia stands in an attractive bay with sandy beaches about forty kilometres east of Iraklion. There are very frequent buses between the two towns. The palace site lies a few kilometres east of the town itself and between the road and the sea. As one approaches it one passes through the residential area which surrounded the palace, some of which has been excavated. At the south end of the palace one meets the fine group of circular stone structures perhaps to be identified as cisterns. In front, and to the west of the central court, are some magazines and a great corridor. Across the central court are another set of magazines, now covered over and in which are preserved many large, complete storage vessels. To the north of the court is the pillar room, probably situated beneath a large dining-room on the upper floor. Beyond this is an open yard grouped around which are rooms which probably formed the domestic quarters of the palace. Tucked away on the west side of the palace is the small suite of rooms identified by Platon as part of the 'royal' quarters.

The great advantage of Mallia is that it has a simple plan which can be readily grasped by the visitor. It is almost as if one is looking at the early stages of construction rather than the remains of the completed palace. As far as we know much of Mallia, in plan if not in construction, dates back to the early palace. It is therefore the nearest that we can get to what the first palaces might have looked like. It is true that to the south of the west court at Phaistos Levi has uncovered part of the MM I complex but overlain as it is by later structures it is difficult to appreciate its significance without the expert and kindly guidance of Professor Levi himself.

SUMMARY

There are in Crete, within easy reach of the visitor who is dependent on public buses for transport, a group of well preserved monuments which illustrate Minoan domestic dwellings, tombs, and palaces of the Early Bronze Age. With the exception of Fournou Korifi, Lebena, and possibly Vasiliki, all the sites are within a day's return journey of Heraklion. Most of the sites are near important monuments of the palatial era and one does not need to urge the student to visit these sites as well. A day's trip to the Mesara is an invaluable experience for those interested in Early Minoan Crete and Kamilari, the Agia Triadha tholoi, and the EM I–II house and MM I palace fragments at Phaistos can all be comfortably accommodated within the time allowed. There are two points that the student is asked to remember. Antiquities must not be removed from archaeological sites, and some of the sites mentioned above have not been fully published yet and photographs should not be taken on these sites. At the time of writing the unpublished sites include MM I palace fragments at Phaistos, Arkhanes tombs, Lebena tholoi, parts of Mallia, and the mansion at Fournou Korifi.

Abbreviations used in the bibliographies

AA	Archäologischer Anzeiger.
AD	Archaiologikon Deltion.
AE	Archaiologiki Ephemeris.
Ann	Annuario della Scuola Archeologica di Atene.
AR	Archaeological Reports.
AS	Anatolian Studies.
BCH	Bulletin de Correspondance Hellénique.
BIAL	Bulletin of the Institute of Archaeology, London.
BICS	Bulletin of the Institute of Classical Studies.
BMB	Bulletin du Musée de Beyrouth.
BPI	Bollettino de Paletnologia Italiana.
BSA	Annual of the British School at Athens.
ILN	Illustrated London News.
JRGZ	Jahrbuch des Römisch-germanische Zentralsmuseum, Mainz.
Jahrb.	Jahrbuch des deutschen archäologischen Instituts.
KC	Kretika Chronika.
PP	La Parola del Passato.
PPS	Proceedings of the Prehistoric Society.
Rev. Arch.	Revue Archéologique.
SMEA	Studi Micenei ed Egeo-Anatolici.
TFMSA	Transactions of the Free Museum of Science and Art.

General bibliography

AABERG, N. (1933) *Bronzezeitliche und Fruheisenzeitliche Chronologie IV* (Stockholm).

ALEXIOU, S. (1951) 'Protominoikai Taphai para to Kanli Kastelli, Heraklion' *KC* 1951.

—(1954) 'Anaskaphai en Katsamba' *Praktika* 1954, 369–76.

—(1958) 'Ein Frühminoisches Grab bei Lebena' *AA* 1958, 1ff.

—(1960) 'New Light on Minoan Dating; Early Minoan Tombs at Lebena' *ILN* Aug. 6th, 1960.

ALBRIGHT, W. F. (1960) *The Archaeology of Palestine* (London).

ALLBOUGH, L. (1953) *Crete (A Case Study of an Undeveloped Area).*

AMIET, P. (1961) *La Glyptique Mesopotamienne* (Paris).

ATKINSON, T. D. (1904) *Excavations at Phylakopi in Melos* (London).

BANTI, L. (1933) 'La Grande Tomba a Tholos di Hagia Triadha' *Ann.* 1933.

BERNABO-BREA, L. (1957) *Sicily before the Greeks* (London).

—(1964) *Poliochni, Citta Preistorica nell'Isola di Lemnos* (Rome).

BLEGEN, C. W. (1921) *Korakou, A Prehistoric Settlement near Corinth* (New York).

—(1928) *Zygouries* (Cambridge, Mass.).

—(1950) *Troy I* (Princeton).

—(1951) *Troy II* (Princeton).

BOARDMAN, J. (1961) *The Cretan Collection in Oxford* (Oxford).

—(1967) *Preclassical* (London).

BORDA, M. (1946) *Arte Cretese Micenia nel Museo Pigorini di Roma* (Rome).

BOSANQUET, R. (1923) *The Unpublished Objects from the Palaikastro Excavations. I* (London).

BOSSERT, E. (1960) 'Die gestempelten Verzierungen auf frühbronzezeitlichen Gefässen de Agäis' *Jahrb.* 75, 1–16.

BOYD-HAWES, H. (1905) 'Excavations in Eastern Crete' *TFMSA* I, 183ff.

—(1908) *Gournia* (Philadelphia).

BRAIDWOOD, R. & L. (1953) 'The Earliest Village Communities of South-Western Asia' *Journal of World History* I, 278ff.

—(1955) 'The Earliest Village Materials of Syro-Cilicia' *PPS* 21, 72ff.

BRANIGAN, K. (1965) 'The Origins of the Hieroglyphic Sign 18' *Kadmos* 4.

—(1965a) 'Four "Miniature Sickles" of Middle Minoan Crete' *KC* 19.

—(1966) 'Byblite Daggers in Cyprus and Crete' *AJA* 70.

—(1966a) 'The Prehistory of Hieroglyphic Signs 12 and 36' *Kadmos* 5.

—(1966b) 'Prehistoric Relations Between Italy and the Aegean' *BPI* 17.

—(1967) 'Further Light on Prehistoric Relations Between Crete and Syria' *AJA* 71.

—(1967a) 'The Early Bronze Age Daggers of Crete' *BSA* 61.

—(1968) *Copper and Bronzework in Early Bronze Age Crete* (Lund).

—(1968a) 'The Mesara Tholoi and Middle Minoan Chronology' *SMEA* 5.

—(1968b) 'A Transitional Phase in Minoan Metallurgy' *BSA* 62.

—(1968c) 'Early Minoan Metallurgy–A Re-appraisal' *Proc. of the Second Creteological Congress, II* (Athens).

—(1968d) 'Silver and Lead in Prepalatial Crete' *AJA* 72.

—(1969) 'The Genesis of the Household Goddess' *SMEA*. 8

—(1969a) 'The Earliest Aegean Scripts–The Prepalatial Background' *Kadmos* 8

—(1969b) 'Early Aegean Hoards of Metalwork' *BSA* 64.

BUCHHOLZ, H. (1959) *Zur Herkunft der Kretischen Doppelaxt* (Munich).

BUISSON, R. (1948) *Baghouz* (Paris).

CADOGAN, G. (1966) 'An Egyptian Flint Knife from Knossos' *BSA* 60.

CALEY, E. (1949) 'On the Prehistoric Use of Arsenical Copper in the Aegean Region' *Hesperia Supp.* 8.

CASKEY, J. (1955) 'Excavations at Lerna 1954' *Hesperia* 24.

—(1960) 'The Early Helladic Period in the Argolid' *Hesperia* 29.

—(1962) 'Excavations in Keos 1960–61' *Hesperia* 31.

—(1964) *Greece, Crete, and the Aegean Islands in the Early Bronze Age* (Cambridge).

—(1964a) 'Excavations in Keos 1963' *Hesperia* 33.

CATLING, H. and KARAGEORGHIS, V. (1960) 'Minoika in Cyprus' *BSA* 55.

CHAPOUTHIER, F. (1936) *Deux Epeés* (Paris).

CHAPOUTHIER, F. and BISSON de la ROQUE, F. (1953) *Le Trésor de Tôd* (Cairo).

CHAPOUTHIER, F. and DEMARGNE, P. (1942) *Fouilles Executées à Mallia Troisième Rapport* (Paris).

—(1962) *Fouilles Executées a Mallia. IV* (Paris).

DAUX, G. (1959) 'Chronique des Fouilles en 1958' *BCH* 83.

—(1960) 'Chroniques des Fouilles. 1959' *BCH* 84.

—(1961) 'Chroniques des Fouilles. 1960' *BCH* 85.

DAWKINS, R. (1903) 'Excavations at Palaikastro II' *BSA* 9.

—(1904) 'Excavations at Palaikastro III' *BSA* 10.

—(1905) 'Excavations at Palaikastro IV' *BSA* 11.

DAWKINS, R. and DROOP, J. P. (1912) 'The Excavations at Phylakopi in Melos' *BSA* 17.

DEMARGNE, P. (1945) *Fouilles Executées à Mallia. Exploration des Nécropoles* (Paris).

DESHAYES, J. (1960) *Les Outils de Bronze del'Indus au Danube* (Paris).

DESHAYES, J. and DESSENNE, A. (1959) *Fouilles Executées a Mallia. Exploration des Maisons et Quartiers d'Habitation* (Paris).

DUCKWORTH, W. (1903) 'Human Remains at Hagios Nikolaos' *BSA* 9.

DUNAND, M. (1937) *Fouilles de Byblos. I* (Paris).

—(1950) 'Fouilles de Byblos' *BMB* 9, 55ff.

—(1954) *Fouilles de Byblos. II* (Paris).

—(1956) 'Fouilles de Byblos' *BMB* 13, 74ff.

EDGAR, C. C. (1897) 'Prehistoric Tombs at Pelos' *BSA* 3.

EHRICH, R. (1954) *Relative Chronologies in Old World Archaeology* 1st Ed. (Chicago).

—(1965) ed. *Relative Chronologies in Old World Archaeology* (Chicago).

EVANS, A. J. (1895) *Cretan Pictographs and the Mycenaean Script* (London).

—(1903) 'The Palace of Knossos. Excavations at Knossos 1903' *BSA* 9.

—(1904) 'The Palace of Knossos. Knossos Excavations 1904' *BSA* 10.

—(1921) *The Palace of Minos. I* (London).

—(1928) *The Palace of Minos. II* (London).

—(1930) *The Palace of Minos. III* (London).

—(1935) *The Palace of Minos. IV* (London).

—EVANS, J. D. (1959) *Malta* (London).

—(1964) 'Excavations in the Neolithic Settlement of Knossos, 1957–60. I' *BSA* 59.

—(1964) 'Excavations in the Neolithic Settlement of Knossos, 1957–60. I' *BSA* 59.

—(1964a) 'Excavations in the Neolithic Mound of Knossos, 1958–60'. *BIAL* 4.

FAURE, P. (1964) *Fonctions des Cavernes Crétoises* (Paris).

—(1966) 'Les Minerais de la Crète Antiques. *Rev. Arch.* 1966.

—(1967) 'Sur Trois Sortes de Sanctuaries Crétois' *BCH* 91.

—(1968) 'Le Problème du Cuivre dans la Crète Antique' *Proc. of Second Creteological Congress, II*.

FRANKFORT, H. (1927) *Studies in Early Pottery of the Near East* (London).

FRODIN, O. and PERSSON, A. (1938) *Asine* (Stockholm).

GARSTANG, J. (1953) *Prehistoric Mersin* (Oxford).

GLOTZ, G. (1921) *La Civilization Minoenne* (Paris).

GOLDMAN, H. (1931) *Excavations at Eutresis in Boeotia* (Cambridge, Mass.).

—(1956) *Excavations at Gözlü Kule, Tarsus II* (Princeton).

GRAHAM, J. (1962) *The Palaces of Crete* (Toronto).

GUIDO, M. (1963) *Sardinia* (London).

HALL, E. H. (1905) 'Early Painted Pottery from Gournia, Crete' *TFMSA* 1905.

—(1907) *The Decorative Art of Crete in the Bronze Age* (Philadelphia).

—(1912) *Excavations in Eastern Crete – Sphoungaras* (Philadelphia).

—(1914) *Excavations in Eastern Crete – Vrokastro* (Philadelphia).

HAZZIDAKIS, J. (1912) 'Tylisos Minoiki' *AE* 1912.

—(1913) 'An Early Minoan Sacred Cave at Arkalokhori' *BSA* 19.

—(1914) 'Protominoikoi Taphoi para to Khorion Gournes' *AD* 1.

—(1921) *Tylissos a l'Époque Minoenne* (Paris).

—(1934) *Les Villas Minoennes de Tylissos* (Paris).

HEATH, M. (1958) 'Early Helladic Clay Sealings from the House of the Tiles at Lerna' *Hesperia* 27.

HIGGINS, R. (1957) 'The Aegina Treasure Reconsidered' *BICS* 1957.

—(1967) *Minoan and Mycenaean Art* (London).

HOGARTH, D. (1901) 'Excavations at Zakro, Crete' *BSA* 7.

HOOD, M. S. F. (1955) 'British Excavations – Chios' *AR* 1955.

—(1960) 'Crete' *AR* 1960.

—(1962) 'Excavations at Emporio in Chios' *Proceedings of the Rome Congress. II* 224–8.

—(1962a) 'Knossos' *AD* 17, 294–6.

—(1962b) 'The Home of the Heroes' in Piggott. S. (ed) *The Dawn of Civilization.*

—(1964) Review of F. Schachermeyr *1964, JHS* 85.

—(1965) 'Minoan Sites in the Far West of Crete' *BSA* 60.

—(1967) *Home of the Heroes* (London).

HOOD, M. S. F. and WARREN, P. (1966) 'Ancient Sites in the Province of Agios Vasilios, Crete' *BSA* 61.

HOOD, M. S. F., WARREN, P., and CADOGAN, G. (1964) 'Travels in Crete, 1962' *BSA* 59.

HUTCHINSON, R. W. (1948) 'Notes on Minoan Chronology' *Antiquity* 22.

—(1954) 'Minoan Chronology Reviewed' *Antiquity* 28.

—(1962) *Prehistoric Crete* (London).

HUXLEY, G. and COLDSTREAM, J. (1966) 'Kythera, First Minoan Colony' *ILN* Aug. 27th, 1966.

KANTOR, H. (1947) 'The Aegean and the Orient in the Second Millennium B.C.' *AJA* 51.

—(1949) *The Aegean and the Orient in the Second Millennium BC* (Bloomington).

KENNA, V. (1960) *Cretan Seals* (Oxford).

—(1968) 'Ancient Crete and the Use of the Cylinder Seal' *AJA* 72.

KENYON, K. (1960) *Archaeology in the Holy Land* (London).

KOEPPEL, R. (1940) *Teleilat el-Ghassul II* (Rome).

KOHLER, E. and RALPH, E. (1961) 'C. 14 Dates for Sites in the Mediterranean' *AJA* 65.

KOSAY, H. (1951) *Les Fouilles d'Alaca Huyuk* (Ankara).

LAMB, W. (1936) *Excavations at Thermi in Lesbos* (Cambridge).

LEVI, D. (1952) 'One of the Richest Finds of Minoan Treasure in Crete' *ILN* Jan. 19th, 1952.

—(1953) 'Uncovering the Oldest Palace of Phaistos' *ILN* Dec. 12th, 1953.

—(1958) 'L'Archivio di Cretule a Festos' *Ann.* 1958.

—(1960) 'Per una Nuova Classificazione della Civilta Minoica' *PP* 15.

—(1962) 'La Tomba a Tholos di Kamilari presso a Festos' *Ann.* 1962.

—(1963) 'New Discoveries on one of the Greatest of Minoan Sites' *ILN* July 27th, 1963.

—(1965) 'Le Varieta della Primitiva Ceramica Cretese' in *Studies in Onore di Liusa Banti.*

—(1967) 'La Conclusions degli Scavi a Festos' *Ann.* 1967.

—(1967a) 'La Campagne 1962–64 a Iasos' *Ann.* 1967.

LLOYD, S. and MELLAART, J. (1955) 'Beycesultan' *AS* 5.

—(1956) 'Beycesultan' *AS* 6.

LLOYD, S. and MELLAART, J. (1957) 'Beycesultan' *AS* 7.

—(1960) 'Beycesultan' *AS* 10.

—(1962) *Beycesultan. I. The Chalcolithic and Early Bronze Age Levels* (London).

MACKENZIE, D. (1908) 'Cretan Palaces. IV' *BSA* 14.

MALLON, A. (1933) *Teleilat el-Ghassul I* (Rome).

MARINATOS, S. (1928) 'Höhlenforschungen in Kreta' *Zeitschrift des Hauptuerbandes deutscher Höholenforscher.*

—(1929) 'Protominoikos Tholotos Taphos para to Khorion Krasi Pediadhos' *AD* 12.

—(1929a) 'To Speos Eileithyes' *Praktika* 1929.

—(1930) 'Anaskaphai en Krete' *Praktika* 1930.

—(1931) 'Duo Proimoi Minoikoi Taphoi ek Vorou Mesaras' *AD* 1931.

—(1932) 'Funde und Forschungen auf Kreta' *AA* 1932.

—(1933) 'Funde und Forschugen auf Kreta' *AA* 1933.

—(1960) *Kreta und das Mykenische Hellas* (English translation available) (Munich).

MATZ, F. (1928) *Die Frühkretischen Siegel* (Berlin).

—(1942) *Forschungen auf Kreta* (Berlin).

—(1962) *Minoan Civilisation : Maturity and Zenith* (Cambridge).

MEGAW, J. V. S. (1966) 'Archaeology in Greece' *AR* 1966.

MELLAART, J. (1959) 'Excavations at Beycesultan 1958. II. The Chalcolithic Sounding' *AS* 9.

—(1959a) 'The Royal Treasure of Dorak' *ILN* Nov. 28th, 1959.

—(1965) *Earliest Civilizations of the Near East* (London).

MILOJCIĆ, V. (1959) 'Ergebnisse der Deutschen Ausgrabungen in Thessalien 1953–1958' *JRGZ* 6.

MONEY-COUTTS, M. (1936) 'A Stone Bowl and Lid from Byblos' *Berytus* 1936.

MONTELIUS, O. (1928) *La Grèce Préclassique* (Stockholm).

General Bibliography

MOSSO, A. (1910) *The Dawn of Mediterranean Civilisation* (London).
MYLONAS, G. (1959) *Agios Kosmas, An Early Bronze Age Settlement and Cemetery in Attica* (Princeton).
MYRES, J. L. (1903) 'The Sanctuary Site of Petsopha' *BSA* 9.
NILSSON, M. (1950) *The Minoan Mycenaean Religion* (Lund).
NOACK, F. (1908) *Ovalhaus und Palast in Kreta* (Berlin).
PALMER, L. R. (1963) *The Find Places of the Knossos Tablets* (Oxford).
PARABENI, R. (1913) 'Scavi nella Necropoli . . . . di Siva' *Ausonia* 8.
PENDLEBURY, J. D. S. (1929) *Aegyptiaca* (Cambridge).
—(1932) 'Two Protopalatial Houses at Knossos' *BSA* 29.
—(1936) 'Excavations in Lasithi' *BSA* 36.
—(1937) *Guide to the Stratigraphical Museum at Knossos* (London).
—(1939) *The Archaeology of Crete* (London).
PENDLEBURY, J. D. S. et al. (1938) 'Excavations in the Plain of Lasithi II' *BSA* 38.
PERNIER, L. (1935) *Il Palazzo Minoico di Festos I* (Rome).
PERSSON, A. W. (1942) *The Religion of Greece in Prehistoric Times* (Berkley/Los Angeles).
PLATON, N. (1947) 'Chronika' *KC* 2.
—(1951) 'To Ieron Maza kai ta Minoika 'Iera Korephes' *KC* 5.
—(1957) 'Chronika' *KC* 11.
—(1964) 'A New Major Minoan Palace Discovered in Crete' *ILN* March 7th, 1964.
POPHAM, M., SACKETT, H., and WARREN, P. (1965) 'Excavations at Palaikastro VI' *BSA* 60.
RENFREW, C. (1964) 'Crete Before Rhadamanthus' *KC* 18.
—(1967) 'Colonialism and Megalithismus' *Antiquity* 41.
—(1967a) 'Cycladic Metallurgy and the Aegean Early Bronze Age' *AJA* 71.
RENFREW, C. and EVANS, J. D. (1968) *Saliagos. A Neolithic Village in the Cyclades* (London).
RENFREW, C. et al. (1965) 'Obsidian in the Aegean' *BSA* 60.
RODDEN, R. (1964) 'A European Link with Chatal Huyuk' *ILN* April 11th, 1964.
—(1964a) 'A European Link with Chatal Huyuk. Pt. II' *ILN* April 18th, 1964.
SAKELLARAKIS, J. (1966) 'The First Untouched Royal Burial Found in Crete' *ILN* March 26th, 1966.
SCHACHERMEYR, F. (1955) *Die Ältesten Kulturen Griechenlands* (Stuttgart).
—(1962) 'Forschungsbericht über die Ausgrabungen und Neufunde zur Agäischen Frühzeit 1957–60' *AA* 1962.
—(1964) *Die Minoische Kultur des Alten Kreta* (Stuttgart).
SCHAEFFER, C. et al. (1962) *Ugaritica IV* (Paris).
SCHLIEMANN, H. (1880) *Ilios* (London).
SEAGER, R. (1905) 'Excavations at Vasiliki, 1904' *TFMSA* I.
—(1907) 'Report of Excavations at Vasiliki, Crete, in 1906' *TFMSA* II.

—(1909) 'Excavations at Mochlos' *AJA* 13.

—(1912) *Excavations on the Island of Mochlos* (Boston and New York).

—(1912a) *Excavations on the Island of Pseira* (Philadelphia).

—(1916) *The Cemetery at Pachyammos* (Philadelphia).

STEVENSON SMITH, W. (1962) *The Old Kingdom in Egypt* (Cambridge).

TARAMELLI, A. (1897) 'The Prehistoric Grotto of Miamu' *AJA* I.

TRUMP, D. (1961) 'The Trefoil Temple at Skorba' *ILN* Dec. 30th, 1961.

—(1966) *Central and Southern Italy Before Rome* (London).

TSOUNTAS, C. (1899) 'Kykladika II' *AE* 1899.

—(1908) *Ai Proistorikai Akropoleis Diminiou kai Sesklo* (Athens).

VANDIER, J. (1937) 'A Propos d'un Dêpot de Provenance Asiatique Trouvé à Tod' *Syria* 1937.

VAN EFFENTERRE, H. (1963) 'Voies et Places Publiques au Nord-Ouest du Palais de Mallia' *BCH* 87.

VICKERY, K. (1936) *Food in Early Greece* (Urbana, Ill.).

WAINWRIGHT, G. A. 'Egyptian Bronze Making' *Antiquity* 17.

WARREN, P. (1965) 'Two Palatial Stone Vases from Knossos' *BSA* 60.

—(1965a) 'The First Minoan Stone Vases and Early Minoan Chronology' *KC* 19.

—(1968) 'A Textile Town–4,500 Years Ago' *ILN* Feb. 17th, 1968.

WARREN, P. (1968a) 'Minoan Stone Vases as Evidence for Minoan Foreign Connections in the Aegean Late Bronze Age' *PPS* 33.

—(1969) 'Minoan Village on Crete' *ILN* Feb. 8th, 1969.

WEINBERG, S. (1947) 'Aegean Chronology; Neolithic Period and Early Bronze Age' *AJA* 51.

—(1962) 'Excavations at Prehistoric Elateia, 1959' *Hesperia* 31.

—(1965) *The Stone Age in the Aegean* (Cambridge).

WILLETTS, R. F. (1962) *Cretan Cults and Festivals* (London/New York).

—(1965) *Ancient Crete. A Social History* (London/Toronto).

WOLDERING, I. (1963) *Egypt. The Art of the Pharaohs* (London).

WOOLLEY, L. (1953) *A Forgotten Kingdom* (London).

XANTHOUDIDES, S. (1906) 'Ek Kretes – Chamaizi' *AE* 1906.

—(1912) 'Cretan Kernoi' *BSA* 18.

—(1918) 'Marathokephalo' *AD* 4, 15–23.

—(1918a) 'Megas Protominoikos Taphos Pyrgos' *AD* 4, 136–70.

—(1924) *The Vaulted Tombs of the Mesara* (London).

XENAKI-SAKELLARIOU, A. (1958) *Les Cachets Minones de la Collection Giamalakis* (Paris).

ZERVOS, C. (1956) *L'Art de la Crète* (Paris).

—(1957) *L'Art des Cyclades* (Paris).

ZOES, A. (1965) 'Phaistiaka' *AE* 1965.

—(1967) *Studies in Minoan Pottery* (Athens).

—(1967a) 'Is there an EM III Period?' *Proc. of Second Creteological Congress, I* (Athens).

Chapter bibliographies

Chapter II (Chronology)
Aaberg *1933*, Alexiou *1958*, *1960*, Branigan *1968a*, Ehrich *1965*, Deshayes *1960*, Hall *1912*, Hutchinson *1948*, *1954*, Levi *1952*, *1953*, *1960* Pendlebury *1937*, Seager *1905*, *1907*, *1912*, Weinberg *1965*, Warren *1965a*, Zoes *1965*, *1967*, *1967a*.

Chapter III (Architecture and Settlements)
Deshayes and Dessenne *1959*, Graham *1962*, Hazzidakis *1934*, Hood *1965*, Hood and Warren *1966*, Hood, Cadogan and Warren *1964*, Levi *1958*, *1967*, Mackenzie *1908*, Pendlebury *1932*, Pernier *1935*, Seager *1907*, *1909*, Taramelli *1897*, Warren *1968*.

Chapter IV (Economy)
Allbough *1953*, Branigan *1967a*, *1968*, *1968b*, *1968c*, *1968d*, *1969b*, Chapouthier and Demargne *1942* (p. 56ff.), Faure *1966*, Marinatos *1929a*, Vickery *1936*, Warren *1965*, *1965a*, *1968*, Hutchinson *1962*, 237ff.

Chapter V (Religion)
Branigan *1965*, *1965a*, *1969*, Buchholz *1959*, Faure *1964*, *1967*, Hazzidakis *1913*, Myres *1903*, Noack *1908*, Platon *1951*, Xanthoudides *1912*, *1924*, *1906*, Nilsson *1950*, Persson *1942*, Willetts *1962*.

Chapter VI (Social Organization)
Duckworth *1903*, Van Effenterre *1963*, Willetts *1965*, Hutchinson *1962* 232ff.

Chapter VII (Art)
Hall *1905*, *1907*, Higgins *1957*, *1967*, Kenna *1960*, Marinatos *1960*, Matz *1928*, *1962*, Platon *1964*, Xenaki-Sakellariou *1958*, Zervos *1956*, *1957*.

Chapter VIII (Funerary Architecture and Ritual)
Alexiou *1951*, *1958*, Branigan *1968a*, Demargne *1945*, Hazzidakis *1914*,

The foundations of palatial Crete
Levi *1962, 1963,* Marinatos *1929, 1931,* Matz *1942,* Parabeni *1913,* Sakellarakis *1966,* Seager *1912,* Xanthoudides *1918, 1918a, 1924.*

Chapter IX (Trade and Communications)
Alexiou *1960,* Blegen *1928,* Branigan *1966, 1966b, 1967, 1968, 1969a,* Catling and Karageorghis *1960,* Cadogan *1966,* Evans *1895,* Huxley and Coldstream *1966,* Kantor *1947,* Kenna *1968,* Money-Coutts *1936,* Renfrew *1964,* Hutchinson *1962,* p. 91ff., Warren *1965a.*

Chapter X (Prepalatial History and Research)
Evans J. D. *1964,* Hood *1962b, 1967,* Levi *1965,* Renfrew *1964,* Schachermeyr *1955, 1964,* Zoes *1967a.*

General books
Caskey *1964,* Evans, A. J. *1921,* Hood *1967,* Hutchinson *1962,* Pendlebury *1939,* Schachermeyr *1964,* Seager *1912,* Xanthoudides *1924.*

Index

Index

Index